LIFE IS STRANGE

– WAVES –

AVAILABLE NOW
LIFE IS STRANGE: DUST
LIFE IS STRANGE: WAVES

COMING SOON
LIFE IS STRANGE VOLUME 3

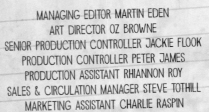

TITAN COMICS

EDITOR
TOLLY MAGGS

SENIOR DESIGNER
ANDREW LEUNG

MANAGING EDITOR MARTIN EDEN
ART DIRECTOR OZ BROWNE
SENIOR PRODUCTION CONTROLLER JACKIE FLOOK
PRODUCTION CONTROLLER PETER JAMES
PRODUCTION ASSISTANT RHIANNON ROY
SALES & CIRCULATION MANAGER STEVE TOTHILL
MARKETING ASSISTANT CHARLIE RASPIN
PUBLICIST IMOGEN HARRIS
ADS & MARKETING ASSISTANT BELLA HOY
COMMERCIAL MANAGER MICHELLE FAIRLAMB
HEAD OF RIGHTS JENNY BOYCE
PUBLISHING DIRECTOR DARRYL TOTHILL
OPERATIONS DIRECTOR LEIGH BAULCH
EXECUTIVE DIRECTOR VIVIAN CHEUNG
PUBLISHER NICK LANDAU

FOR RIGHTS INFORMATION CONTACT JENNY.BOYCE@TITANEMAIL.COM

THANK YOU TO JON M BROOKE, ROXANE DOMALAIN, SCOTT BLOWS, ANDREW JAMES, AND
TO ALL AT SQUARE ENIX. THANK YOU TO THE DONTNOD TEAM FOR ORIGINATING THESE WONDERFUL
CHARACTERS, AND DECK NINE GAMES FOR EXPANDING THEIR WORLD.

LIFE IS STRANGE: WAVES
ISBN: 9781787730885
FP VARIANT ISBN: 9781787734142

COLLECTS LIFE IS STRANGE #5-8

CHAPTER OPENER ART BY VERONICA FISH AND CLAUDIA LEONARDI
CHAPTER 5 CLOSING GAME ART BY WILL OFFER

PUBLISHED BY TITAN COMICS,
A DIVISION OF TITAN PUBLISHING GROUP, LTD. 144 SOUTHWARK STREET, LONDON, SE1 0UP

A CIP CATALOGUE FOR THIS TITLE IS AVAILABLE FROM THE BRITISH LIBRARY
FIRST EDITION OCTOBER 2019
10 9 8 7 6 5 4 3 2 1

WWW.TITAN-COMICS.COM
BECOME A FAN ON FACEBOOK.COM/COMICSTITAN | FOLLOW US ON TWITTER @COMICSTITAN

$e=MC^2$

T 127941

LIFE IS STRANGE

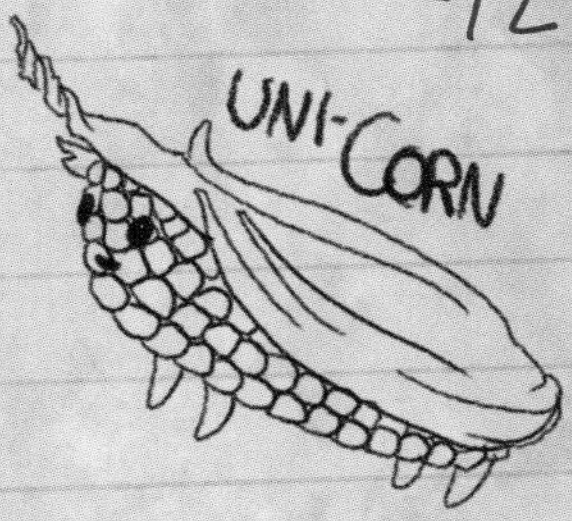
UNI-CORN

- WAVES -

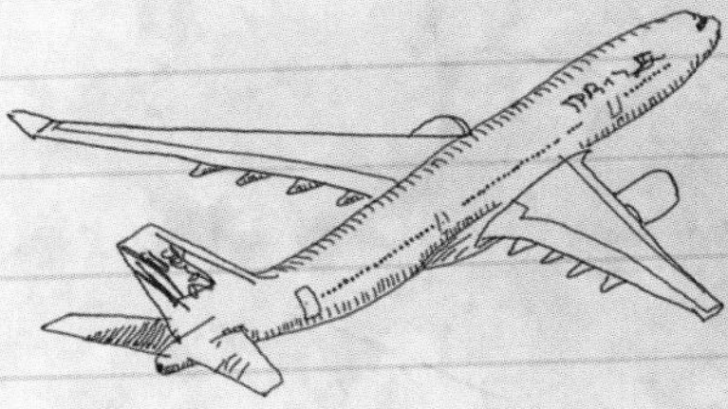

WRITTEN BY
EMMA VIECELI

ARTWORK BY
CLAUDIA LEONARDI

COLORS BY
ANDREA IZZO

LETTERS BY
RICHARD STARKINGS & COMICRAFT'S
JIMMY BETANCOURT

ORIGINAL STORY AND CHARACTERS BY
RAOUL BARBET, JEAN-LUC CANO
AND MICHEL KOCH.

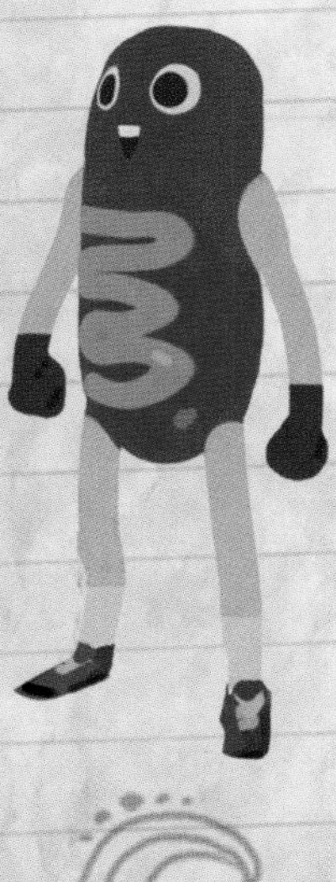

PREVIOUSLY...

Mysteriously gifted with the power to rewind time, Max Caulfield used her new abilities to reconnect with her oldest friend, Chloe Price, and to bring to justice the murderers of Chloe's closest confidante, Rachel Amber. Max's abilities came at a cost, however: if Max altered the original timeline - in which Chloe died of a gunshot wound - a hurricane would destroy their hometown, Arcadia Bay. In one reality, our Max chose to save Chloe's life, sacrificing Arcadia Bay. A year later, to save herself from a flux of possibilities that was tearing her apart, Max jumped into a new timeline, reconciling the disparate shards of herself in the process. Max may now be whole, but she's far from unscathed. In an ocean of possibilities, where does she go from here?

In one timeline, Max sacrificed Arcadia Bay to save Chloe. Since then, the pair had been living in Max's parents' house in Seattle for nearly a year.

Max hadn't used her powers since the night of the storm. But when she started slipping between timelines, or strings of reality, Max and Chloe set course for Arcadia Bay in search of answers.

The pair found a Prescott-funded restoration effort in full swing, attempting to breathe life back into the remains of Arcadia Bay in time for the one-year anniversary of its destruction.

Max continued to flicker between a multitude of possible timelines - it was out of her control. could feel the currents of time pulling her ap

RING
RING

In memory of
Max Caulfield
1995 - 2008

The flickers became faster, more intense. Max was pulled through a maelstrom of possibilities, each flicker taking more and more out of her. She eventually learned that the only way out... was through.

Max realized that she had to reunite all the fractured parts of herself before reality itself washed her away. Max and Chloe opened their hearts to one another... before Max took a leap of faith.

ith a photo from before her time at Blackwell Academy as r lodestar, Max dived into the whorl of timelines she calls he transect to find a string untouched by her time travel ventures. She reached out for the brightest light...

... and found herself on the shore of somewhere entirely new. Santa Monica, California. A timeline where both Chloe AND Rachel were alive! But what will Max find in this new timeline?

CHAPTER 1

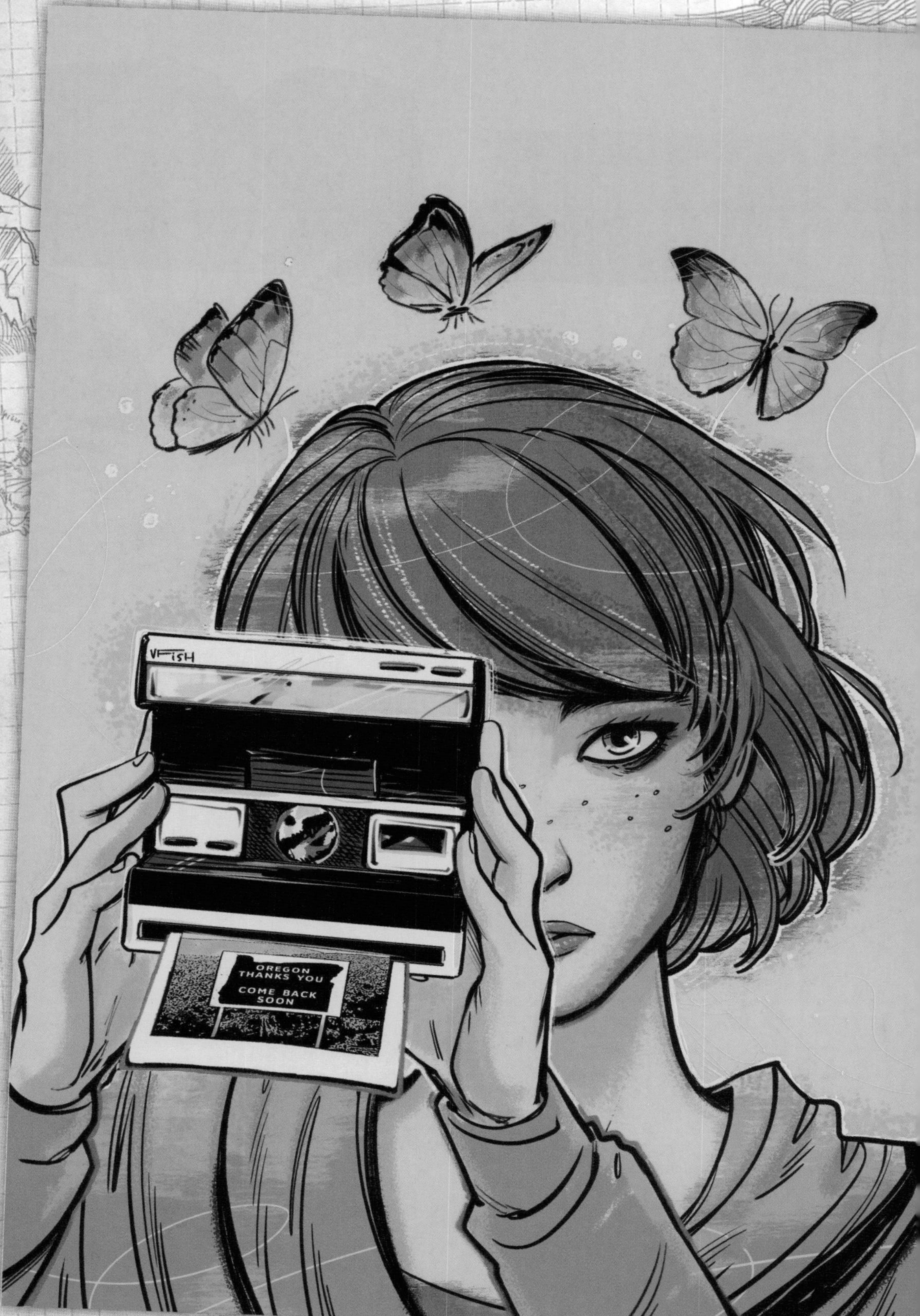
OREGON
THANKS YOU
COME BACK
SOON

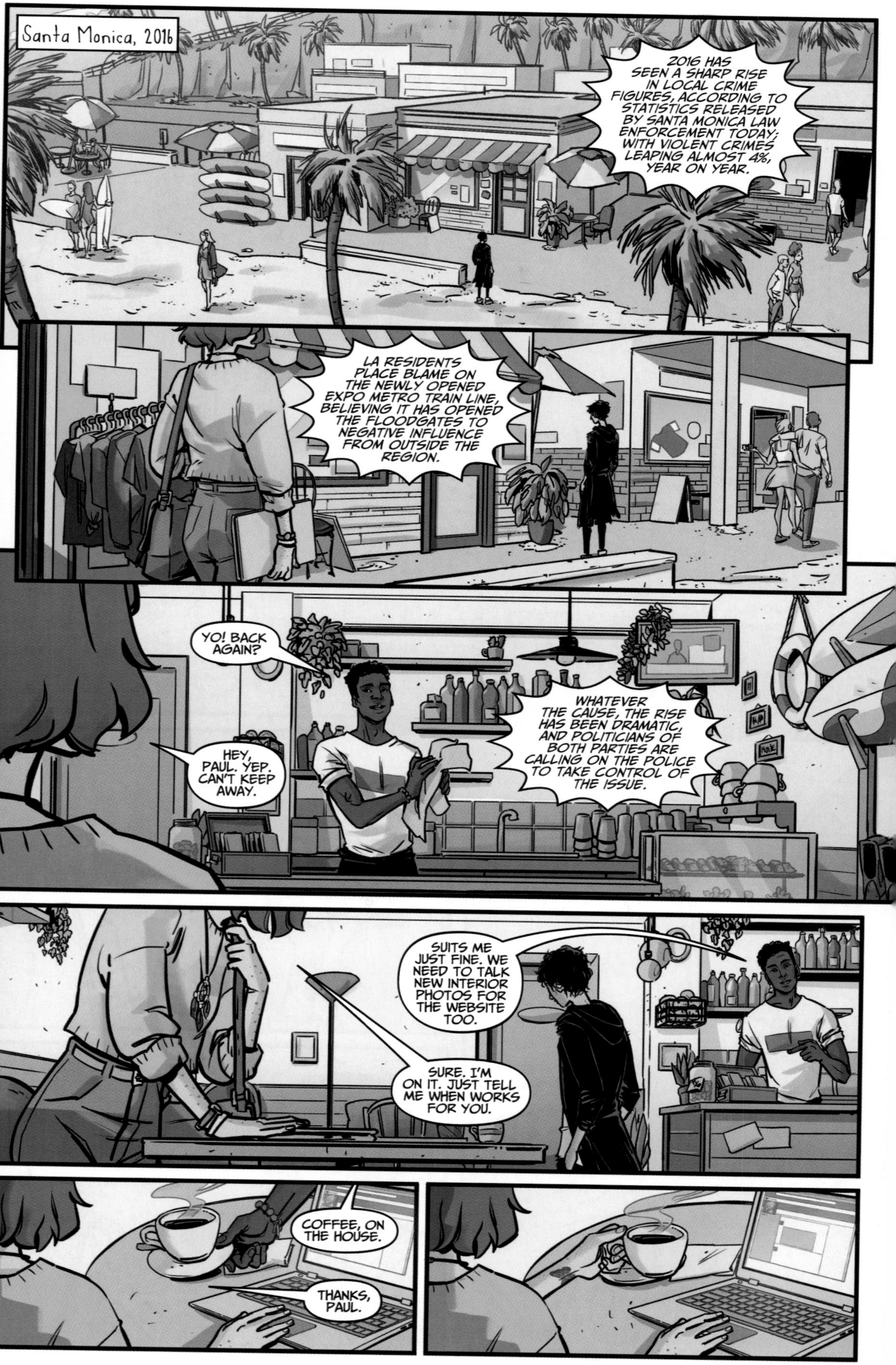
Santa Monica, 2016
2016 HAS SEEN A SHARP RISE IN LOCAL CRIME FIGURES, ACCORDING TO STATISTICS RELEASED BY SANTA MONICA LAW ENFORCEMENT TODAY; WITH VIOLENT CRIMES LEAPING ALMOST 4%, YEAR ON YEAR.
LA RESIDENTS PLACE BLAME ON THE NEWLY OPENED EXPO METRO TRAIN LINE, BELIEVING IT HAS OPENED THE FLOODGATES TO NEGATIVE INFLUENCE FROM OUTSIDE THE REGION.
YO! BACK AGAIN?
HEY, PAUL. YEP. CAN'T KEEP AWAY.
WHATEVER THE CAUSE, THE RISE HAS BEEN DRAMATIC, AND POLITICIANS OF BOTH PARTIES ARE CALLING ON THE POLICE TO TAKE CONTROL OF THE ISSUE.
SUITS ME JUST FINE. WE NEED TO TALK NEW INTERIOR PHOTOS FOR THE WEBSITE TOO.
SURE. I'M ON IT. JUST TELL ME WHEN WORKS FOR YOU.
COFFEE, ON THE HOUSE.
THANKS, PAUL.

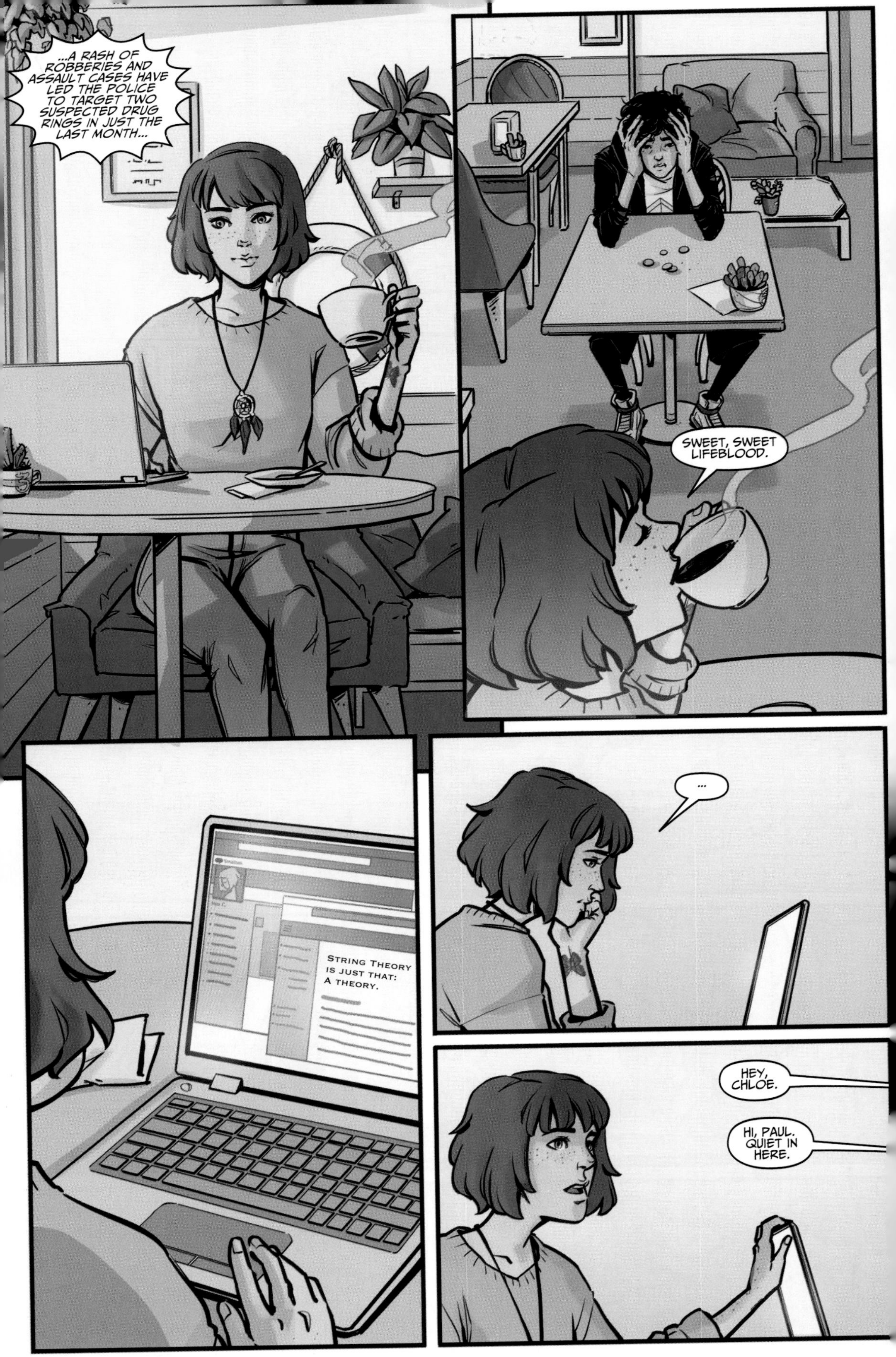
...A RASH OF ROBBERIES AND ASSAULT CASES HAVE LED THE POLICE TO TARGET TWO SUSPECTED DRUG RINGS IN JUST THE LAST MONTH...
SWEET, SWEET LIFEBLOOD.
String Theory is just that: A theory.
...
HEY, CHLOE.
HI, PAUL. QUIET IN HERE.

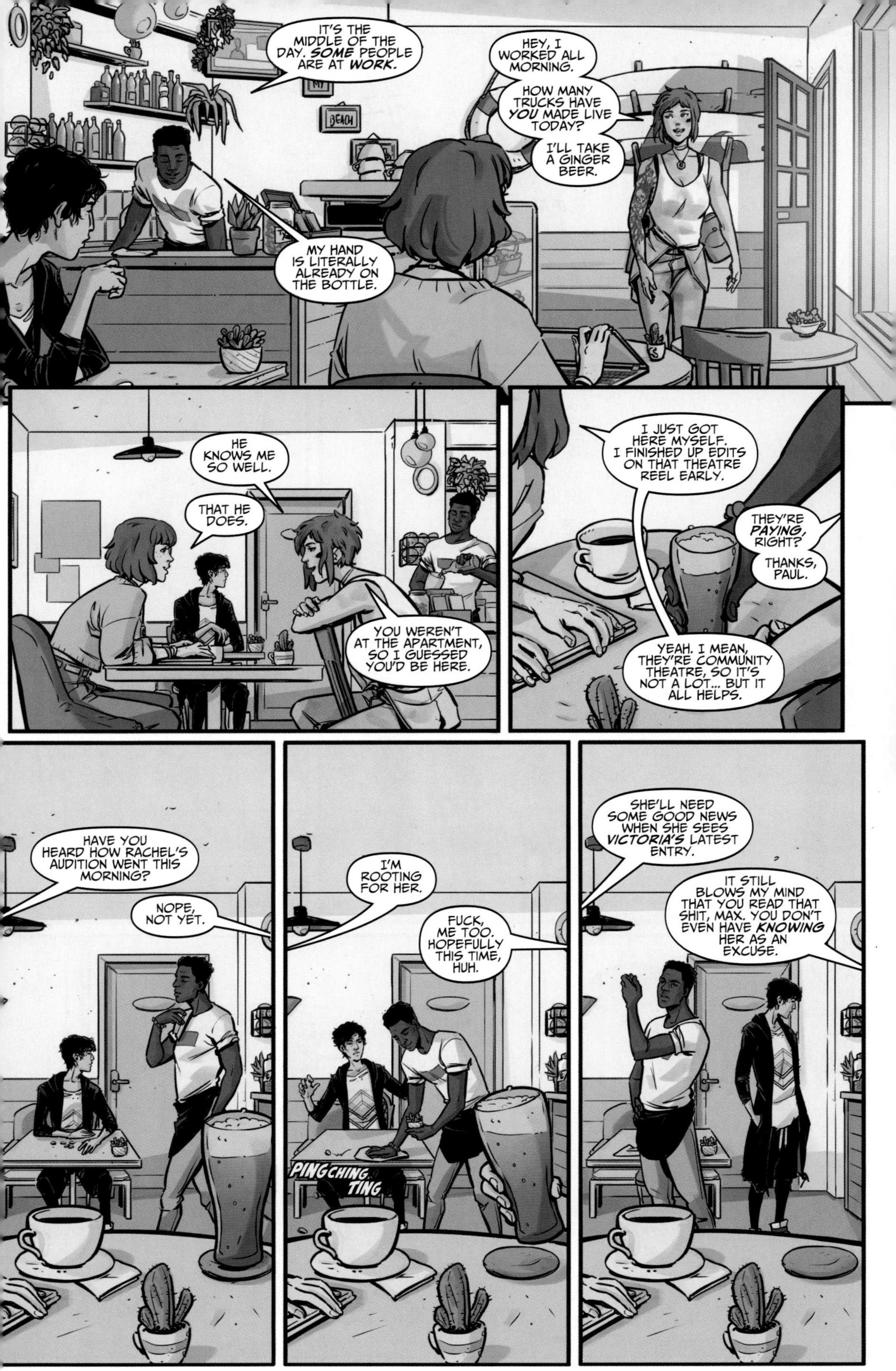
IT'S THE MIDDLE OF THE DAY. SOME PEOPLE ARE AT WORK.
MY HAND IS LITERALLY ALREADY ON THE BOTTLE.
HEY, I WORKED ALL MORNING.
HOW MANY TRUCKS HAVE YOU MADE LIVE TODAY?
I'LL TAKE A GINGER BEER.
BEACH
HE KNOWS ME SO WELL.
THAT HE DOES.
YOU WEREN'T AT THE APARTMENT, SO I GUESSED YOU'D BE HERE.
I JUST GOT HERE MYSELF. I FINISHED UP EDITS ON THAT THEATRE REEL EARLY.
THEY'RE PAYING, RIGHT?
THANKS, PAUL.
YEAH. I MEAN, THEY'RE COMMUNITY THEATRE, SO IT'S NOT A LOT... BUT IT ALL HELPS.
HAVE YOU HEARD HOW RACHEL'S AUDITION WENT THIS MORNING?
NOPE, NOT YET.
I'M ROOTING FOR HER.
FUCK, ME TOO. HOPEFULLY THIS TIME, HUH.
PING CHING TING
SHE'LL NEED SOME GOOD NEWS WHEN SHE SEES VICTORIA'S LATEST ENTRY.
IT STILL BLOWS MY MIND THAT YOU READ THAT SHIT, MAX. YOU DON'T EVEN HAVE KNOWING HER AS AN EXCUSE.

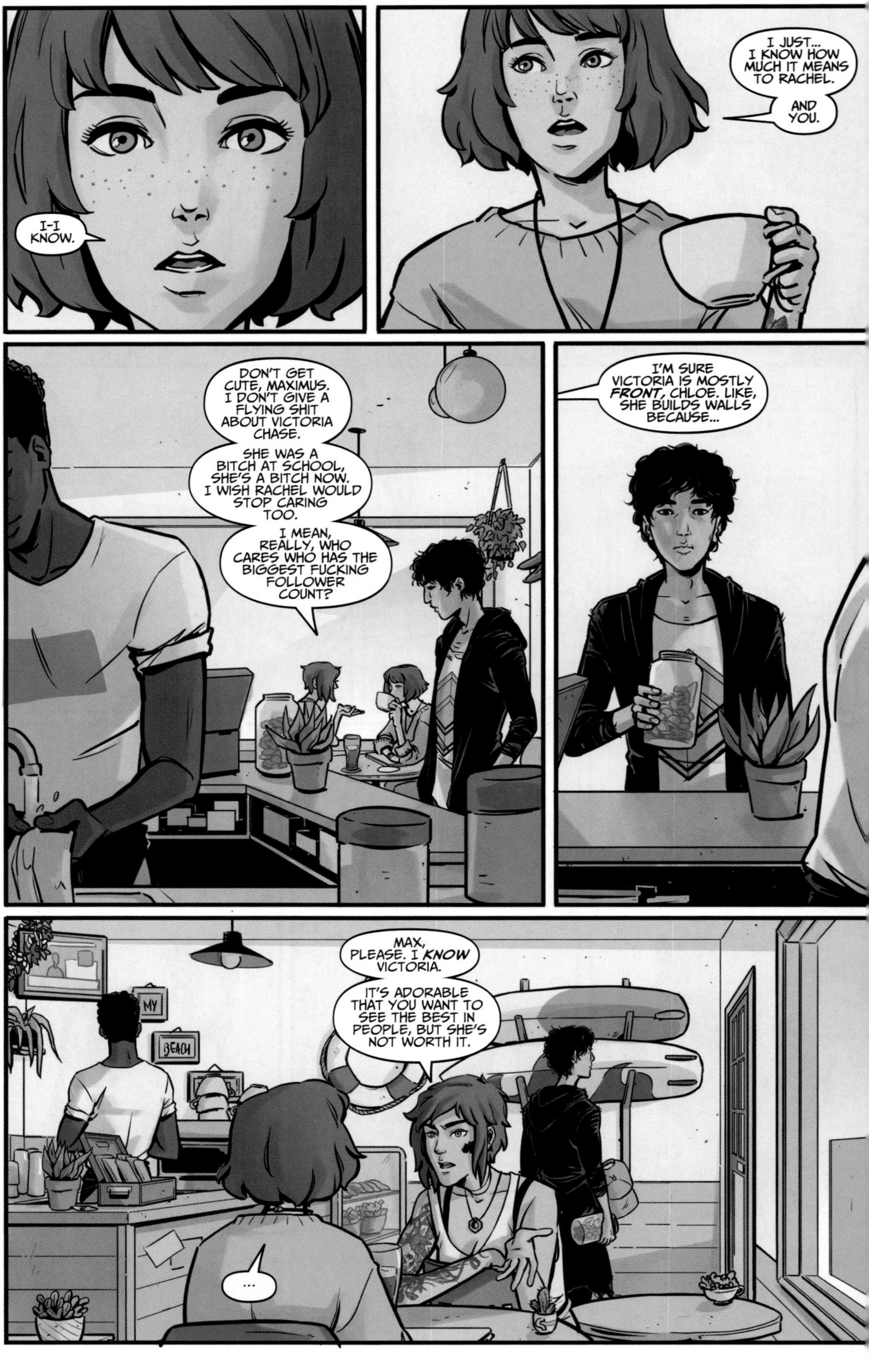
I-I KNOW.
I JUST... I KNOW HOW MUCH IT MEANS TO RACHEL.
AND YOU.
DON'T GET CUTE, MAXIMUS. I DON'T GIVE A FLYING SHIT ABOUT VICTORIA CHASE.
SHE WAS A BITCH AT SCHOOL, SHE'S A BITCH NOW. I WISH RACHEL WOULD STOP CARING TOO.
I MEAN, REALLY, WHO CARES WHO HAS THE BIGGEST FUCKING FOLLOWER COUNT?
I'M SURE VICTORIA IS MOSTLY ***FRONT***, CHLOE. LIKE, SHE BUILDS WALLS BECAUSE...
MAX, PLEASE. I ***KNOW*** VICTORIA.
IT'S ADORABLE THAT YOU WANT TO SEE THE BEST IN PEOPLE, BUT SHE'S NOT WORTH IT.
...
MY
BEACH

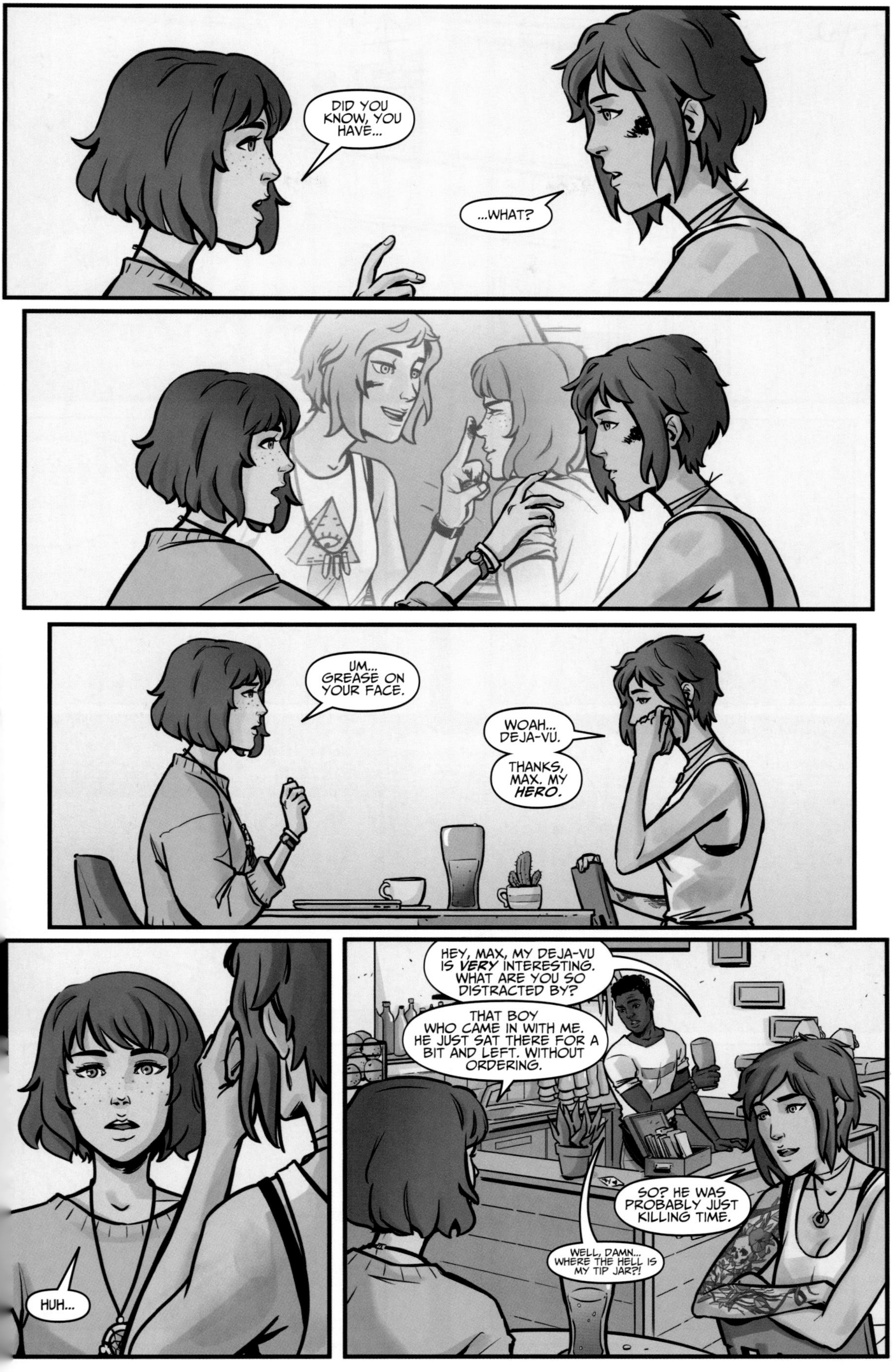
DID YOU KNOW, YOU HAVE...
...WHAT?
UM... GREASE ON YOUR FACE.
WOAH... DEJA-VU.
THANKS, MAX. MY *HERO*.
HUH...
HEY, MAX, MY DEJA-VU IS *VERY* INTERESTING. WHAT ARE YOU SO DISTRACTED BY?
THAT BOY WHO CAME IN WITH ME. HE JUST SAT THERE FOR A BIT AND LEFT. WITHOUT ORDERING.
SO? HE WAS PROBABLY JUST KILLING TIME.
WELL, DAMN... WHERE THE HELL IS MY TIP JAR?!

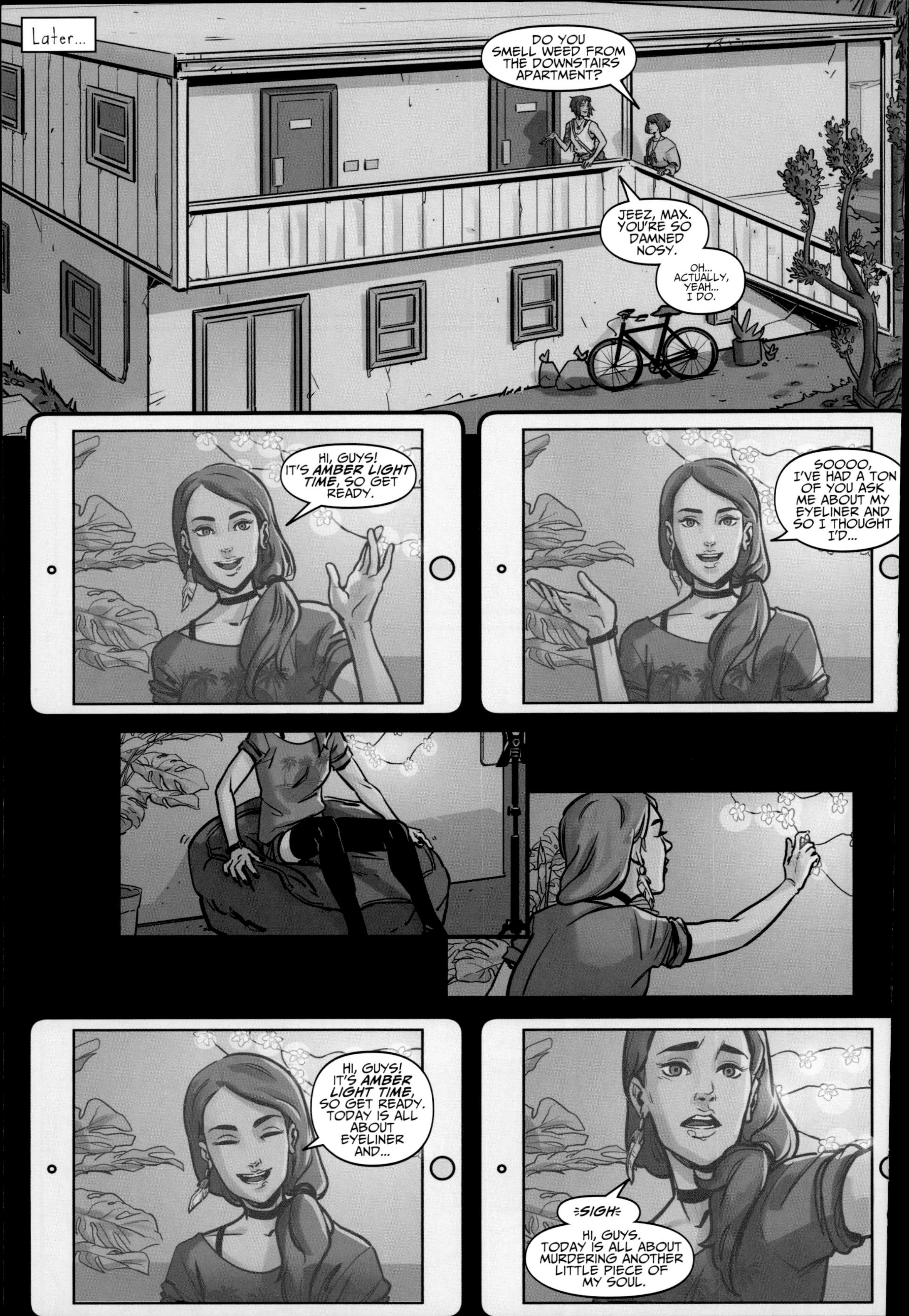
Later...
DO YOU SMELL WEED FROM THE DOWNSTAIRS APARTMENT?
JEEZ, MAX. YOU'RE SO DAMNED NOSY.
OH... ACTUALLY, YEAH... I DO.
HI, GUYS! IT'S AMBER LIGHT TIME, SO GET READY.
SOOOO, I'VE HAD A TON OF YOU ASK ME ABOUT MY EYELINER AND SO I THOUGHT I'D...
HI, GUYS! IT'S AMBER LIGHT TIME, SO GET READY. TODAY IS ALL ABOUT EYELINER AND...
SIGH
HI, GUYS. TODAY IS ALL ABOUT MURDERING ANOTHER LITTLE PIECE OF MY SOUL.

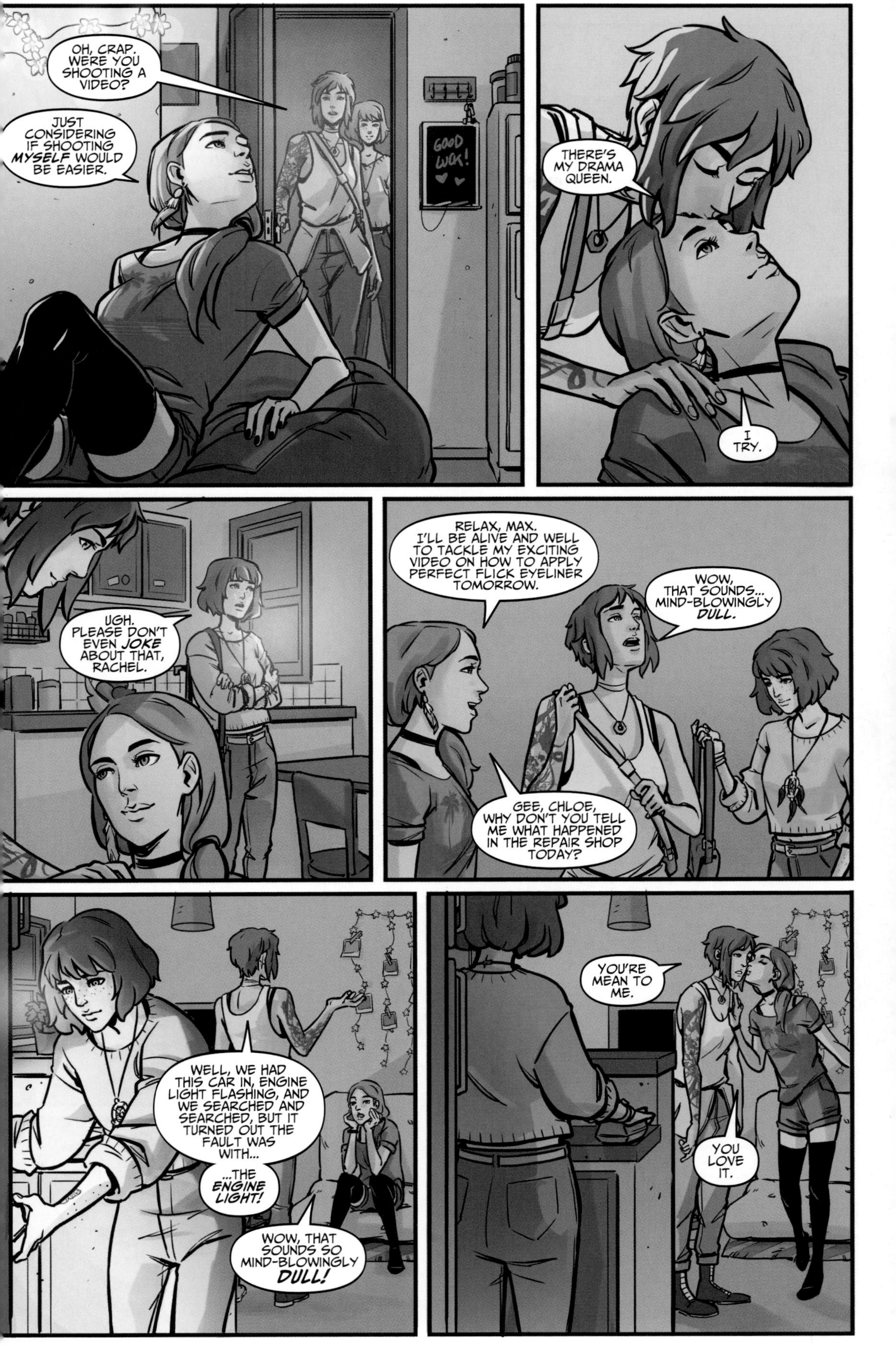
OH, CRAP. WERE YOU SHOOTING A VIDEO?
JUST CONSIDERING IF SHOOTING MYSELF WOULD BE EASIER.
GOOD LUCK!
THERE'S MY DRAMA QUEEN.
I TRY.
UGH. PLEASE DON'T EVEN JOKE ABOUT THAT, RACHEL.
RELAX, MAX. I'LL BE ALIVE AND WELL TO TACKLE MY EXCITING VIDEO ON HOW TO APPLY PERFECT FLICK EYELINER TOMORROW.
WOW, THAT SOUNDS... MIND-BLOWINGLY DULL.
GEE, CHLOE, WHY DON'T YOU TELL ME WHAT HAPPENED IN THE REPAIR SHOP TODAY?
WELL, WE HAD THIS CAR IN, ENGINE LIGHT FLASHING, AND WE SEARCHED AND SEARCHED, BUT IT TURNED OUT THE FAULT WAS WITH...
...THE ENGINE LIGHT!
WOW, THAT SOUNDS SO MIND-BLOWINGLY DULL!
YOU'RE MEAN TO ME.
YOU LOVE IT.

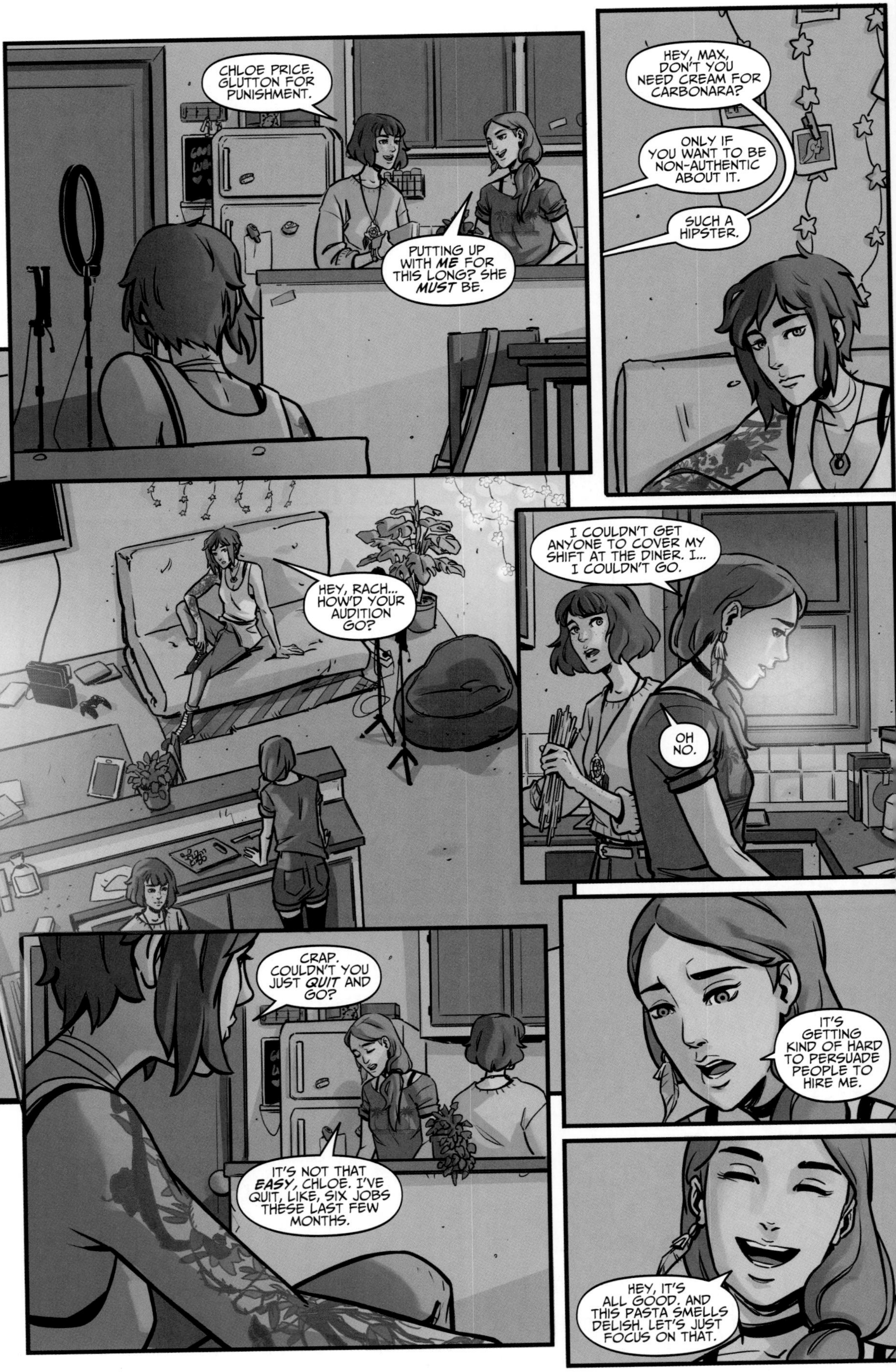
CHLOE PRICE. GLUTTON FOR PUNISHMENT.
PUTTING UP WITH **ME** FOR THIS LONG? SHE **MUST** BE.
HEY, MAX, DON'T YOU NEED CREAM FOR CARBONARA?
ONLY IF YOU WANT TO BE NON-AUTHENTIC ABOUT IT.
SUCH A HIPSTER.
HEY, RACH... HOW'D YOUR AUDITION GO?
I COULDN'T GET ANYONE TO COVER MY SHIFT AT THE DINER. I... I COULDN'T GO.
OH NO.
CRAP. COULDN'T YOU JUST **QUIT** AND GO?
IT'S NOT THAT **EASY**, CHLOE. I'VE QUIT, LIKE, SIX JOBS THESE LAST FEW MONTHS.
IT'S GETTING KIND OF HARD TO PERSUADE PEOPLE TO HIRE ME.
HEY, IT'S ALL GOOD. AND THIS PASTA SMELLS DELISH. LET'S JUST FOCUS ON THAT.

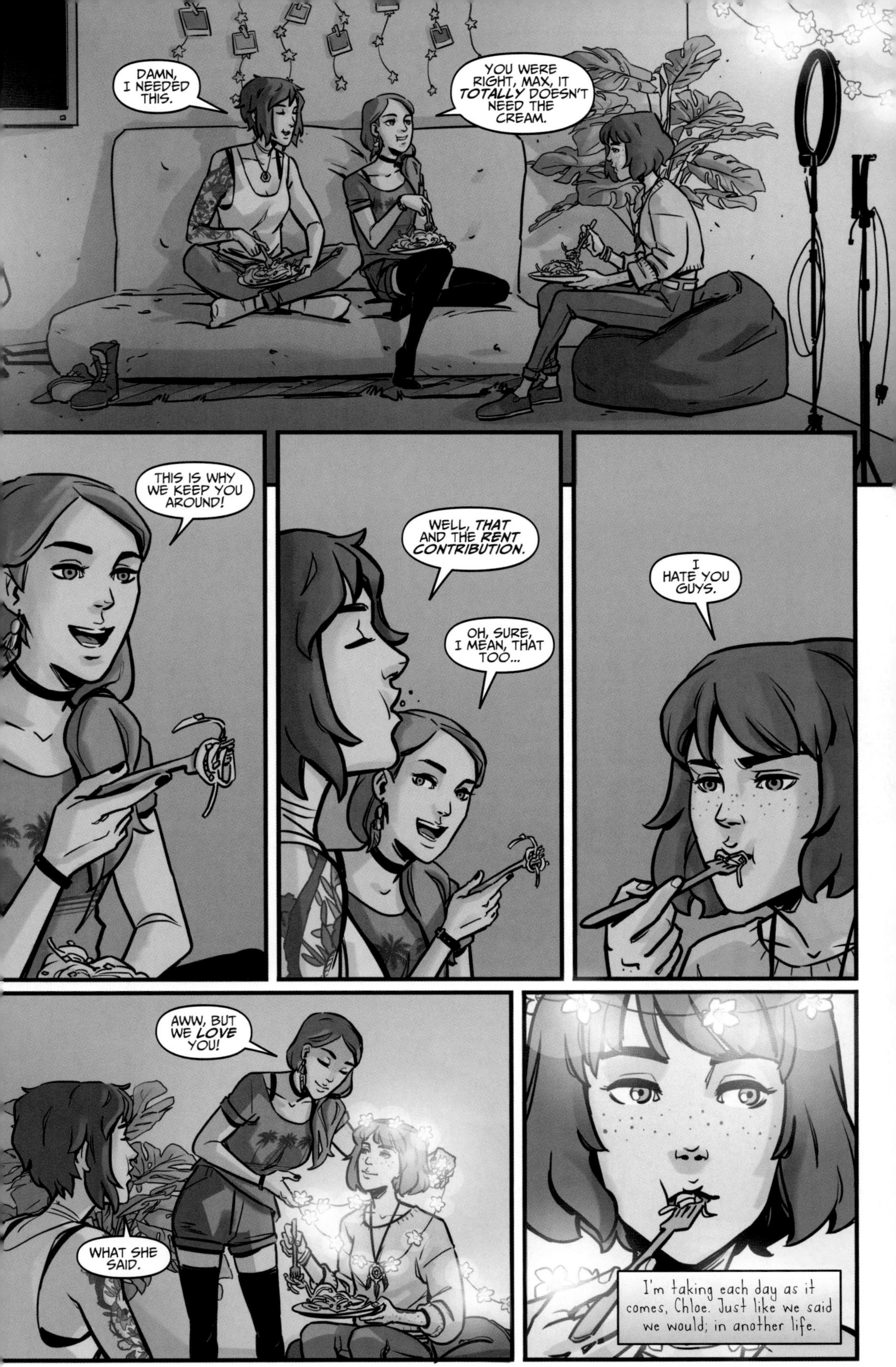
DAMN, I NEEDED THIS.
YOU WERE RIGHT, MAX, IT TOTALLY DOESN'T NEED THE CREAM.
THIS IS WHY WE KEEP YOU AROUND!
WELL, THAT AND THE RENT CONTRIBUTION.
OH, SURE, I MEAN, THAT TOO...
I HATE YOU GUYS.
AWW, BUT WE LOVE YOU!
WHAT SHE SAID.
I'm taking each day as it comes, Chloe. Just like we said we would; in another life.

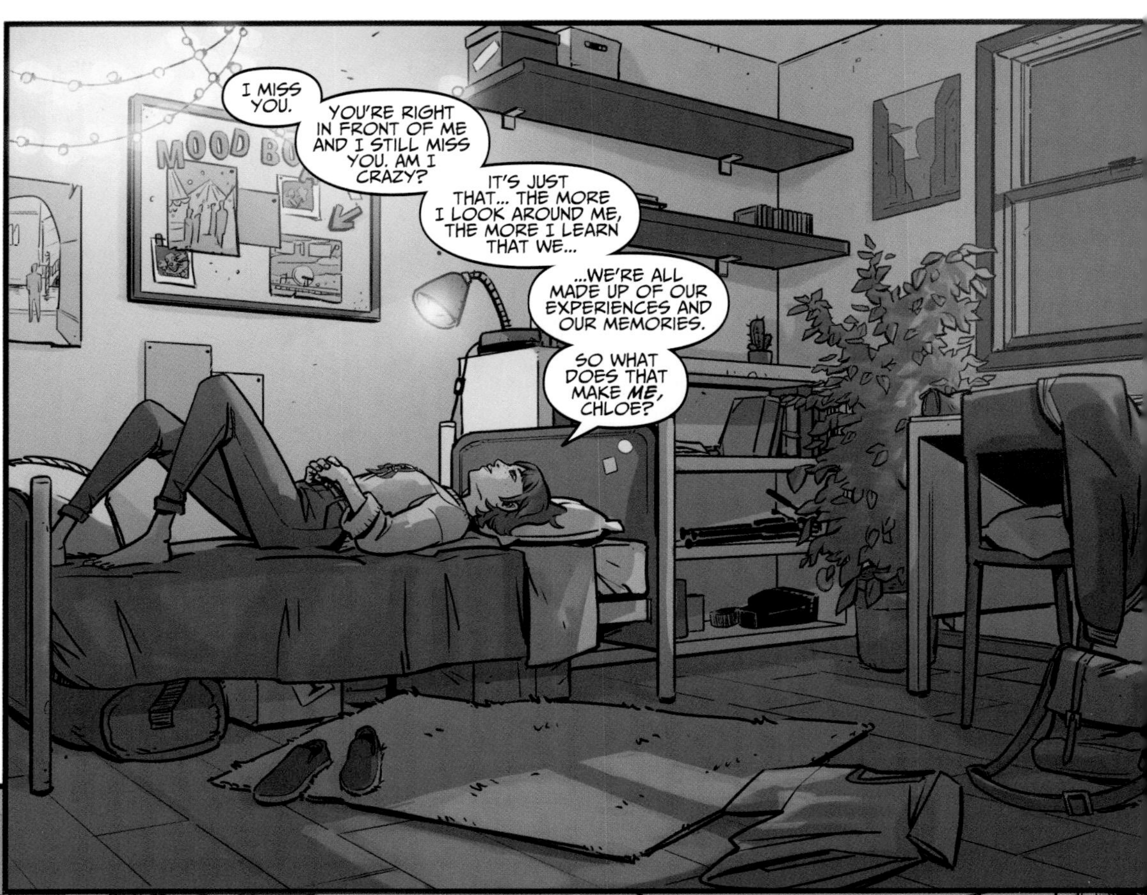
I MISS YOU.
YOU'RE RIGHT IN FRONT OF ME AND I STILL MISS YOU. AM I CRAZY?
IT'S JUST THAT... THE MORE I LOOK AROUND ME, THE MORE I LEARN THAT WE...
...WE'RE ALL MADE UP OF OUR EXPERIENCES AND OUR MEMORIES.
SO WHAT DOES THAT MAKE *ME*, CHLOE?

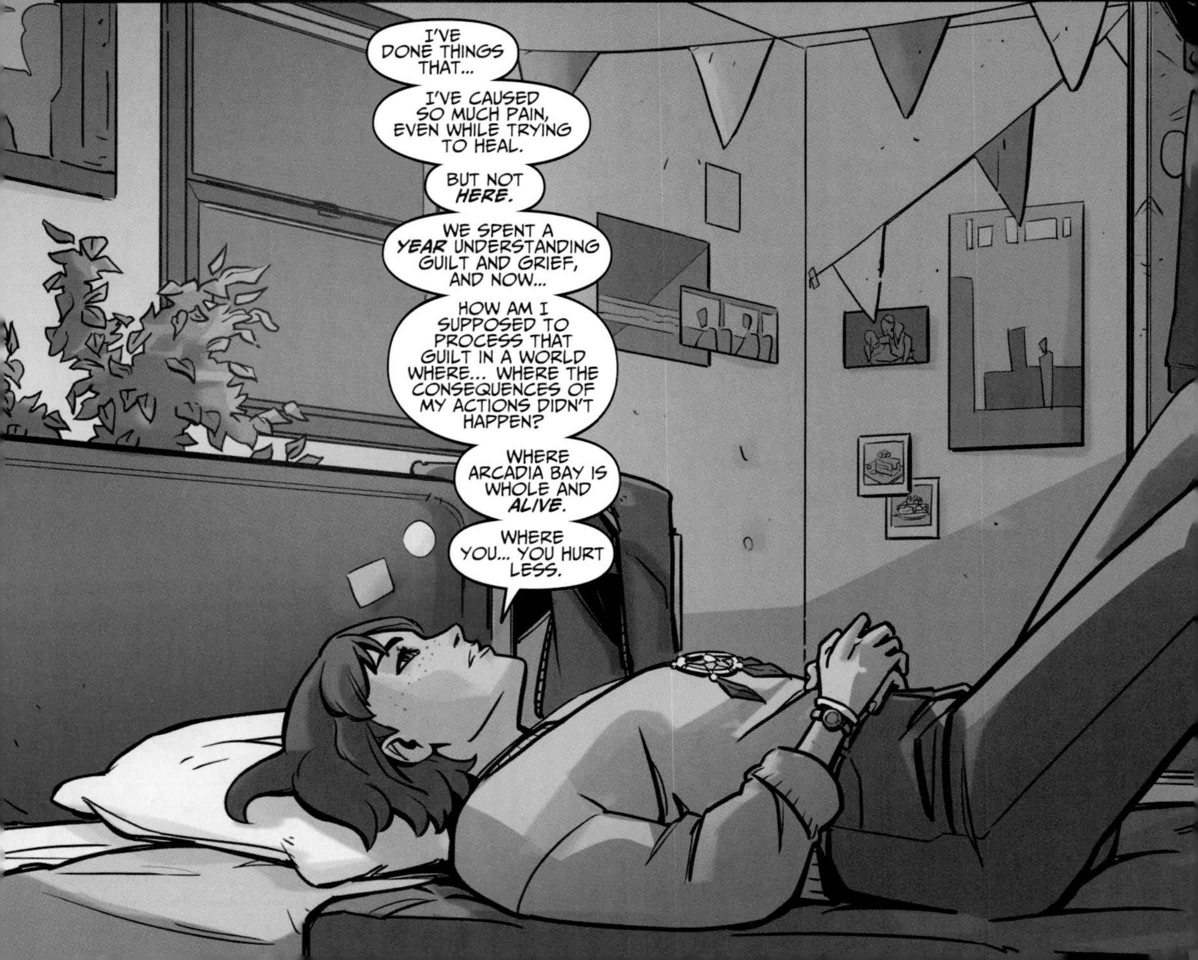
I'VE DONE THINGS THAT...
I'VE CAUSED SO MUCH PAIN, EVEN WHILE TRYING TO HEAL.
BUT NOT *HERE.*
WE SPENT A *YEAR* UNDERSTANDING GUILT AND GRIEF, AND NOW...
HOW AM I SUPPOSED TO PROCESS THAT GUILT IN A WORLD WHERE... WHERE THE CONSEQUENCES OF MY ACTIONS DIDN'T HAPPEN?
WHERE ARCADIA BAY IS WHOLE AND *ALIVE*.
WHERE YOU... YOU HURT LESS.

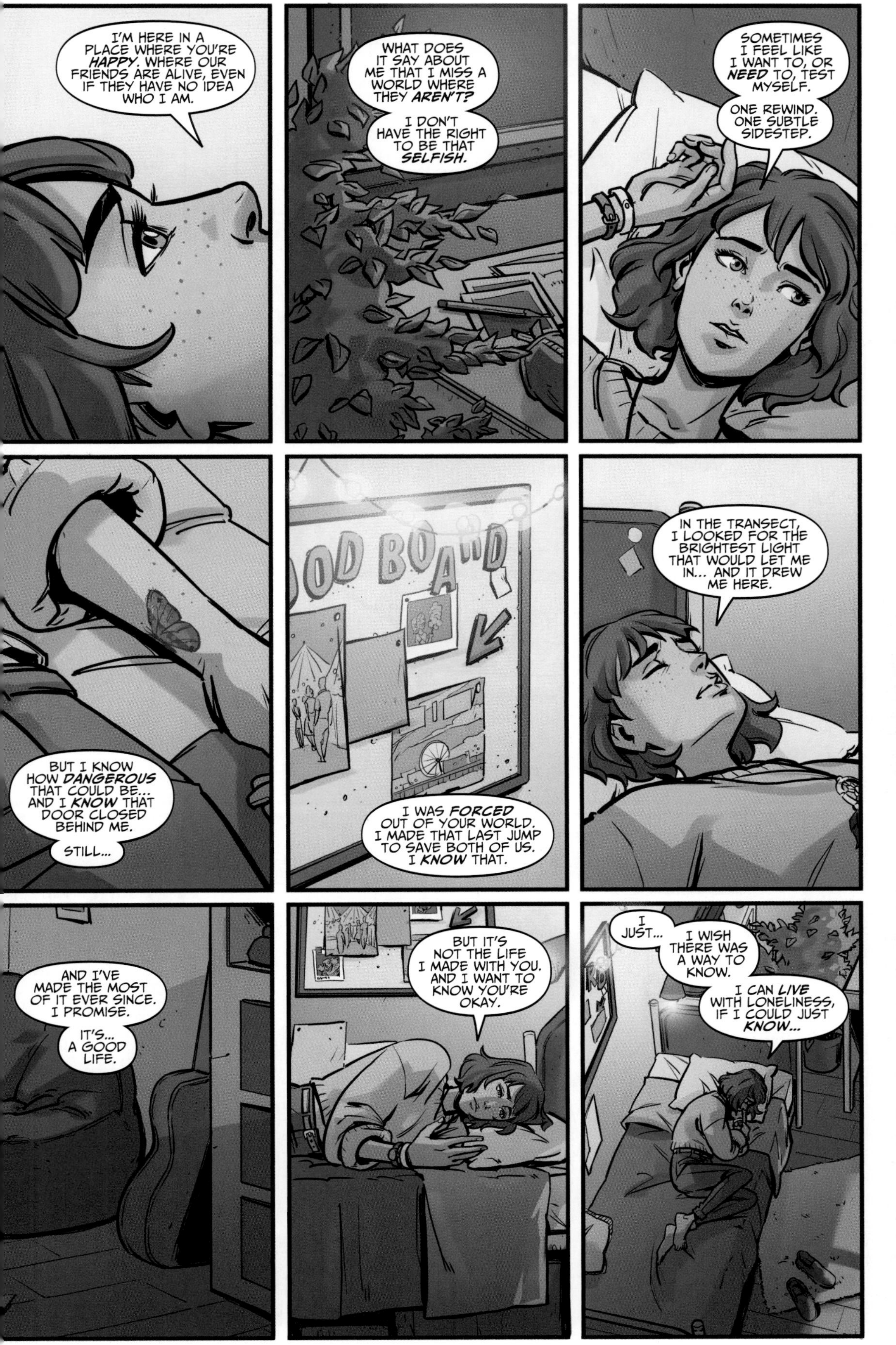
I'M HERE IN A PLACE WHERE YOU'RE **HAPPY**. WHERE OUR FRIENDS ARE ALIVE, EVEN IF THEY HAVE NO IDEA WHO I AM.
WHAT DOES IT SAY ABOUT ME THAT I MISS A WORLD WHERE THEY **AREN'T?**
I DON'T HAVE THE RIGHT TO BE THAT **SELFISH.**
SOMETIMES I FEEL LIKE I WANT TO, OR **NEED** TO, TEST MYSELF.
ONE REWIND. ONE SUBTLE SIDESTEP.
BUT I KNOW HOW **DANGEROUS** THAT COULD BE... AND I **KNOW** THAT DOOR CLOSED BEHIND ME.
STILL...
OOD BOARD
I WAS **FORCED** OUT OF YOUR WORLD. I MADE THAT LAST JUMP TO SAVE BOTH OF US. I **KNOW** THAT.
IN THE TRANSECT, I LOOKED FOR THE BRIGHTEST LIGHT THAT WOULD LET ME IN... AND IT DREW ME HERE.
AND I'VE MADE THE MOST OF IT EVER SINCE. I PROMISE.
IT'S... A GOOD LIFE.
BUT IT'S NOT THE LIFE I MADE WITH YOU. AND I WANT TO KNOW YOU'RE OKAY.
I JUST...
I WISH THERE WAS A WAY TO KNOW.
I CAN **LIVE** WITH LONELINESS, IF I COULD JUST **KNOW...**

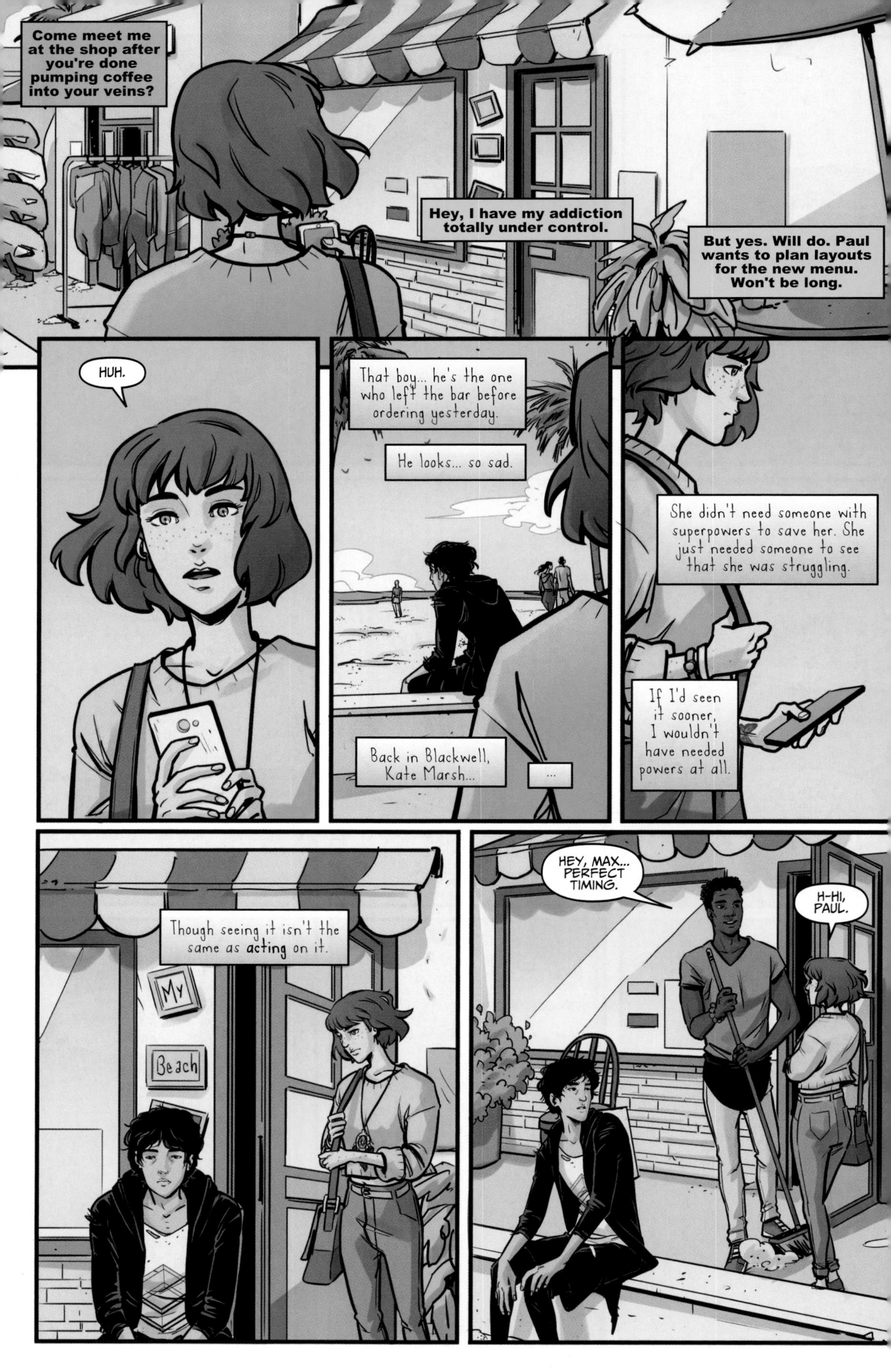
Come meet me at the shop after you're done pumping coffee into your veins?
Hey, I have my addiction totally under control.
But yes. Will do. Paul wants to plan layouts for the new menu. Won't be long.
HUH.
That boy... he's the one who left the bar before ordering yesterday.
He looks... so sad.
Back in Blackwell, Kate Marsh...
...
She didn't need someone with superpowers to save her. She just needed someone to see that she was struggling.
If I'd seen it sooner, I wouldn't have needed powers at all.
Though seeing it isn't the same as acting on it.
My
Beach
HEY, MAX... PERFECT TIMING.
H-HI, PAUL.

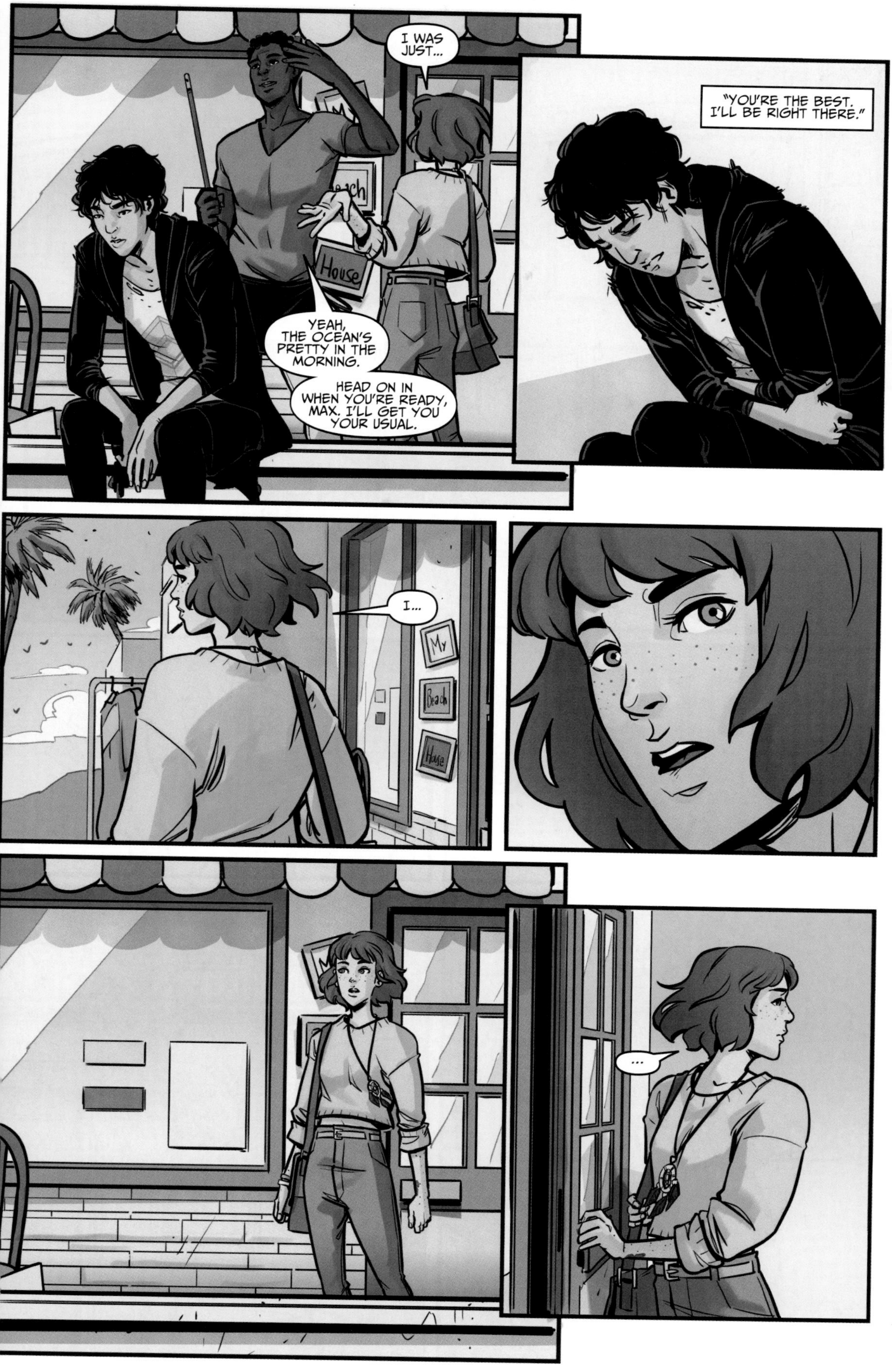
I WAS JUST...
YEAH, THE OCEAN'S PRETTY IN THE MORNING.
HEAD ON IN WHEN YOU'RE READY, MAX. I'LL GET YOU YOUR USUAL.
"YOU'RE THE BEST. I'LL BE RIGHT THERE."
I...
...

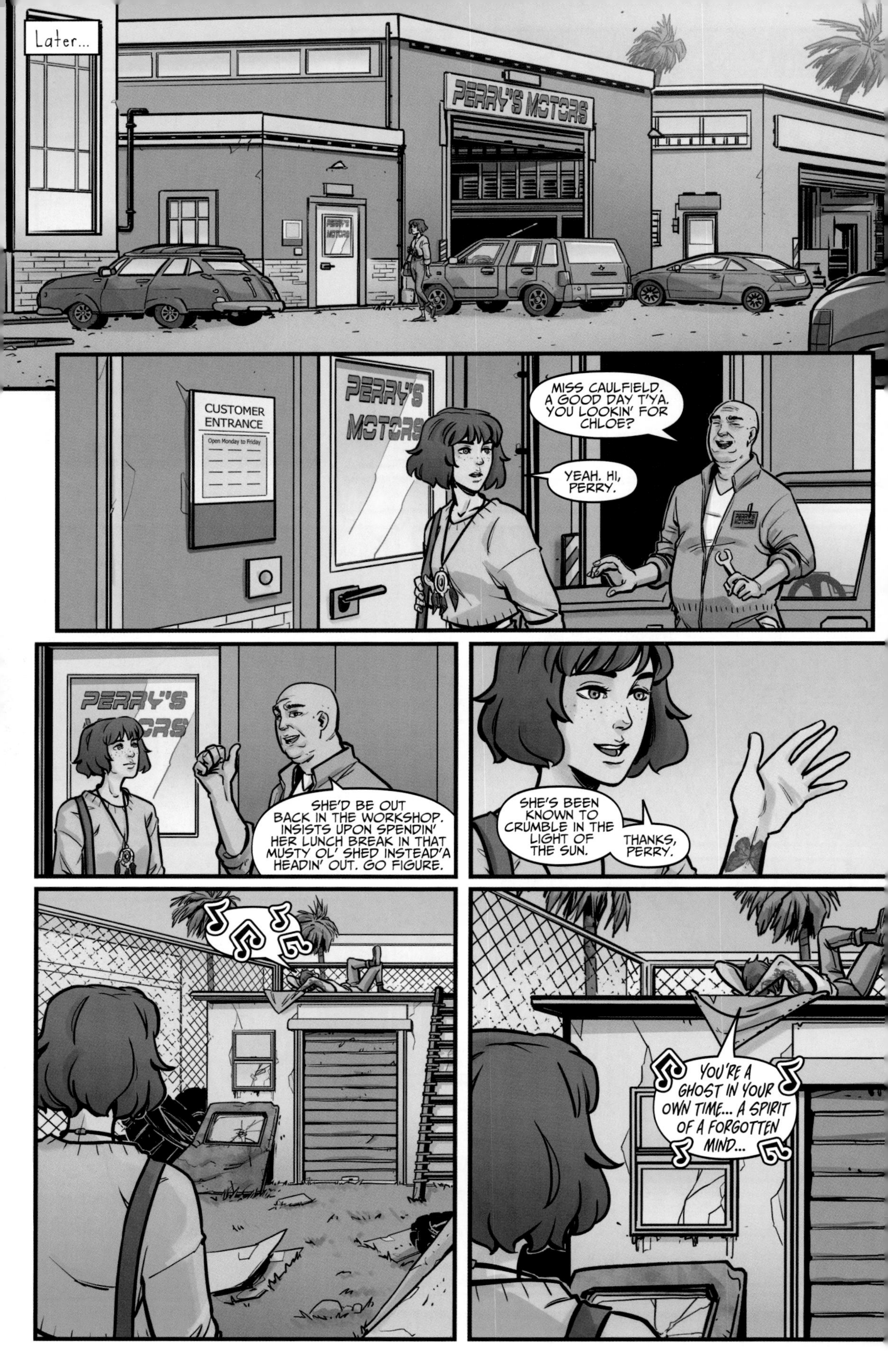
Later...
PERRY'S MOTORS
CUSTOMER ENTRANCE
Open Monday to Friday
MISS CAULFIELD. A GOOD DAY T'YA. YOU LOOKIN' FOR CHLOE?
YEAH. HI, PERRY.
SHE'D BE OUT BACK IN THE WORKSHOP. INSISTS UPON SPENDIN' HER LUNCH BREAK IN THAT MUSTY OL' SHED INSTEAD'A HEADIN' OUT. GO FIGURE.
SHE'S BEEN KNOWN TO CRUMBLE IN THE LIGHT OF THE SUN.
THANKS, PERRY.
YOU'RE A GHOST IN YOUR OWN TIME... A SPIRIT OF A FORGOTTEN MIND...

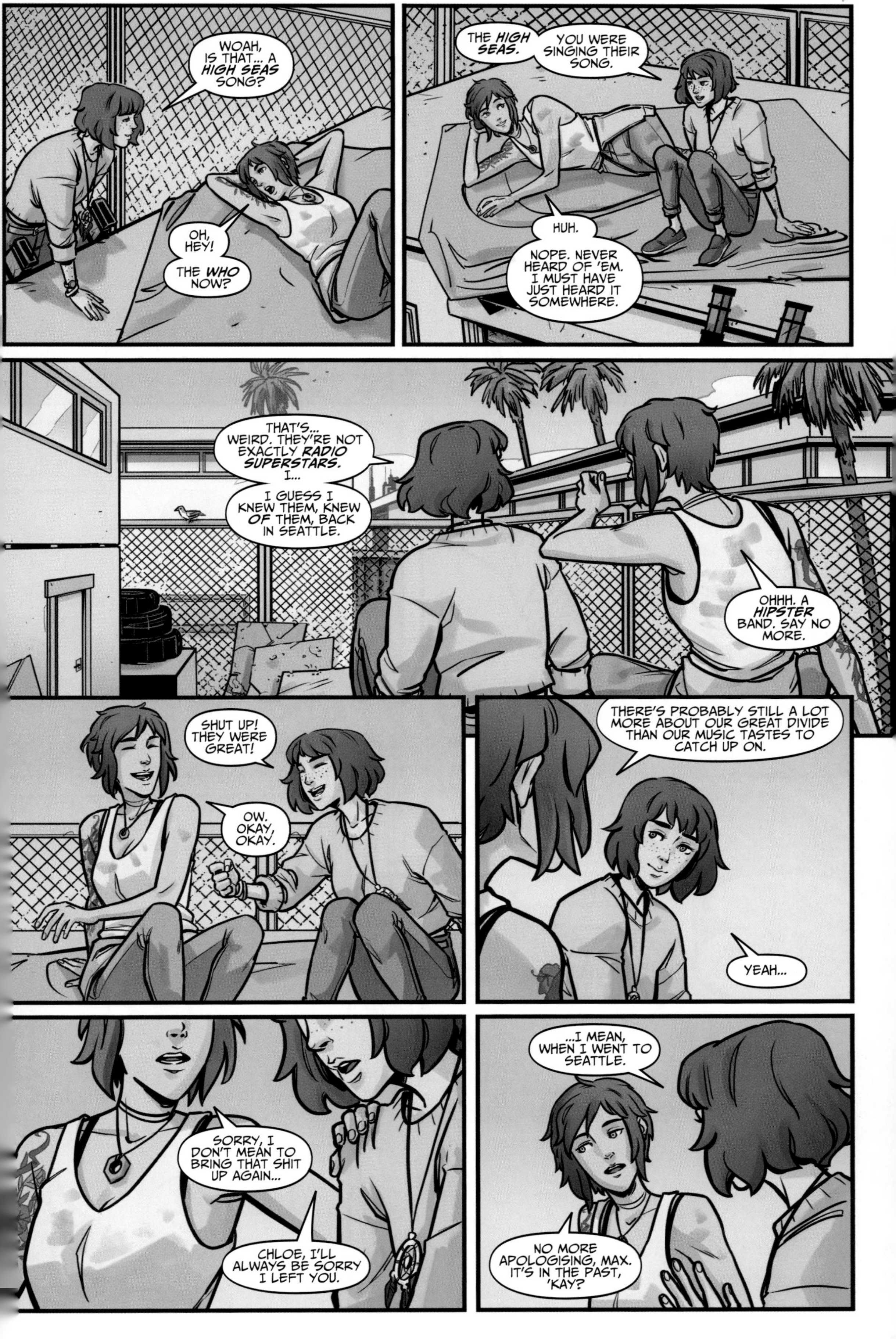
WOAH, IS THAT... A HIGH SEAS SONG?
OH, HEY!
THE WHO NOW?
THE HIGH SEAS.
YOU WERE SINGING THEIR SONG.
HUH.
NOPE. NEVER HEARD OF 'EM. I MUST HAVE JUST HEARD IT SOMEWHERE.
THAT'S... WEIRD. THEY'RE NOT EXACTLY RADIO SUPERSTARS. I...
I GUESS I KNEW THEM, KNEW OF THEM, BACK IN SEATTLE.
OHHH. A HIPSTER BAND. SAY NO MORE.
SHUT UP! THEY WERE GREAT!
OW. OKAY, OKAY.
THERE'S PROBABLY STILL A LOT MORE ABOUT OUR GREAT DIVIDE THAN OUR MUSIC TASTES TO CATCH UP ON.
YEAH...
SORRY, I DON'T MEAN TO BRING THAT SHIT UP AGAIN...
CHLOE, I'LL ALWAYS BE SORRY I LEFT YOU.
...I MEAN, WHEN I WENT TO SEATTLE.
NO MORE APOLOGISING, MAX. IT'S IN THE PAST, 'KAY?

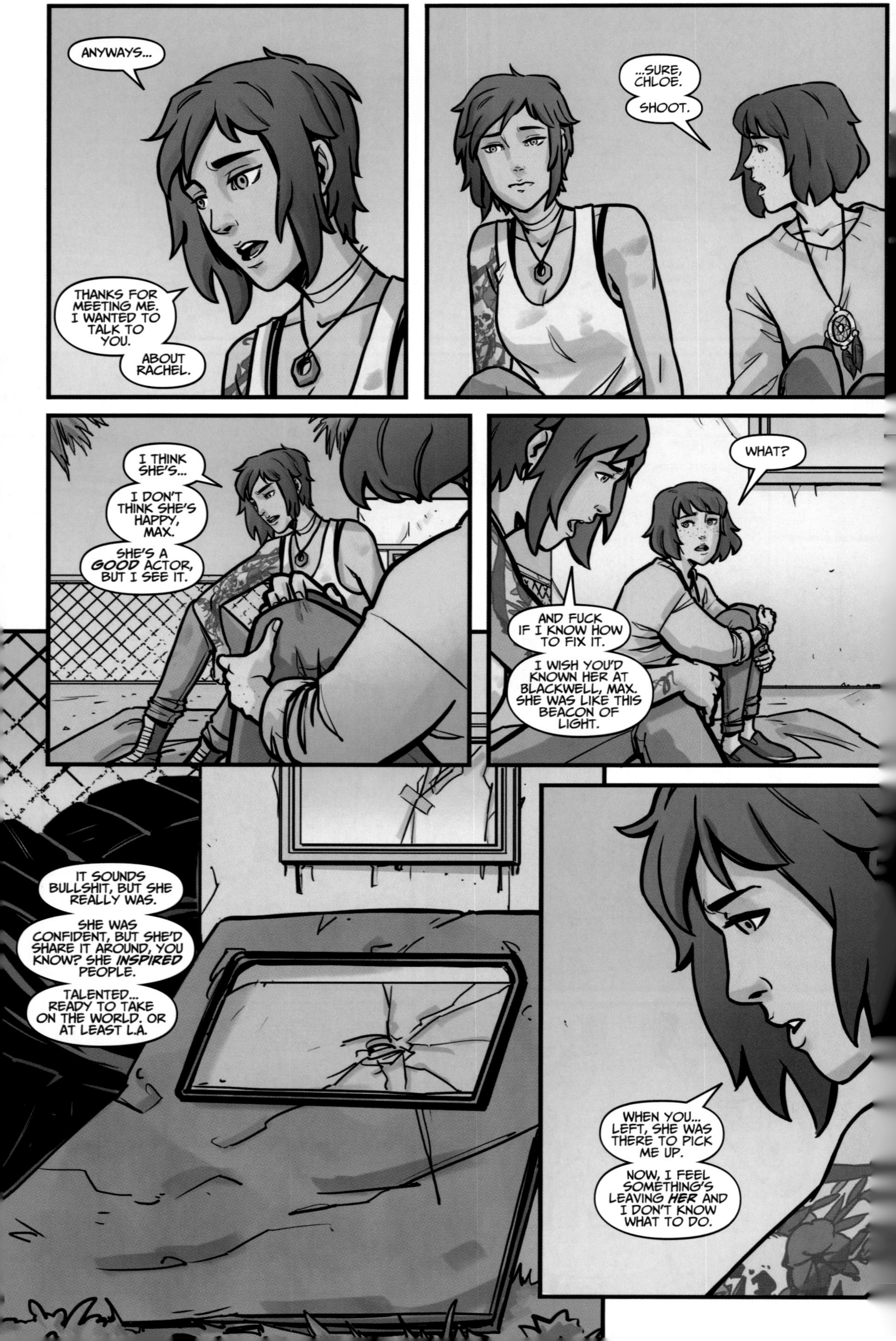
ANYWAYS...
THANKS FOR MEETING ME. I WANTED TO TALK TO YOU.
ABOUT RACHEL.
...SURE, CHLOE.
SHOOT.
I THINK SHE'S...
I DON'T THINK SHE'S HAPPY, MAX.
SHE'S A GOOD ACTOR, BUT I SEE IT.
WHAT?
AND FUCK IF I KNOW HOW TO FIX IT.
I WISH YOU'D KNOWN HER AT BLACKWELL, MAX. SHE WAS LIKE THIS BEACON OF LIGHT.
IT SOUNDS BULLSHIT, BUT SHE REALLY WAS.
SHE WAS CONFIDENT, BUT SHE'D SHARE IT AROUND, YOU KNOW? SHE INSPIRED PEOPLE.
TALENTED... READY TO TAKE ON THE WORLD. OR AT LEAST L.A.
WHEN YOU... LEFT, SHE WAS THERE TO PICK ME UP.
NOW, I FEEL SOMETHING'S LEAVING HER AND I DON'T KNOW WHAT TO DO.

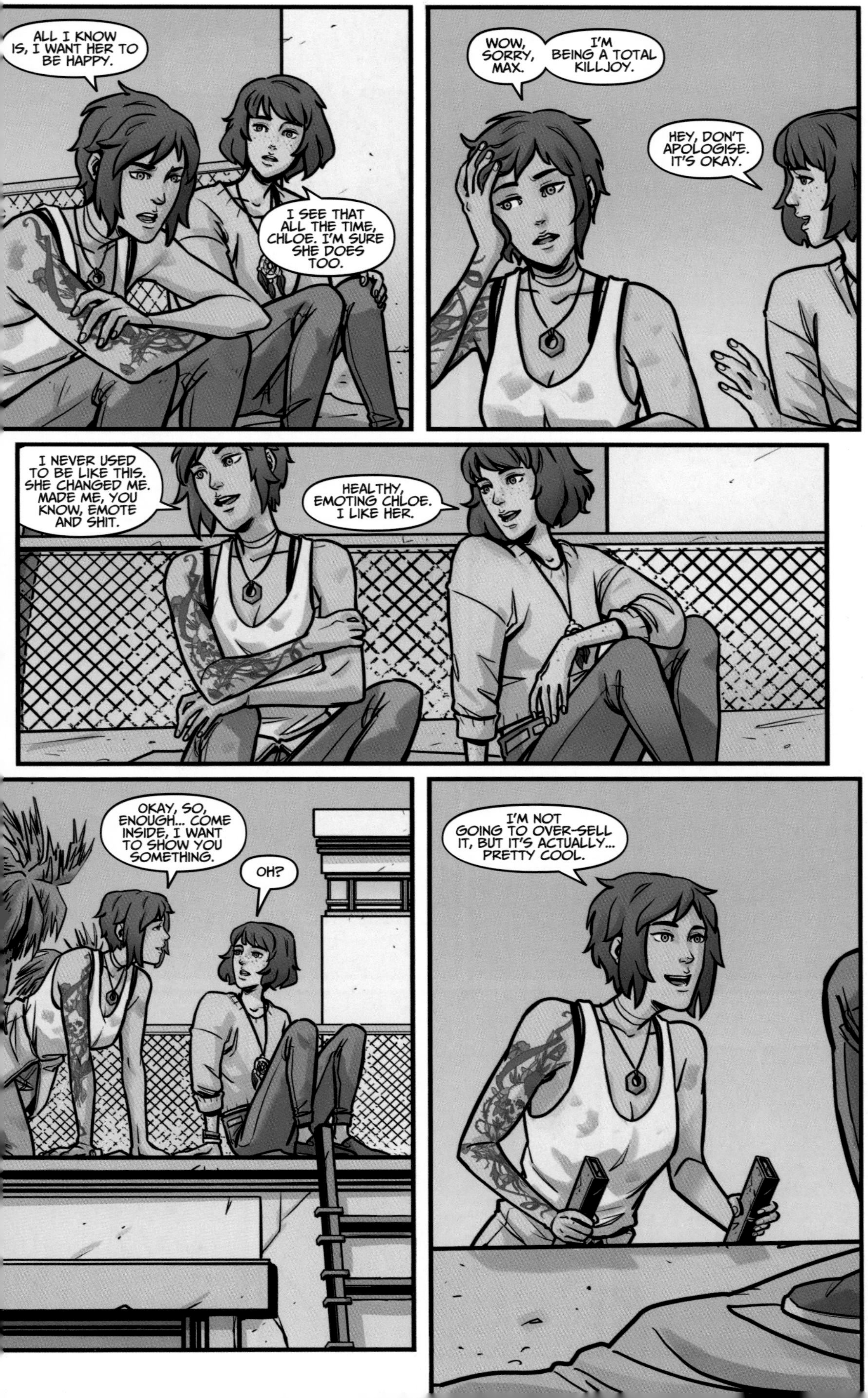
ALL I KNOW IS, I WANT HER TO BE HAPPY.
I SEE THAT ALL THE TIME, CHLOE. I'M SURE SHE DOES TOO.
WOW, SORRY, MAX.
I'M BEING A TOTAL KILLJOY.
HEY, DON'T APOLOGISE. IT'S OKAY.
I NEVER USED TO BE LIKE THIS. SHE CHANGED ME. MADE ME, YOU KNOW, EMOTE AND SHIT.
HEALTHY, EMOTING CHLOE. I LIKE HER.
OKAY, SO, ENOUGH... COME INSIDE, I WANT TO SHOW YOU SOMETHING.
OH?
I'M NOT GOING TO OVER-SELL IT, BUT IT'S ACTUALLY... PRETTY COOL.

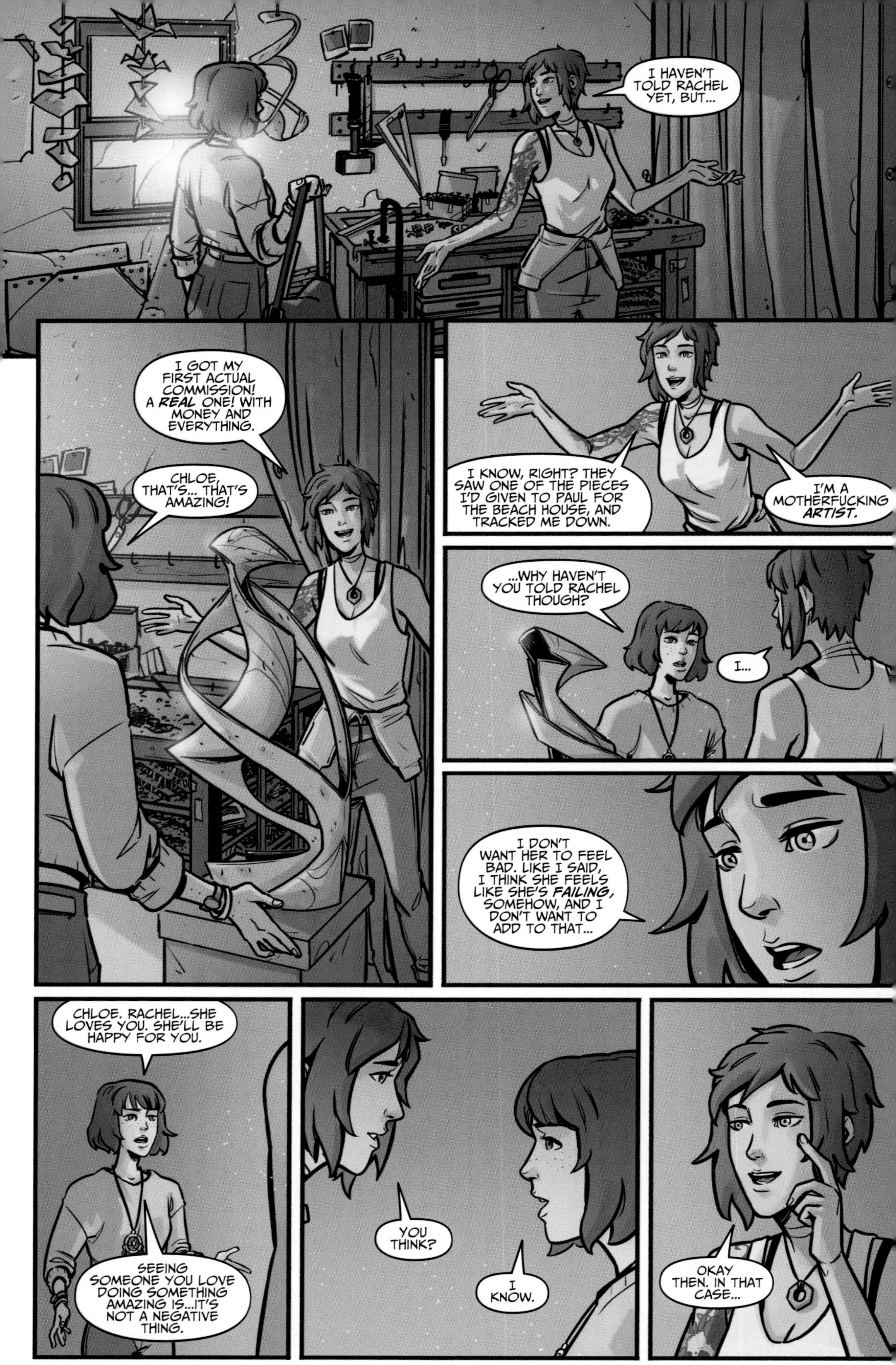
I HAVEN'T TOLD RACHEL YET, BUT...
I GOT MY FIRST ACTUAL COMMISSION! A *REAL* ONE! WITH MONEY AND EVERYTHING.
CHLOE, THAT'S... THAT'S AMAZING!
I KNOW, RIGHT? THEY SAW ONE OF THE PIECES I'D GIVEN TO PAUL FOR THE BEACH HOUSE, AND TRACKED ME DOWN.
I'M A MOTHERFUCKING *ARTIST.*
...WHY HAVEN'T YOU TOLD RACHEL THOUGH?
I...
I DON'T WANT HER TO FEEL BAD. LIKE I SAID, I THINK SHE FEELS LIKE SHE'S *FAILING,* SOMEHOW, AND I DON'T WANT TO ADD TO THAT...
CHLOE. RACHEL...SHE LOVES YOU. SHE'LL BE HAPPY FOR YOU.
SEEING SOMEONE YOU LOVE DOING SOMETHING AMAZING IS...IT'S NOT A NEGATIVE THING.
YOU THINK?
I KNOW.
OKAY THEN. IN THAT CASE...

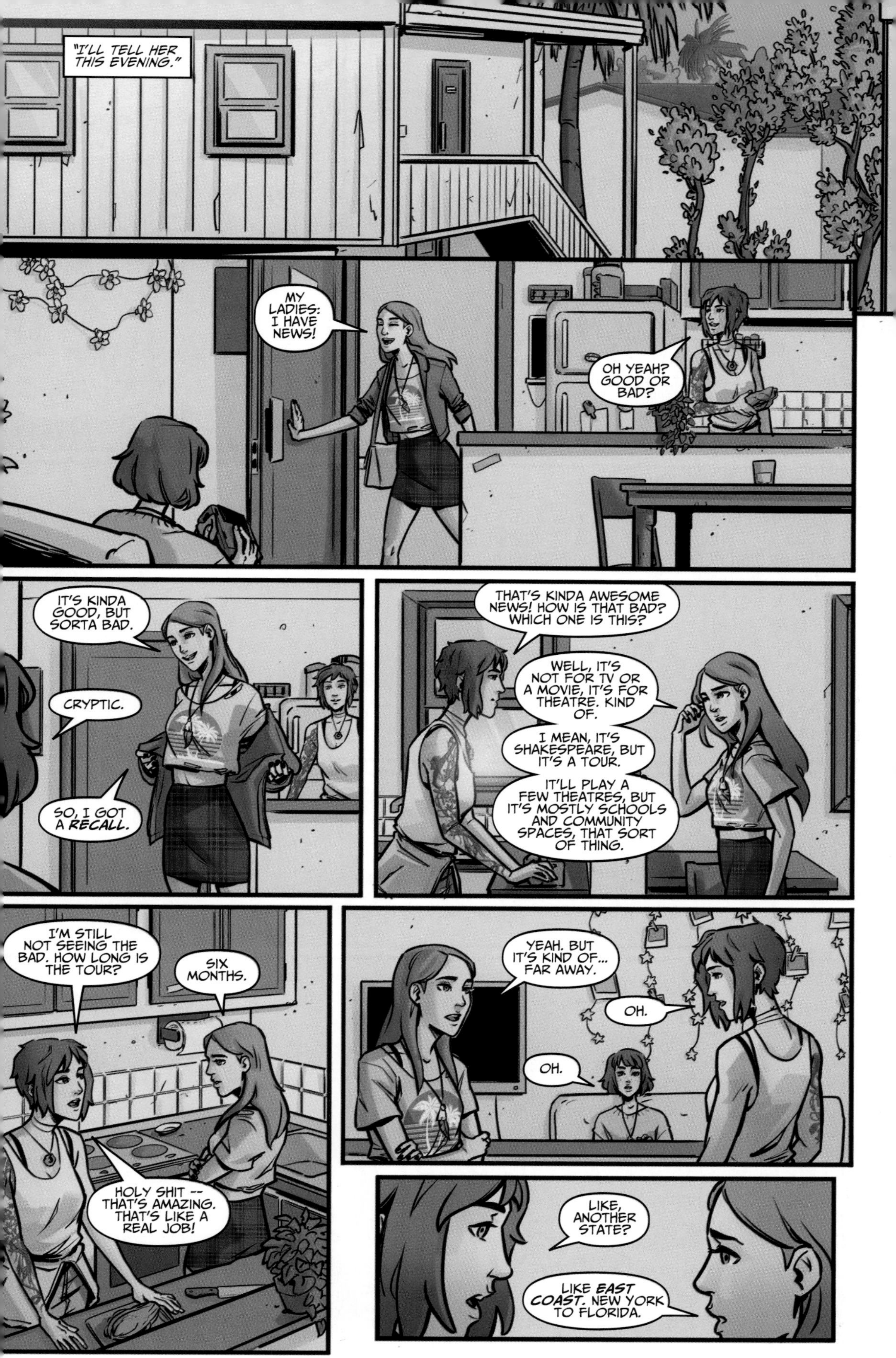
"I'LL TELL HER THIS EVENING."
MY LADIES: I HAVE NEWS!
OH YEAH? GOOD OR BAD?
IT'S KINDA GOOD, BUT SORTA BAD.
CRYPTIC.
SO, I GOT A **RECALL**.
THAT'S KINDA AWESOME NEWS! HOW IS THAT BAD? WHICH ONE IS THIS?
WELL, IT'S NOT FOR TV OR A MOVIE, IT'S FOR THEATRE. KIND OF.
I MEAN, IT'S SHAKESPEARE, BUT IT'S A TOUR.
IT'LL PLAY A FEW THEATRES, BUT IT'S MOSTLY SCHOOLS AND COMMUNITY SPACES, THAT SORT OF THING.
I'M STILL NOT SEEING THE BAD. HOW LONG IS THE TOUR?
SIX MONTHS.
HOLY SHIT -- THAT'S AMAZING. THAT'S LIKE A REAL JOB!
YEAH. BUT IT'S KIND OF... FAR AWAY.
OH.
OH.
LIKE, ANOTHER STATE?
LIKE **EAST COAST.** NEW YORK TO FLORIDA.

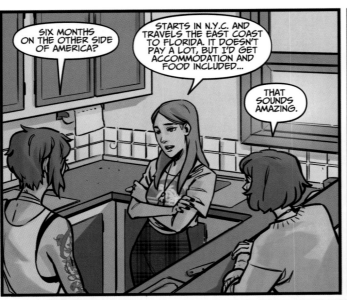

SIX MONTHS ON THE OTHER SIDE OF AMERICA?

STARTS IN N.Y.C. AND TRAVELS THE EAST COAST TO FLORIDA. IT DOESN'T PAY A LOT, BUT I'D GET ACCOMMODATION AND FOOD INCLUDED...

THAT SOUNDS AMAZING.

SIX MONTHS...

ON THE OTHER SIDE OF THE U.S., NOT THE *WORLD*. AND IT'S JUST SIX MONTHS.

PHONES EXIST. VIDEO CHAT EXISTS.

CHLOE -- I NEED THIS. I NEED TO TRY.

I GET THAT. BUT SO FAR AWAY? ALL WE DID TO GET HERE, TO BUILD LIVES HERE...

THIS WAS OUR NEW CHAPTER AND YOU'RE--

AND IT'S BEEN GREAT! AND IT'S STILL *GONNA* BE GREAT. A BOOK HAS A *LOT* OF CHAPTERS, CHLOE. THIS ISN'T ABOUT RUNNING *AWAY* FROM ANYTHING...

LEAST OF ALL YOU.

IT'S ABOUT MOVING *TOWARD* SOMETHING.

LOOK, YOU GUYS CAN'T IMAGINE WHAT IT'S LIKE TO FEEL THAT THERE'S ANOTHER LIFE OUT THERE YOU COULD BE LIVING AND IT'S... IT'S NOT HERE.

I CAN...

YOU ALREADY SAID YES TO THE RECALL, DIDN'T YOU.

...YEAH.

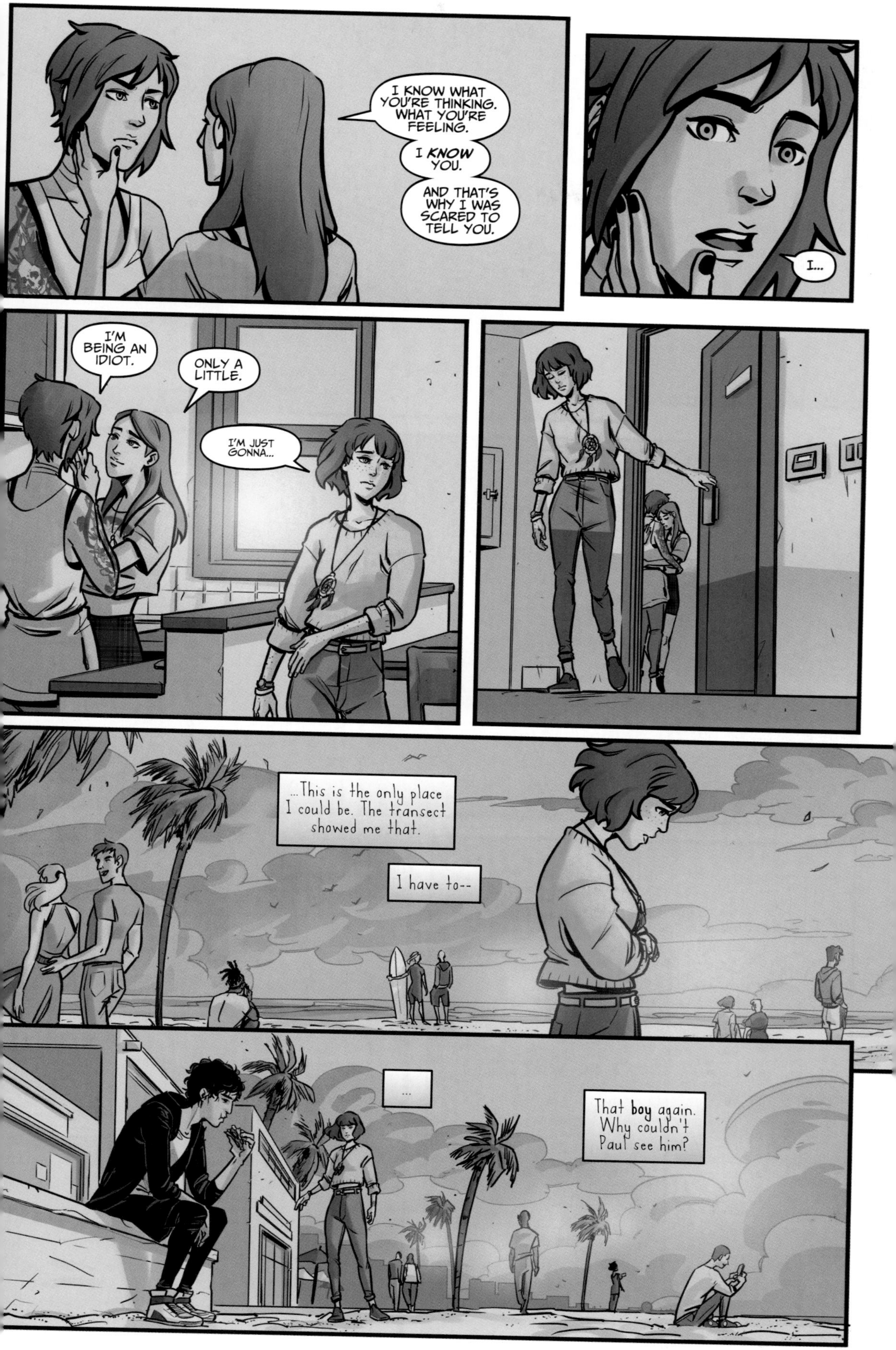
I KNOW WHAT YOU'RE THINKING. WHAT YOU'RE FEELING.
I KNOW YOU.
AND THAT'S WHY I WAS SCARED TO TELL YOU.
I...
I'M BEING AN IDIOT.
ONLY A LITTLE.
I'M JUST GONNA...
...This is the only place I could be. The transect showed me that.
I have to--
...
That boy again. Why couldn't Paul see him?

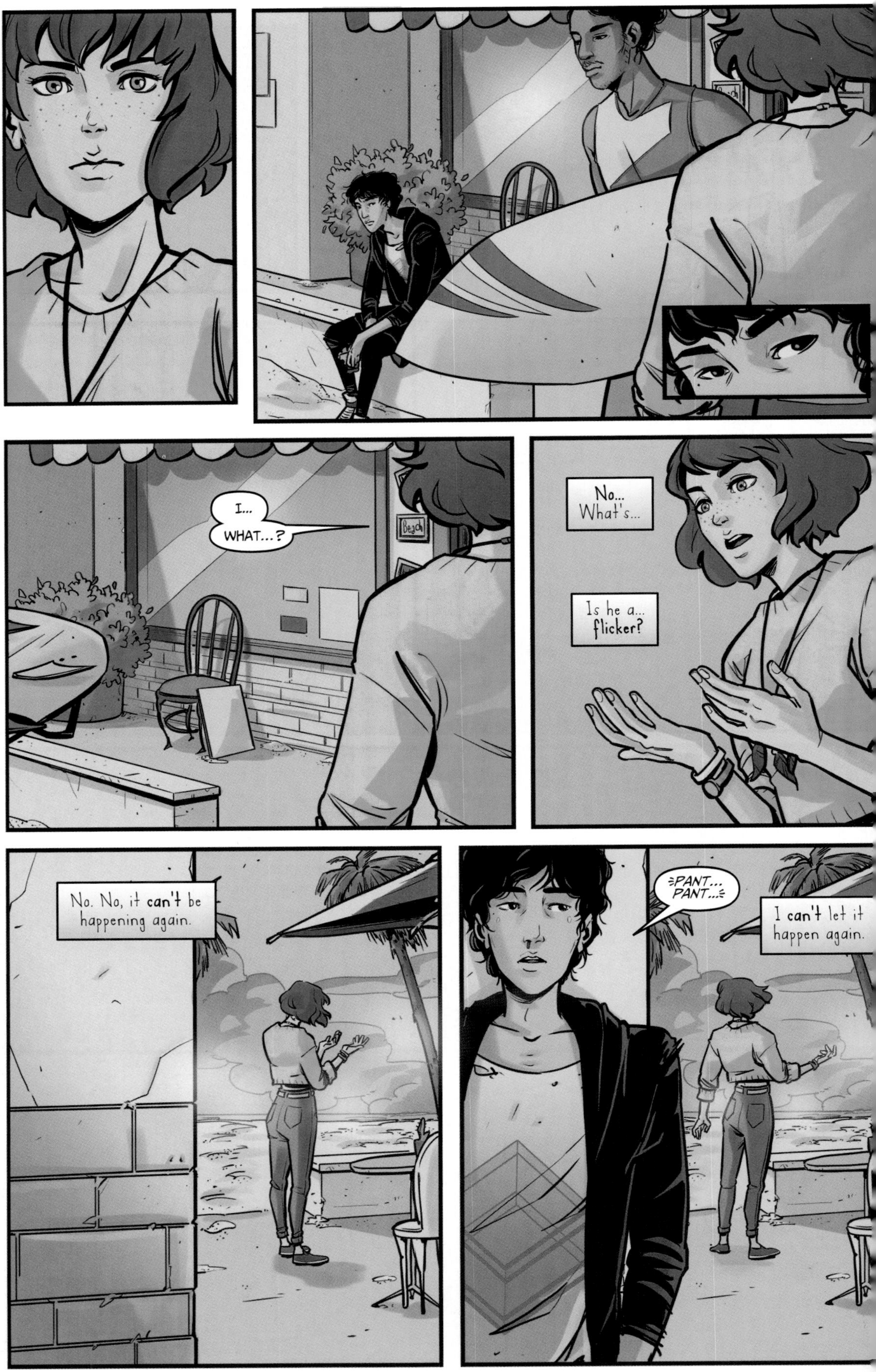
Beach
I...
WHAT...?
No...
What's...
Is he a...
flicker?
No. No, it can't be
happening again.
PANT...
PANT...
I can't let it
happen again.

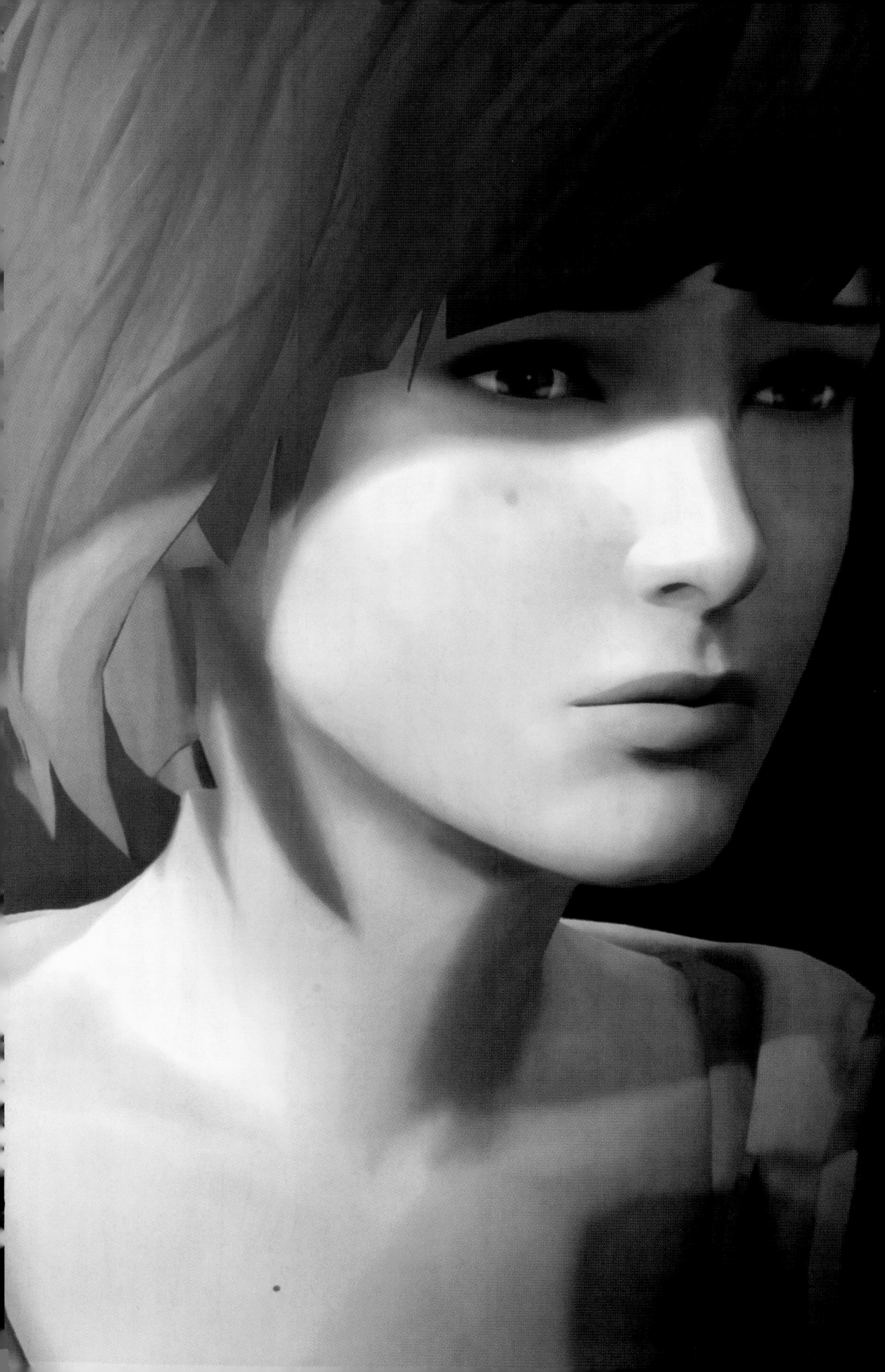

CHAPTER 2

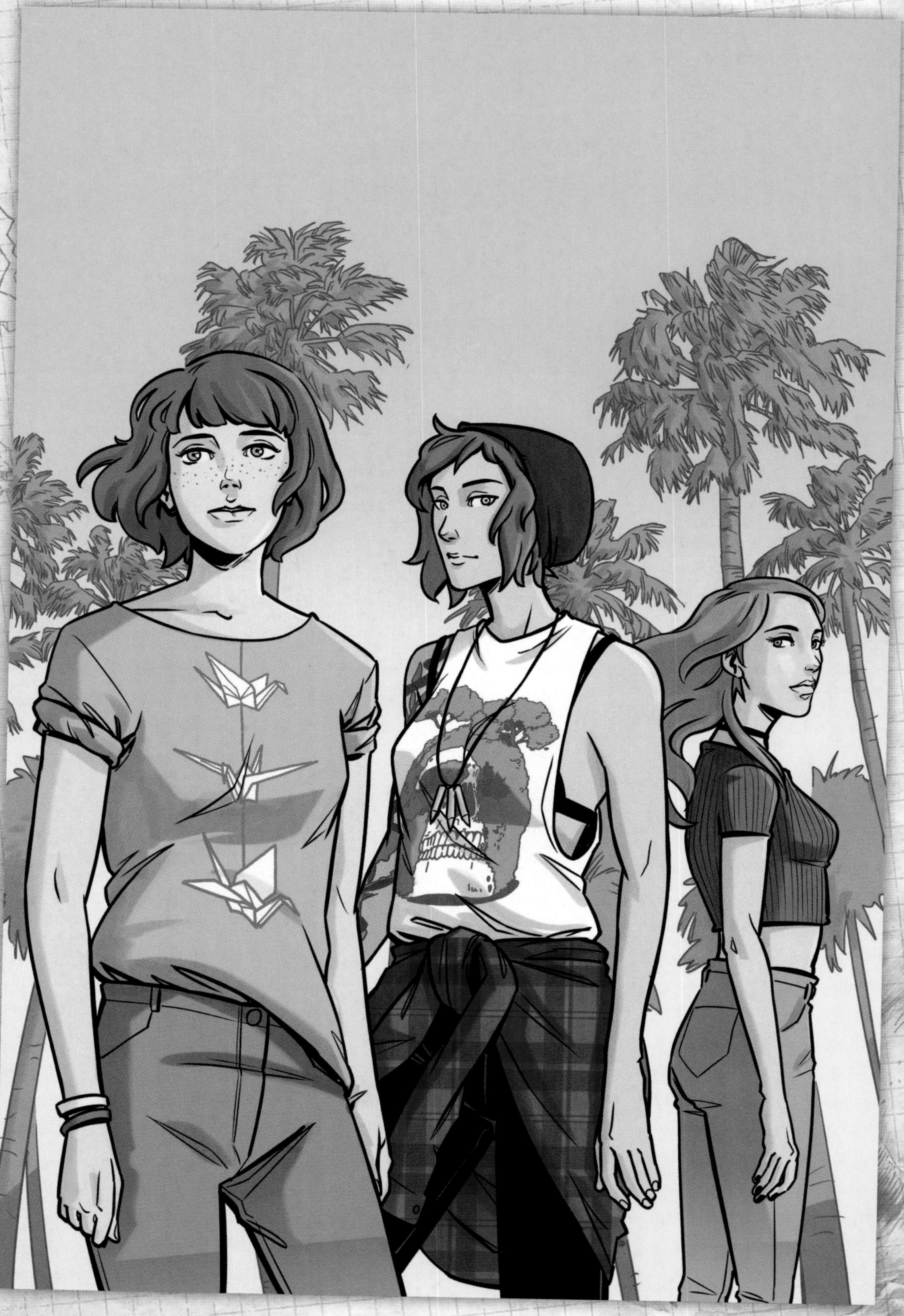

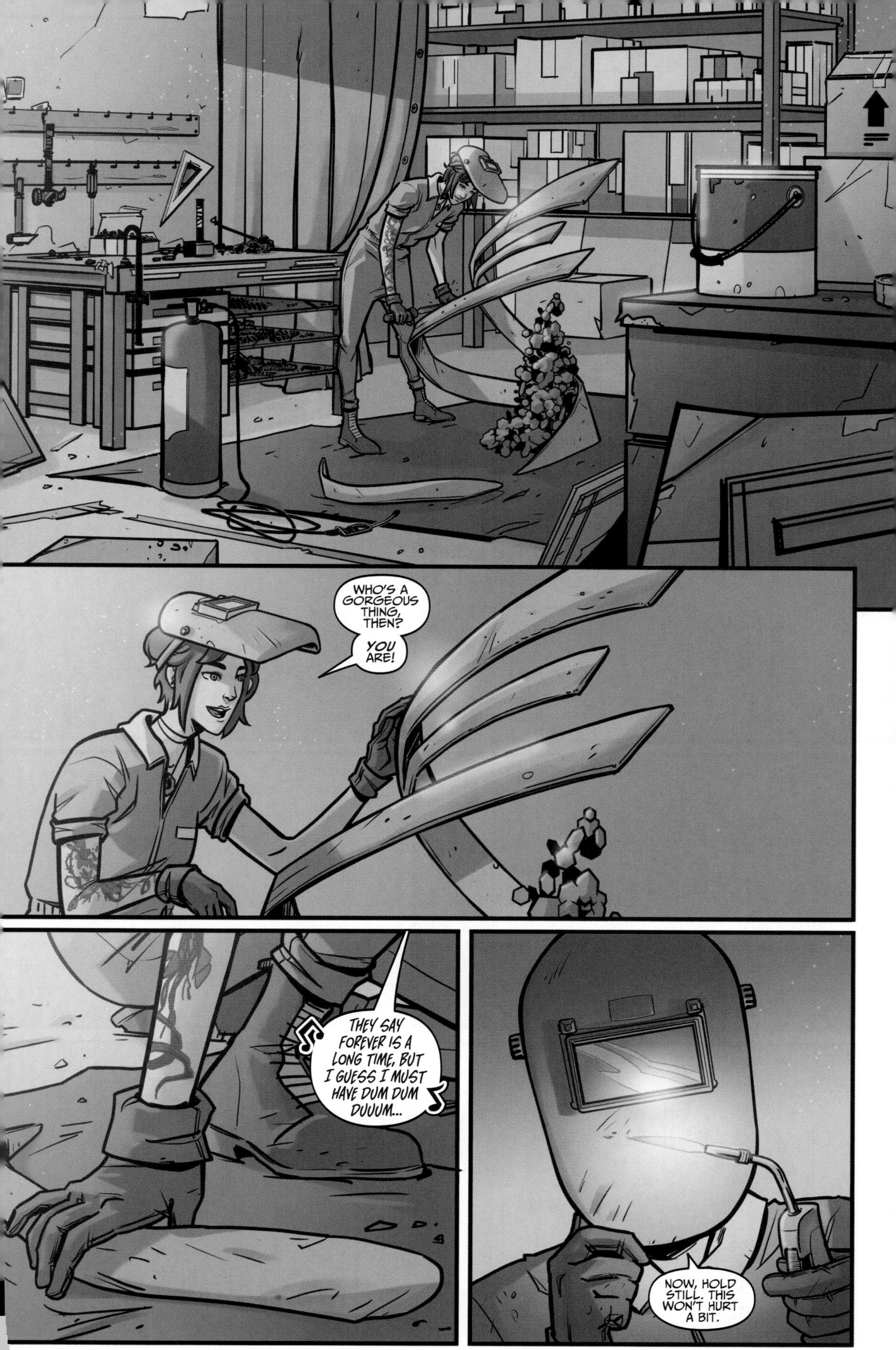
WHO'S A GORGEOUS THING, THEN?
YOU ARE!
THEY SAY FOREVER IS A LONG TIME, BUT I GUESS I MUST HAVE DUM DUM DUUUM...
NOW, HOLD STILL. THIS WON'T HURT A BIT.

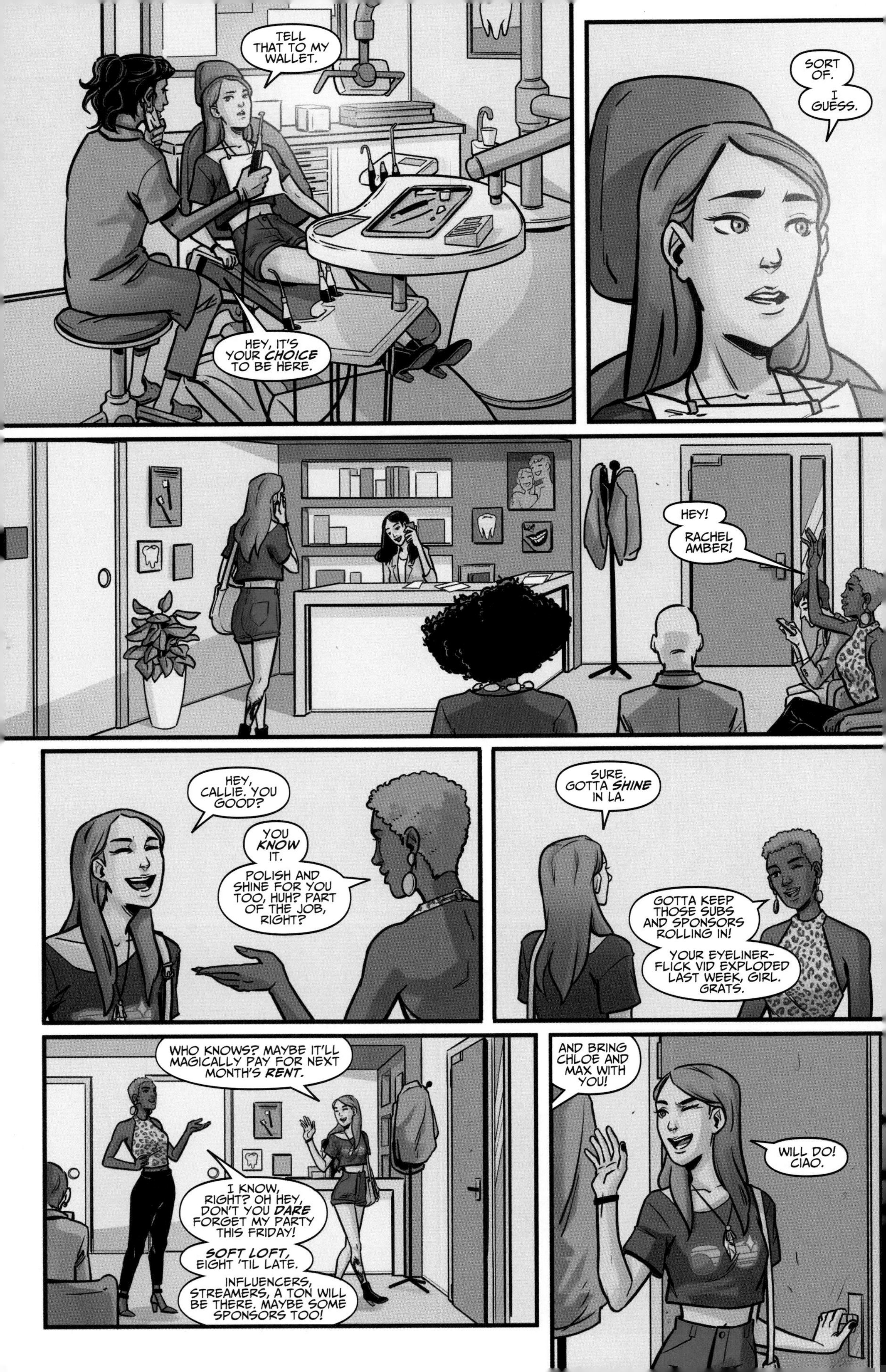
TELL THAT TO MY WALLET.
HEY, IT'S YOUR CHOICE TO BE HERE.
SORT OF.
I GUESS.
HEY!
RACHEL AMBER!
HEY, CALLIE. YOU GOOD?
YOU KNOW IT.
POLISH AND SHINE FOR YOU TOO, HUH? PART OF THE JOB, RIGHT?
SURE. GOTTA SHINE IN LA.
GOTTA KEEP THOSE SUBS AND SPONSORS ROLLING IN!
YOUR EYELINER-FLICK VID EXPLODED LAST WEEK, GIRL. GRATS.
WHO KNOWS? MAYBE IT'LL MAGICALLY PAY FOR NEXT MONTH'S RENT.
I KNOW, RIGHT? OH HEY, DON'T YOU DARE FORGET MY PARTY THIS FRIDAY!
SOFT LOFT, EIGHT 'TIL LATE.
INFLUENCERS, STREAMERS, A TON WILL BE THERE. MAYBE SOME SPONSORS TOO!
AND BRING CHLOE AND MAX WITH YOU!
WILL DO! CIAO.

HEY.

I THINK YOU KNOW THERE'S NO WAY I'M GOING *NEAR* THAT PARTY.

THE WAY I FEEL RECENTLY, I'M NOT SURE I'LL BE GOING EITHER, DON'T WORRY.

I'M EXHAUSTED FROM THE EFFORT, HONESTLY.

AREN'T SOME OF THEM YOUR FRIENDS?

THE WORD *FRIEND* GETS PRETTY COMPLICATED IN THAT CIRCLE.

IN A DIFFERENT LIFE, I THINK I'D STILL BE VERY MUCH ONE OF THEM.

AS IT IS, I FEEL LESS AND LESS LIKE I *BELONG* IN THAT WORLD.

HMM.

SO, WHAT CHANGED?

HONESTLY?

...CHLOE.

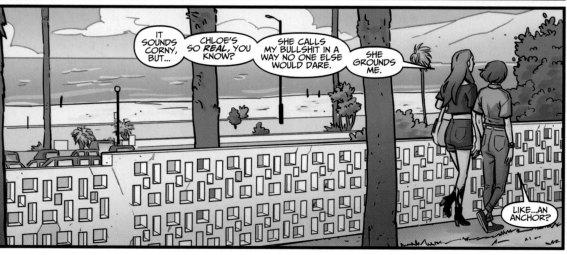

IT SOUNDS CORNY, BUT...

CHLOE'S SO *REAL*, YOU KNOW?

SHE CALLS MY BULLSHIT IN A WAY NO ONE ELSE WOULD DARE.

SHE GROUNDS ME.

LIKE...AN ANCHOR?

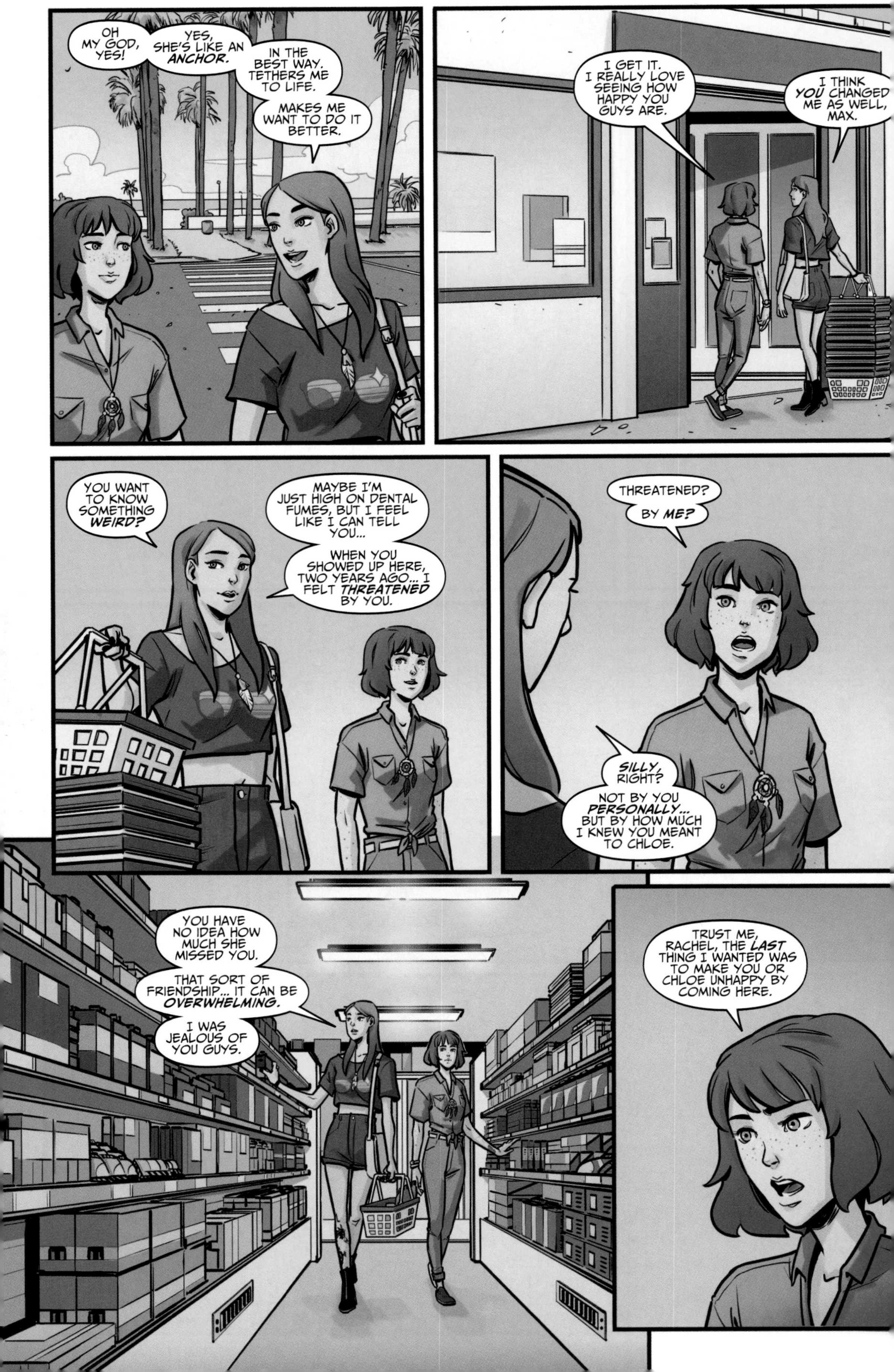
OH MY GOD, YES!
YES, SHE'S LIKE AN ***ANCHOR.***
IN THE BEST WAY. TETHERS ME TO LIFE.
MAKES ME WANT TO DO IT BETTER.
I GET IT. I REALLY LOVE SEEING HOW HAPPY YOU GUYS ARE.
I THINK ***YOU*** CHANGED ME AS WELL, MAX.
YOU WANT TO KNOW SOMETHING ***WEIRD?***
MAYBE I'M JUST HIGH ON DENTAL FUMES, BUT I FEEL LIKE I CAN TELL YOU...
WHEN YOU SHOWED UP HERE, TWO YEARS AGO... I FELT ***THREATENED*** BY YOU.
THREATENED?
BY ***ME?***
SILLY, RIGHT?
NOT BY YOU ***PERSONALLY...*** BUT BY HOW MUCH I KNEW YOU MEANT TO CHLOE.
YOU HAVE NO IDEA HOW MUCH SHE MISSED YOU.
THAT SORT OF FRIENDSHIP... IT CAN BE ***OVERWHELMING.***
I WAS JEALOUS OF YOU GUYS.
TRUST ME, RACHEL, THE ***LAST*** THING I WANTED WAS TO MAKE YOU OR CHLOE UNHAPPY BY COMING HERE.

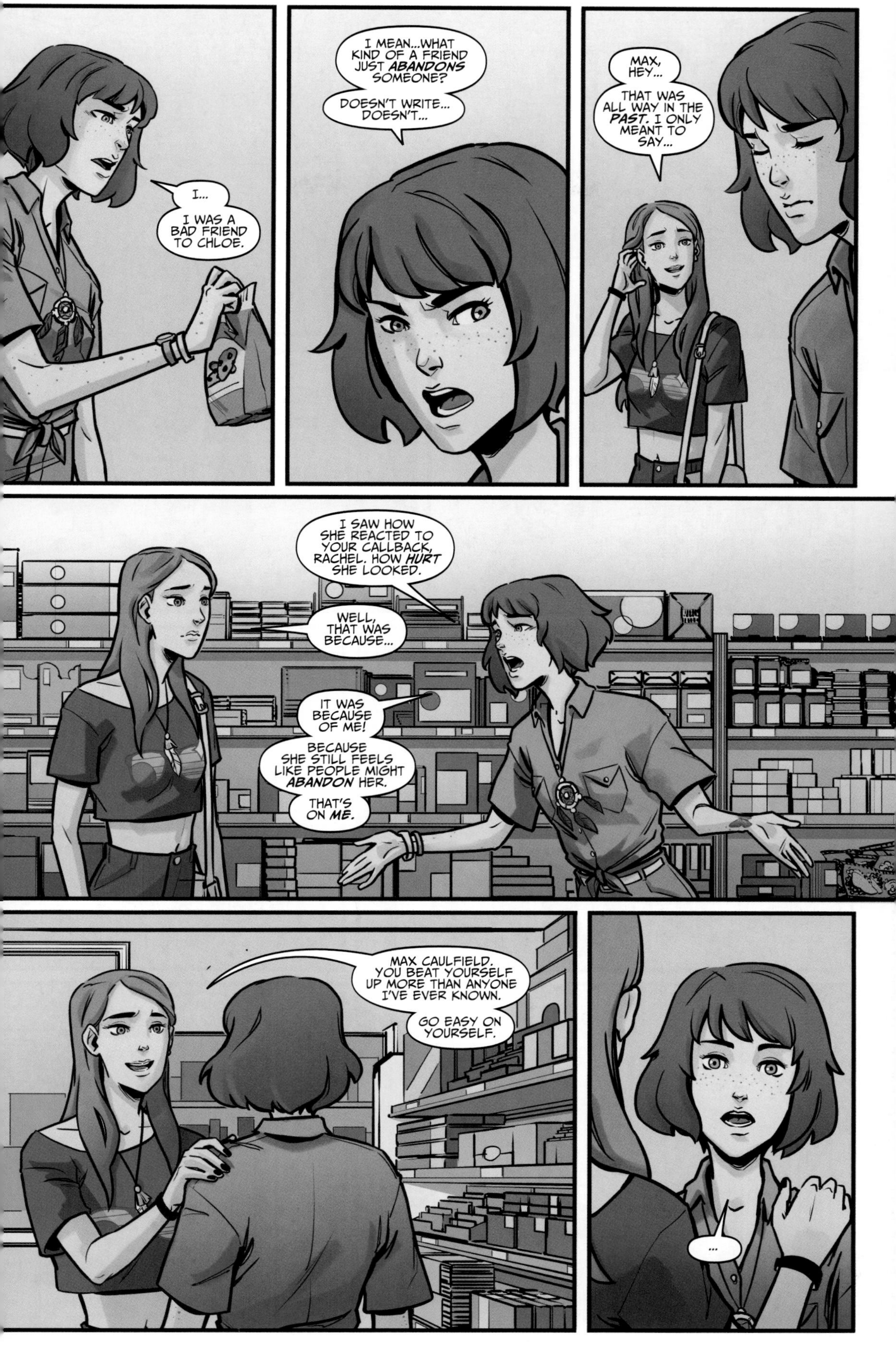
I...
I WAS A BAD FRIEND TO CHLOE.
I MEAN...WHAT KIND OF A FRIEND JUST ABANDONS SOMEONE?
DOESN'T WRITE... DOESN'T...
MAX, HEY...
THAT WAS ALL WAY IN THE PAST. I ONLY MEANT TO SAY...
I SAW HOW SHE REACTED TO YOUR CALLBACK, RACHEL. HOW HURT SHE LOOKED.
WELL, THAT WAS BECAUSE...
IT WAS BECAUSE OF ME!
BECAUSE SHE STILL FEELS LIKE PEOPLE MIGHT ABANDON HER.
THAT'S ON ME.
MAX CAULFIELD. YOU BEAT YOURSELF UP MORE THAN ANYONE I'VE EVER KNOWN.
GO EASY ON YOURSELF.
...

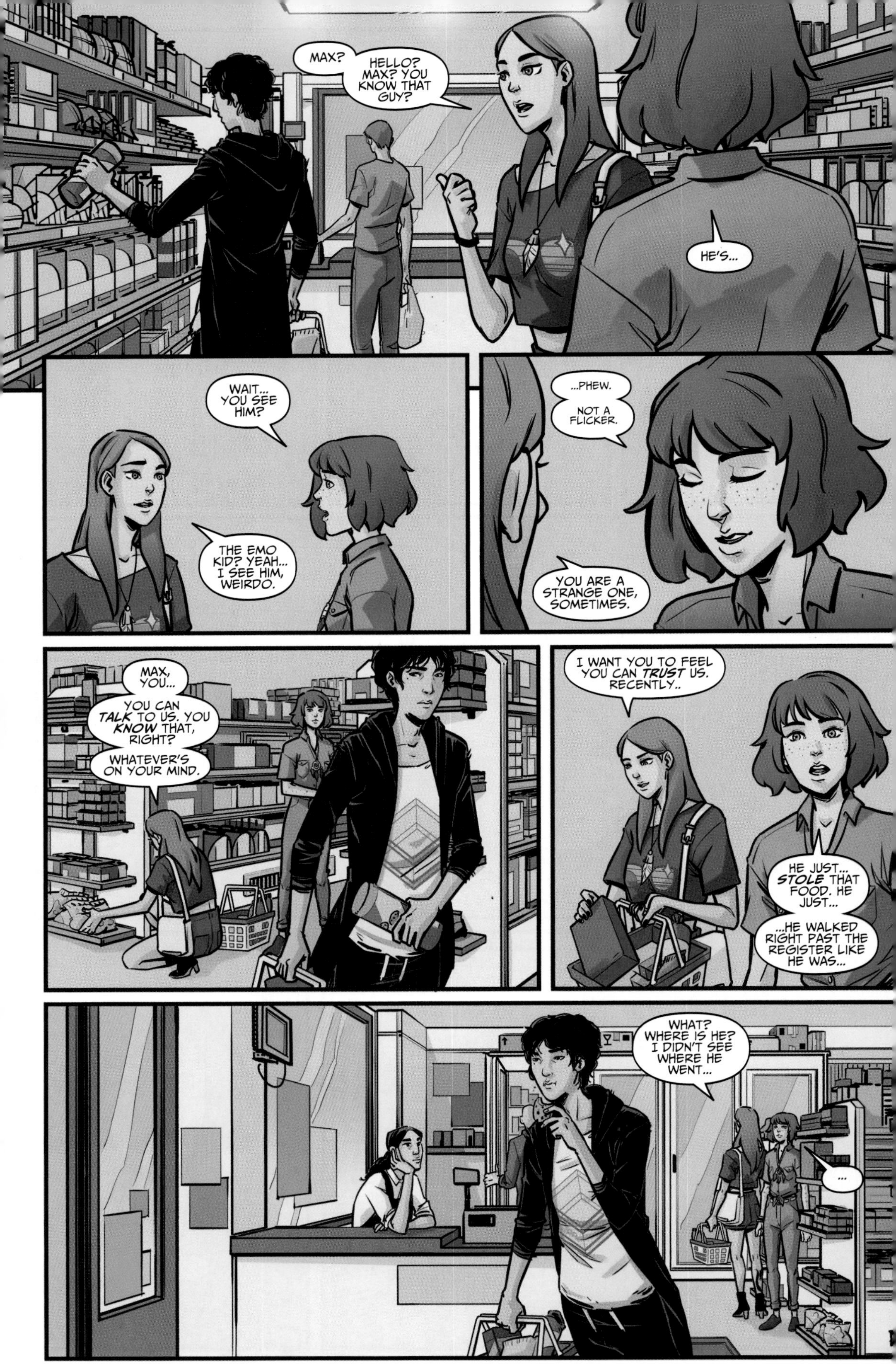
MAX?
HELLO? MAX? YOU KNOW THAT GUY?
HE'S...
WAIT... YOU SEE HIM?
THE EMO KID? YEAH... I SEE HIM, WEIRDO.
...PHEW.
NOT A FLICKER.
YOU ARE A STRANGE ONE, SOMETIMES.
MAX, YOU...
YOU CAN TALK TO US. YOU KNOW THAT, RIGHT?
WHATEVER'S ON YOUR MIND.
I WANT YOU TO FEEL YOU CAN TRUST US. RECENTLY..
HE JUST... STOLE THAT FOOD. HE JUST...
...HE WALKED RIGHT PAST THE REGISTER LIKE HE WAS...
WHAT? WHERE IS HE? I DIDN'T SEE WHERE HE WENT...
...

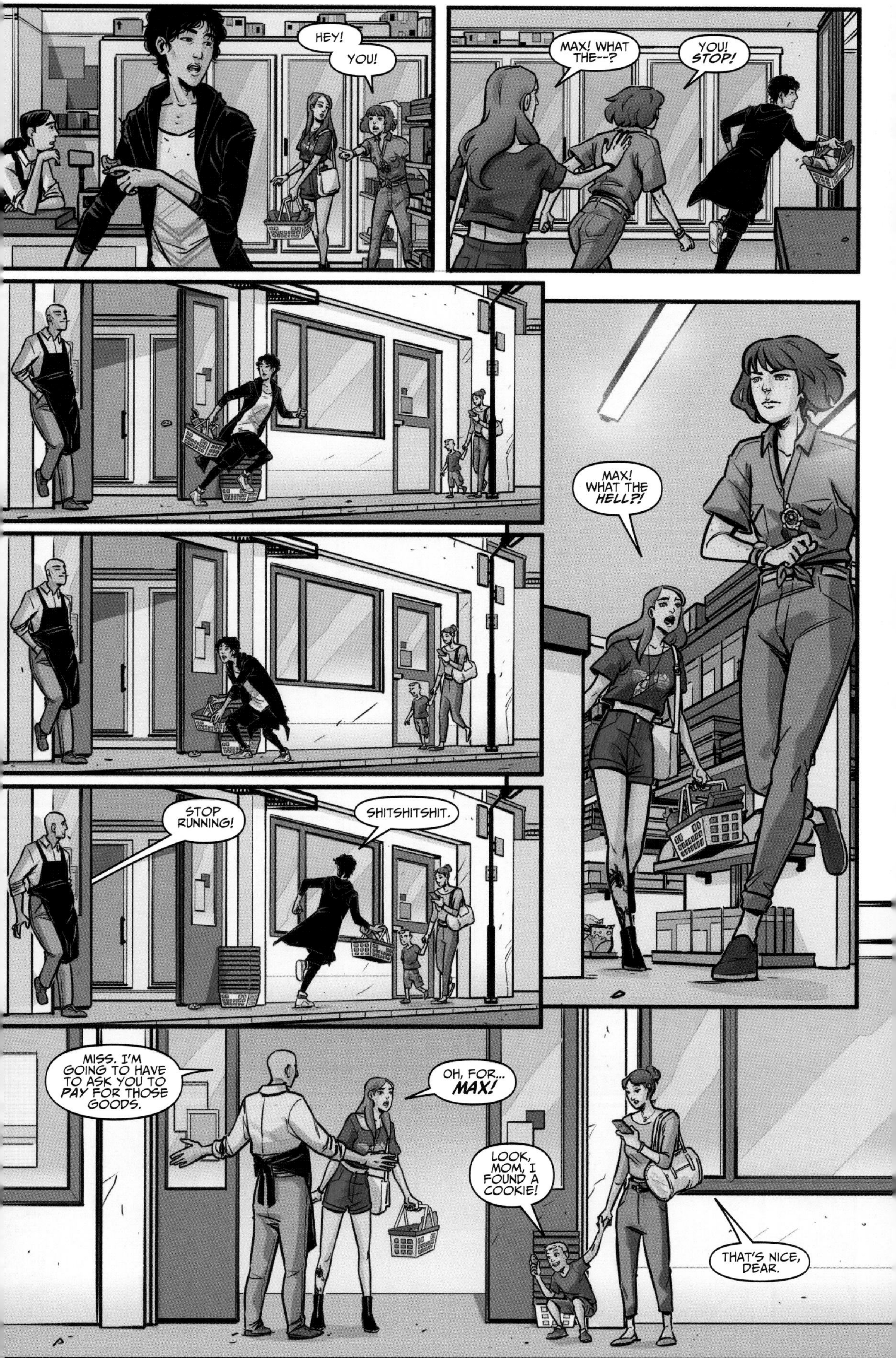
HEY!
YOU!
MAX! WHAT THE--?
YOU! STOP!
MAX! WHAT THE HELL?!
STOP RUNNING!
SHITSHITSHIT.
MISS. I'M GOING TO HAVE TO ASK YOU TO PAY FOR THOSE GOODS.
OH, FOR... MAX!
LOOK, MOM, I FOUND A COOKIE!
THAT'S NICE, DEAR.

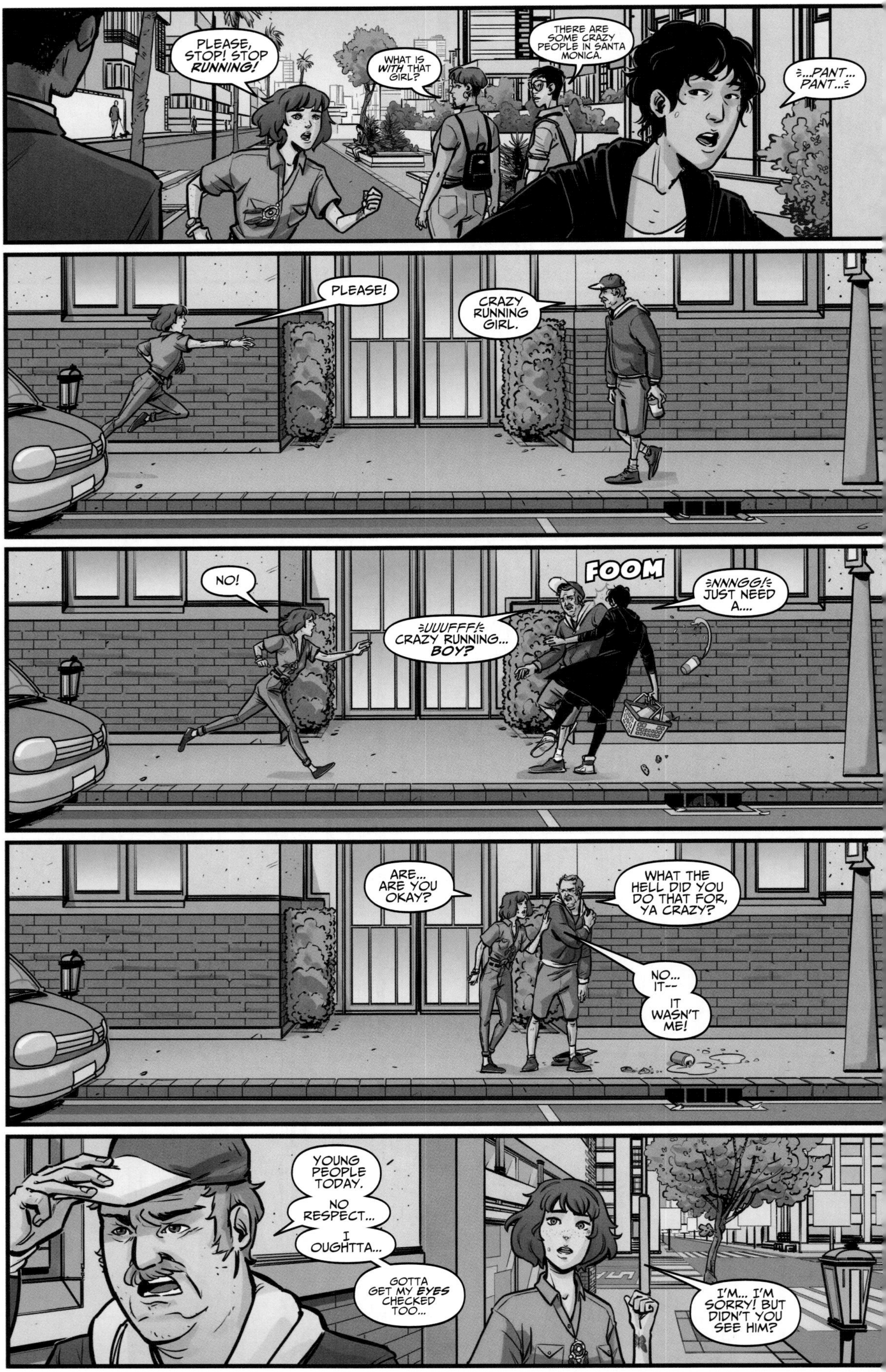

PLEASE, STOP! STOP RUNNING!
WHAT IS WITH THAT GIRL?
THERE ARE SOME CRAZY PEOPLE IN SANTA MONICA.
...PANT... PANT...
PLEASE!
CRAZY RUNNING GIRL.
NO!
FOOM
UUUFFF! CRAZY RUNNING... BOY?
NNNGG! JUST NEED A....
ARE... ARE YOU OKAY?
WHAT THE HELL DID YOU DO THAT FOR, YA CRAZY?
NO... IT--
IT WASN'T ME!
YOUNG PEOPLE TODAY.
NO RESPECT...
I OUGHTTA...
GOTTA GET MY EYES CHECKED TOO...
I'M... I'M SORRY! BUT DIDN'T YOU SEE HIM?

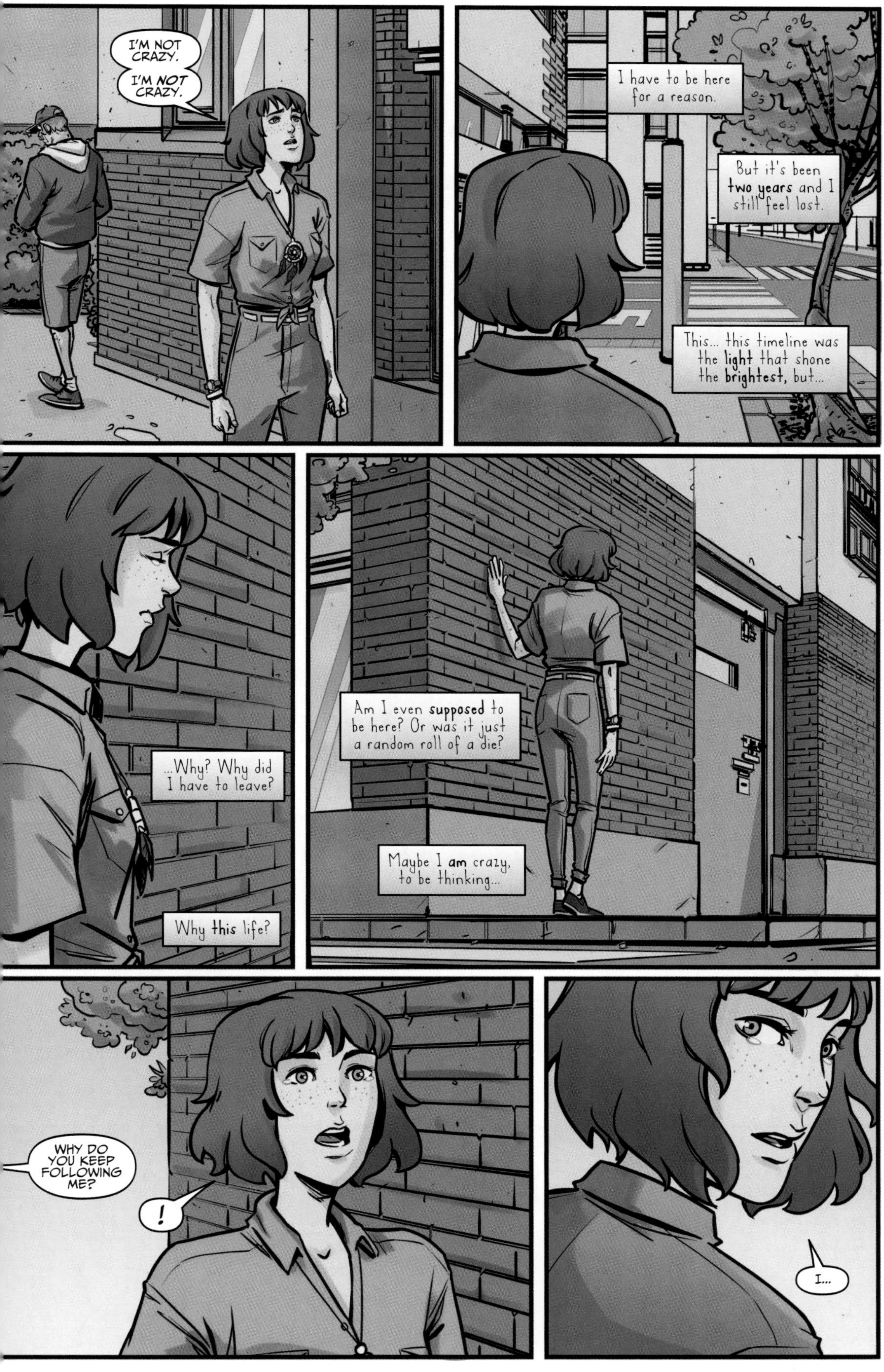
I'M NOT CRAZY.
I'M NOT CRAZY.
I have to be here for a reason.
But it's been two years and I still feel lost.
This... this timeline was the light that shone the brightest, but...
...Why? Why did I have to leave?
Why this life?
Am I even supposed to be here? Or was it just a random roll of a die?
Maybe I am crazy, to be thinking...
WHY DO YOU KEEP FOLLOWING ME?
!
I...

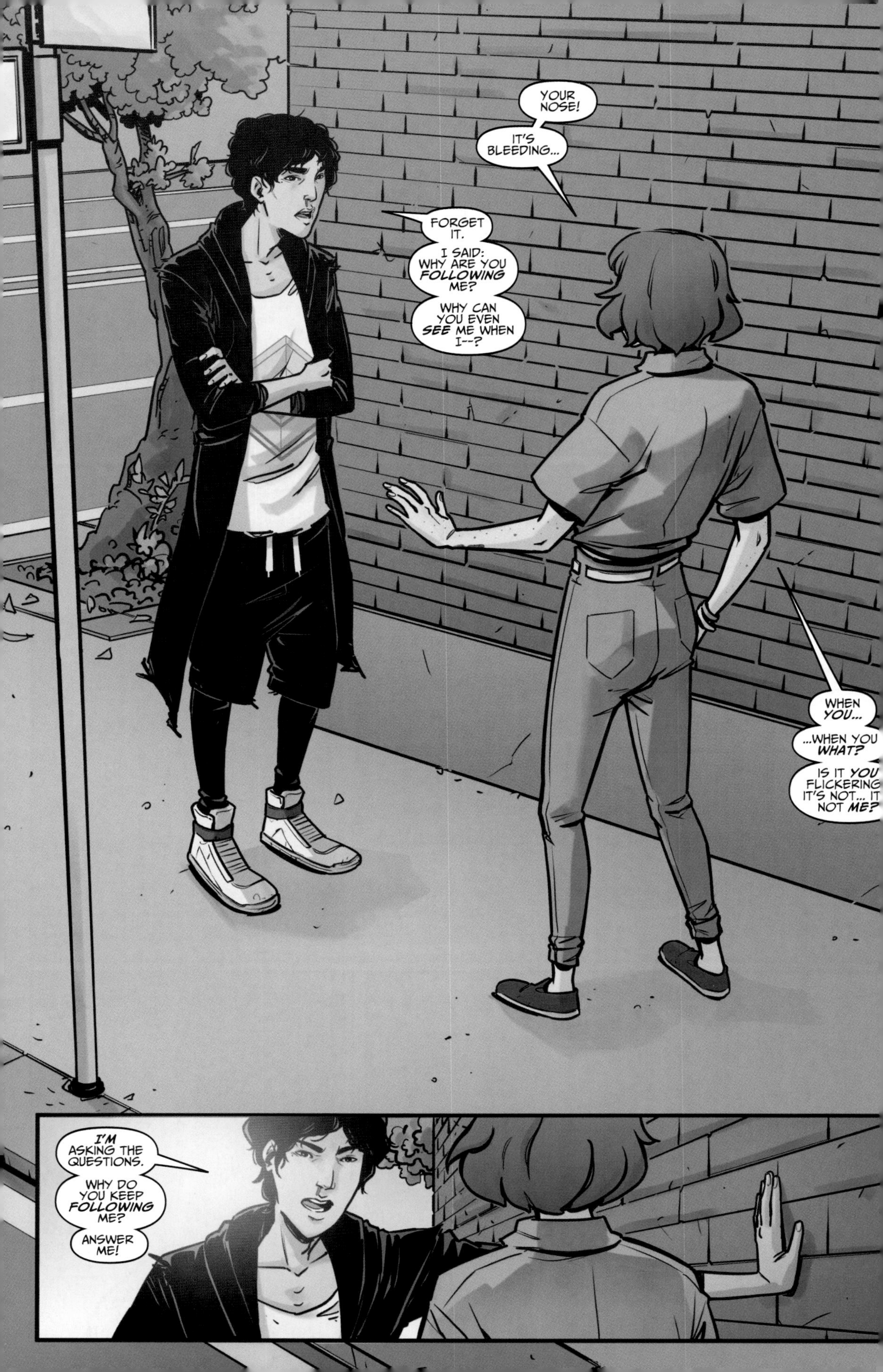
YOUR NOSE!
IT'S BLEEDING...
FORGET IT.
I SAID: WHY ARE YOU FOLLOWING ME?
WHY CAN YOU EVEN SEE ME WHEN I--?
WHEN YOU...
...WHEN YOU WHAT?
IS IT YOU FLICKERING IT'S NOT... IT NOT ME?
I'M ASKING THE QUESTIONS.
WHY DO YOU KEEP FOLLOWING ME?
ANSWER ME!

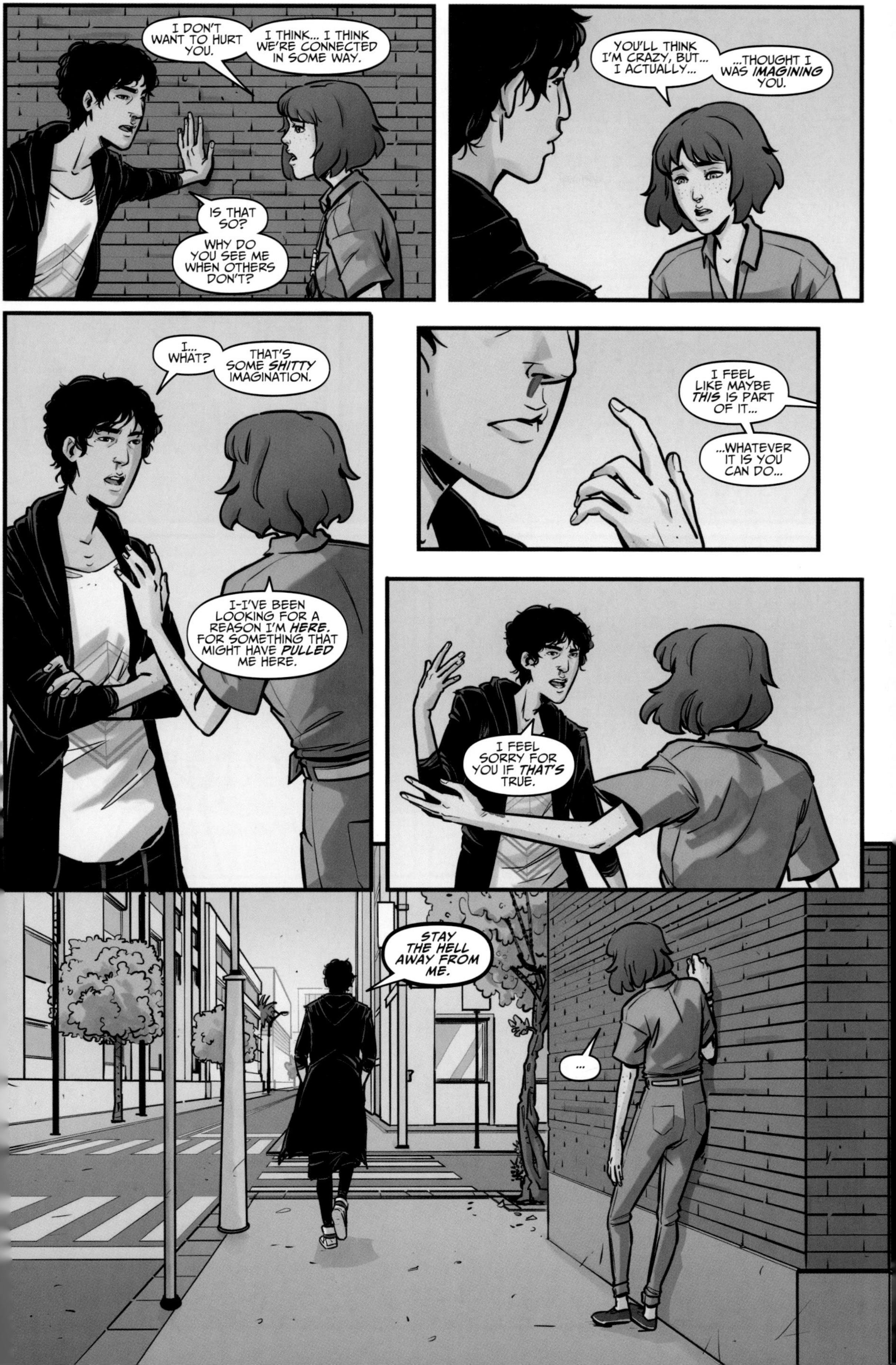

I DON'T WANT TO HURT YOU.
I THINK... I THINK WE'RE CONNECTED IN SOME WAY.
IS THAT SO?
WHY DO YOU SEE ME WHEN OTHERS DON'T?
YOU'LL THINK I'M CRAZY, BUT... I ACTUALLY...
...THOUGHT I WAS *IMAGINING* YOU.
I... WHAT?
THAT'S SOME *SHITTY* IMAGINATION.
I-I'VE BEEN LOOKING FOR A REASON I'M *HERE*. FOR SOMETHING THAT MIGHT HAVE *PULLED* ME HERE.
I FEEL LIKE MAYBE *THIS* IS PART OF IT...
...WHATEVER IT IS YOU CAN DO...
I FEEL SORRY FOR YOU IF *THAT'S* TRUE.
STAY THE HELL AWAY FROM ME.
...

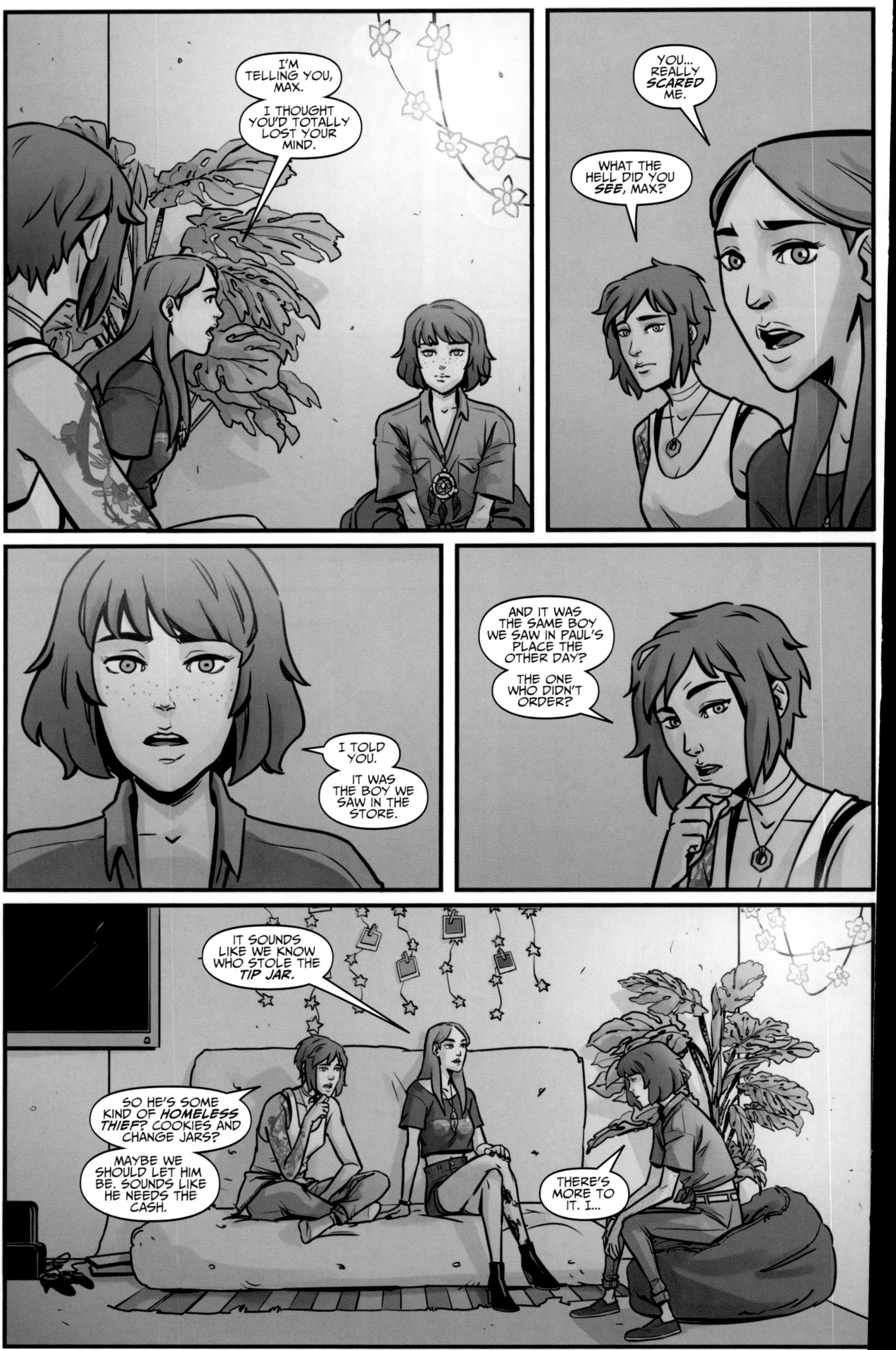
I'M TELLING YOU, MAX.
I THOUGHT YOU'D TOTALLY LOST YOUR MIND.
YOU... REALLY *SCARED* ME.
WHAT THE HELL DID YOU *SEE*, MAX?
I TOLD YOU.
IT WAS THE BOY WE SAW IN THE STORE.
AND IT WAS THE SAME BOY WE SAW IN PAUL'S PLACE THE OTHER DAY?
THE ONE WHO DIDN'T ORDER?
IT SOUNDS LIKE WE KNOW WHO STOLE THE *TIP JAR.*
SO HE'S SOME KIND OF *HOMELESS THIEF*? COOKIES AND CHANGE JARS?
MAYBE WE SHOULD LET HIM BE. SOUNDS LIKE HE NEEDS THE CASH.
THERE'S MORE TO IT. I...

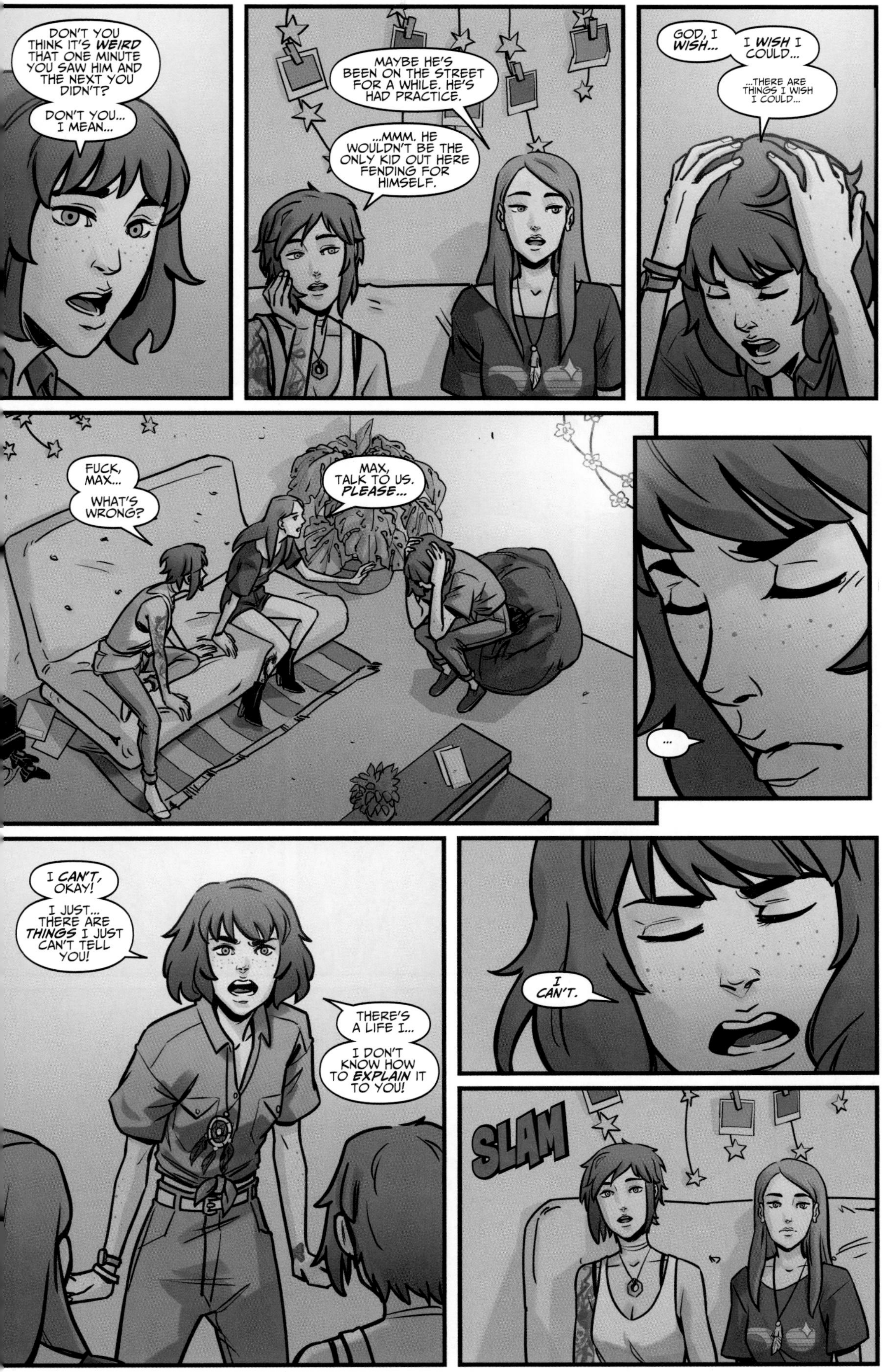
DON'T YOU THINK IT'S WEIRD THAT ONE MINUTE YOU SAW HIM AND THE NEXT YOU DIDN'T?
DON'T YOU... I MEAN...
MAYBE HE'S BEEN ON THE STREET FOR A WHILE. HE'S HAD PRACTICE.
...MMM. HE WOULDN'T BE THE ONLY KID OUT HERE FENDING FOR HIMSELF.
GOD, I WISH...
I WISH I COULD...
...THERE ARE THINGS I WISH I COULD...
FUCK, MAX...
WHAT'S WRONG?
MAX, TALK TO US. PLEASE...
...
I CAN'T, OKAY!
I JUST... THERE ARE THINGS I JUST CAN'T TELL YOU!
THERE'S A LIFE I...
I DON'T KNOW HOW TO EXPLAIN IT TO YOU!
I CAN'T.
SLAM

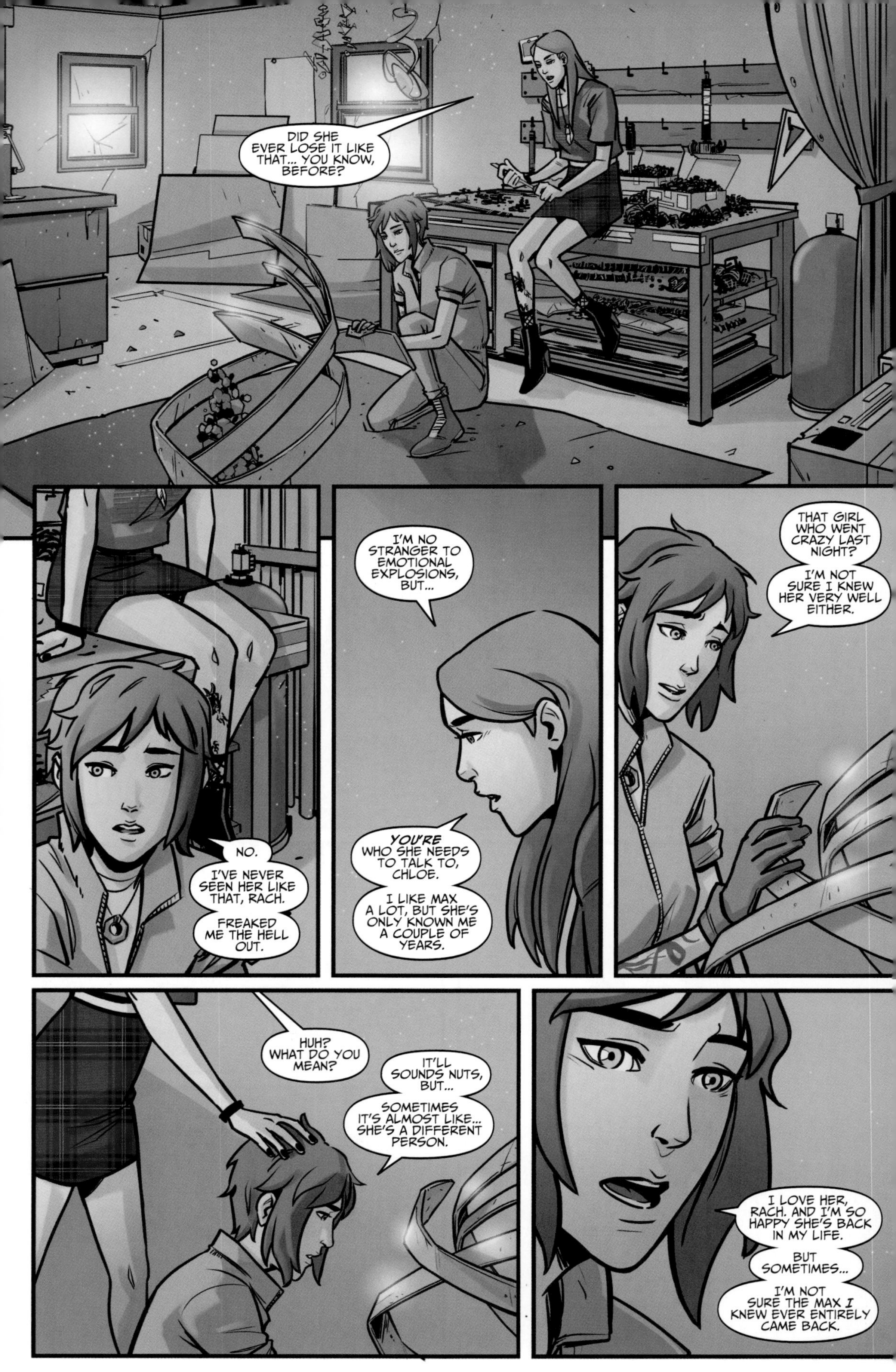

DID SHE EVER LOSE IT LIKE THAT... YOU KNOW, BEFORE?
NO.
I'VE NEVER SEEN HER LIKE THAT, RACH.
FREAKED ME THE HELL OUT.
I'M NO STRANGER TO EMOTIONAL EXPLOSIONS, BUT...
YOU'RE WHO SHE NEEDS TO TALK TO, CHLOE.
I LIKE MAX A LOT, BUT SHE'S ONLY KNOWN ME A COUPLE OF YEARS.
THAT GIRL WHO WENT CRAZY LAST NIGHT?
I'M NOT SURE I KNEW HER VERY WELL EITHER.
HUH? WHAT DO YOU MEAN?
IT'LL SOUNDS NUTS, BUT...
SOMETIMES IT'S ALMOST LIKE... SHE'S A DIFFERENT PERSON.
I LOVE HER, RACH. AND I'M SO HAPPY SHE'S BACK IN MY LIFE.
BUT SOMETIMES...
I'M NOT SURE THE MAX *I* KNEW EVER ENTIRELY CAME BACK.

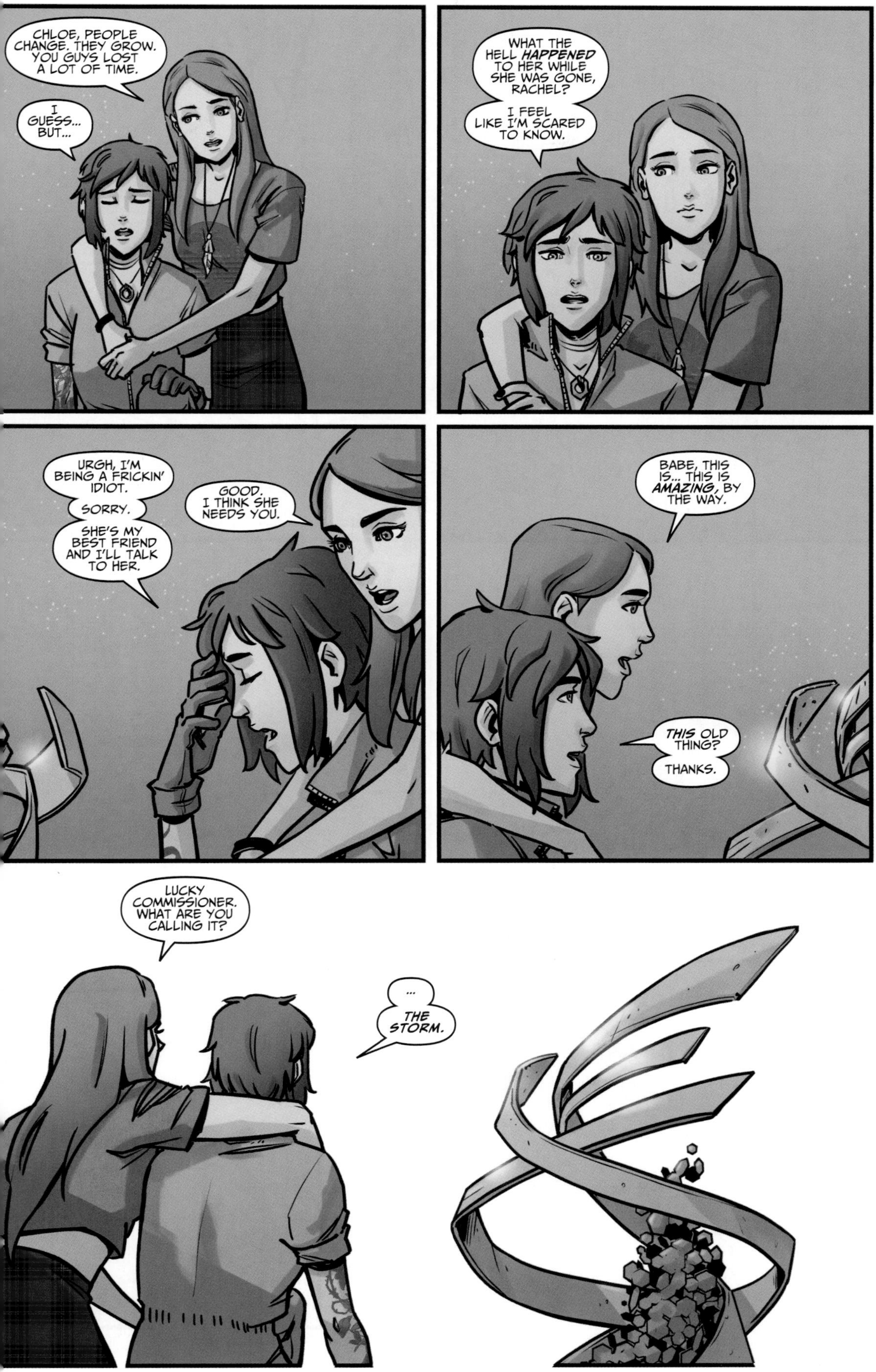
CHLOE, PEOPLE CHANGE. THEY GROW. YOU GUYS LOST A LOT OF TIME.
I GUESS... BUT...
WHAT THE HELL HAPPENED TO HER WHILE SHE WAS GONE, RACHEL?
I FEEL LIKE I'M SCARED TO KNOW.
URGH, I'M BEING A FRICKIN' IDIOT.
SORRY.
SHE'S MY BEST FRIEND AND I'LL TALK TO HER.
GOOD. I THINK SHE NEEDS YOU.
BABE, THIS IS... THIS IS AMAZING, BY THE WAY.
THIS OLD THING?
THANKS.
LUCKY COMMISSIONER. WHAT ARE YOU CALLING IT?
...
THE STORM.

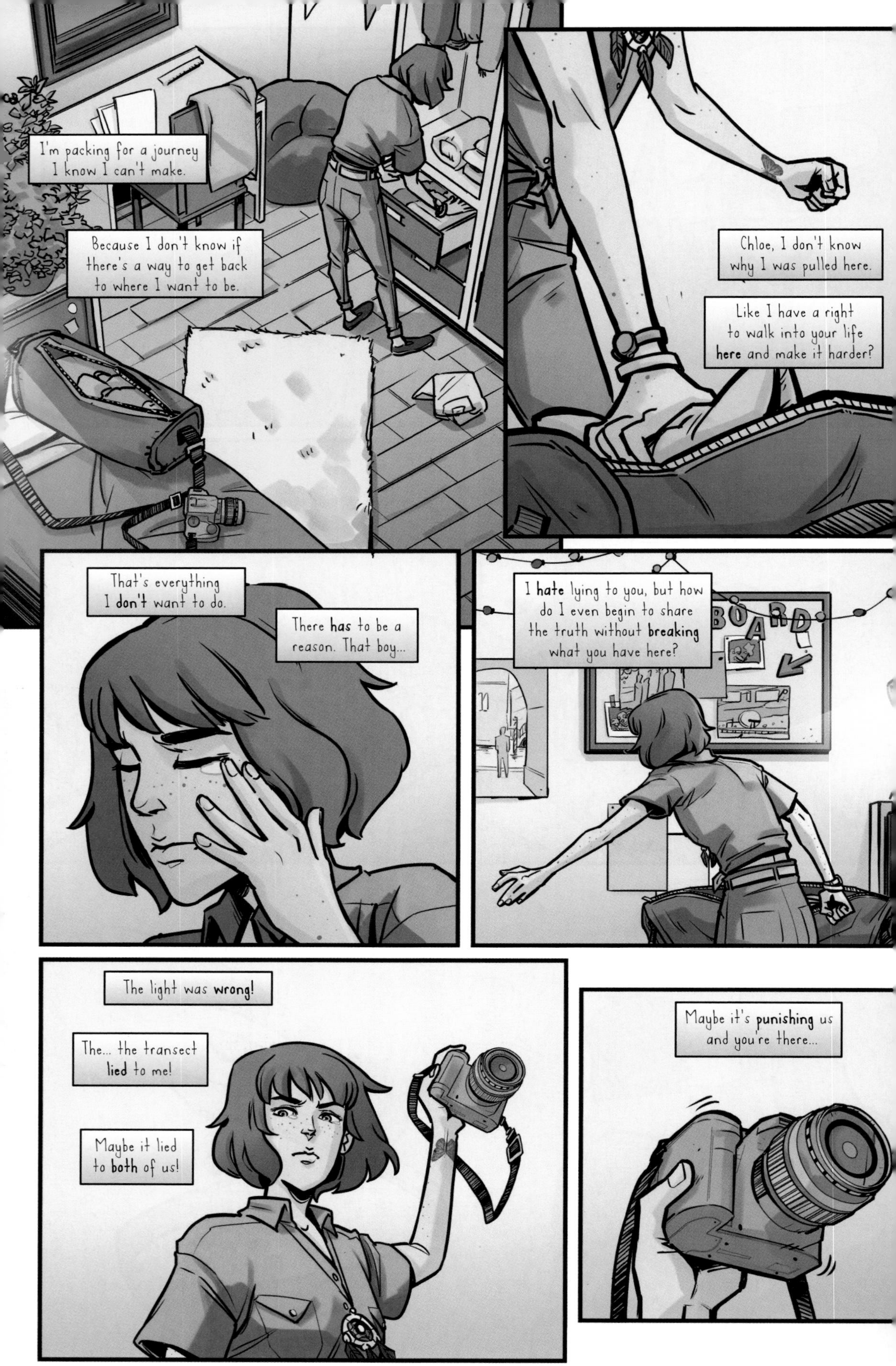
I'm packing for a journey I know I can't make.
Because I don't know if there's a way to get back to where I want to be.
Chloe, I don't know why I was pulled here.
Like I have a right to walk into your life **here** and make it harder?
That's everything I **don't** want to do.
There **has** to be a reason. That boy...
I **hate** lying to you, but how do I even begin to share the truth without **breaking** what you have here?
BOARD
The light was **wrong**!
The... the transect **lied** to me!
Maybe it lied to **both** of us!
Maybe it's **punishing** us and you're there...

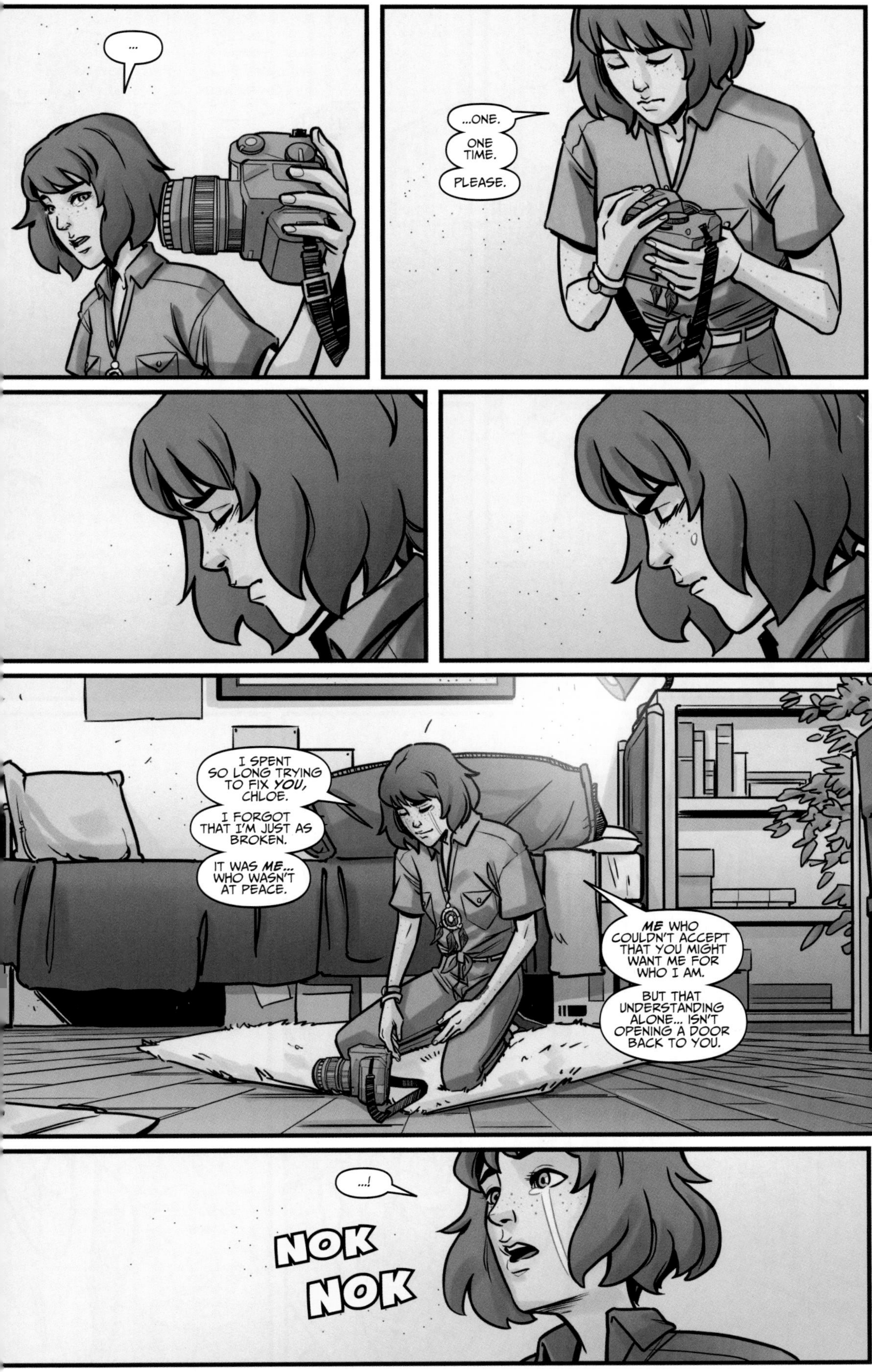
...
...ONE.
ONE TIME.
PLEASE.
I SPENT SO LONG TRYING TO FIX YOU, CHLOE.
I FORGOT THAT I'M JUST AS BROKEN.
IT WAS ME... WHO WASN'T AT PEACE.
ME WHO COULDN'T ACCEPT THAT YOU MIGHT WANT ME FOR WHO I AM.
BUT THAT UNDERSTANDING ALONE... ISN'T OPENING A DOOR BACK TO YOU.
...!
NOK
NOK

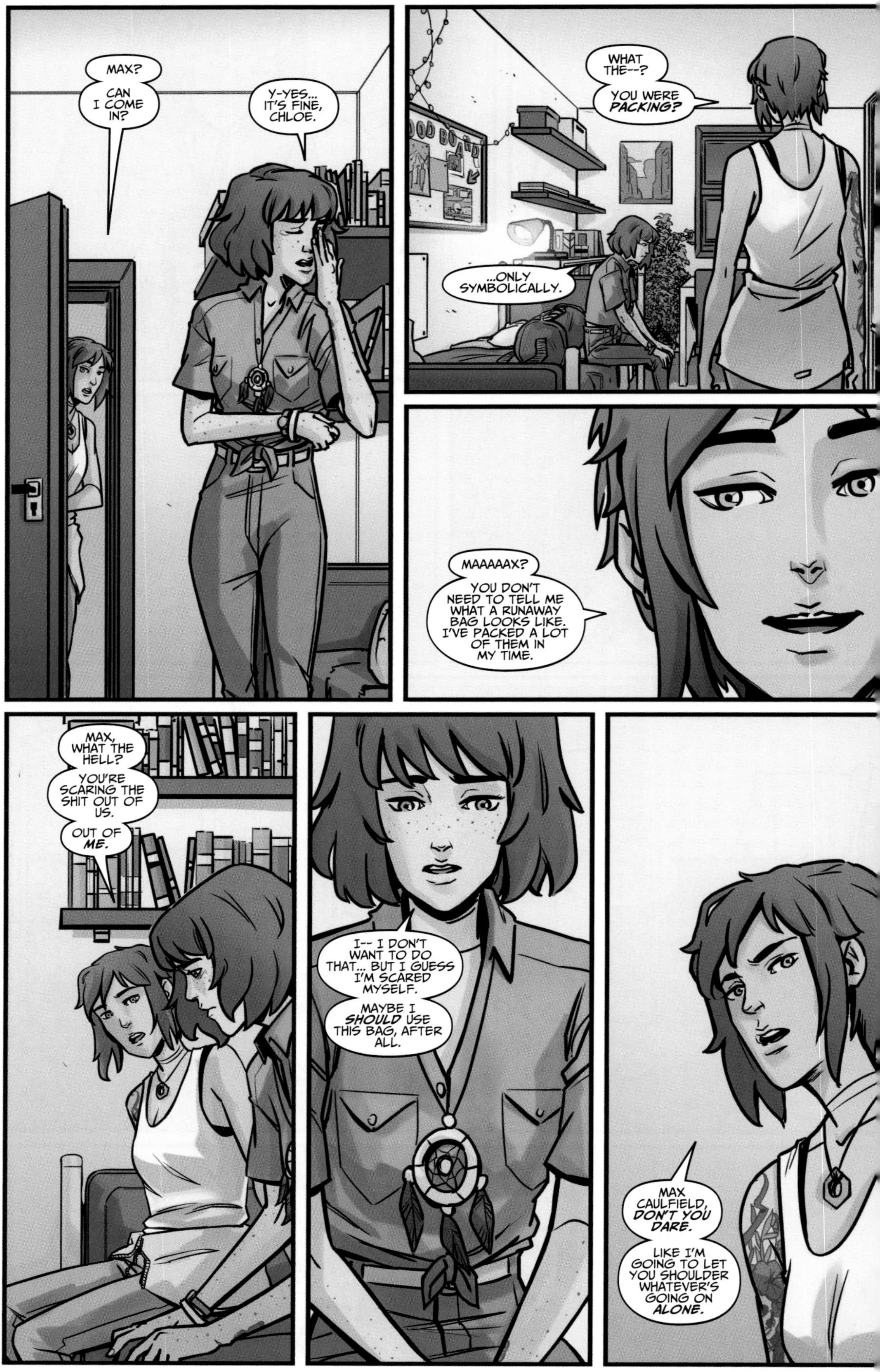
MAX?
CAN I COME IN?
Y-YES... IT'S FINE, CHLOE.
WHAT THE--?
YOU WERE PACKING?
...ONLY SYMBOLICALLY.
MAAAAAX?
YOU DON'T NEED TO TELL ME WHAT A RUNAWAY BAG LOOKS LIKE. I'VE PACKED A LOT OF THEM IN MY TIME.
MAX, WHAT THE HELL?
YOU'RE SCARING THE SHIT OUT OF US.
OUT OF ME.
I-- I DON'T WANT TO DO THAT... BUT I GUESS I'M SCARED MYSELF.
MAYBE I SHOULD USE THIS BAG, AFTER ALL.
MAX CAULFIELD, DON'T YOU DARE.
LIKE I'M GOING TO LET YOU SHOULDER WHATEVER'S GOING ON ALONE.

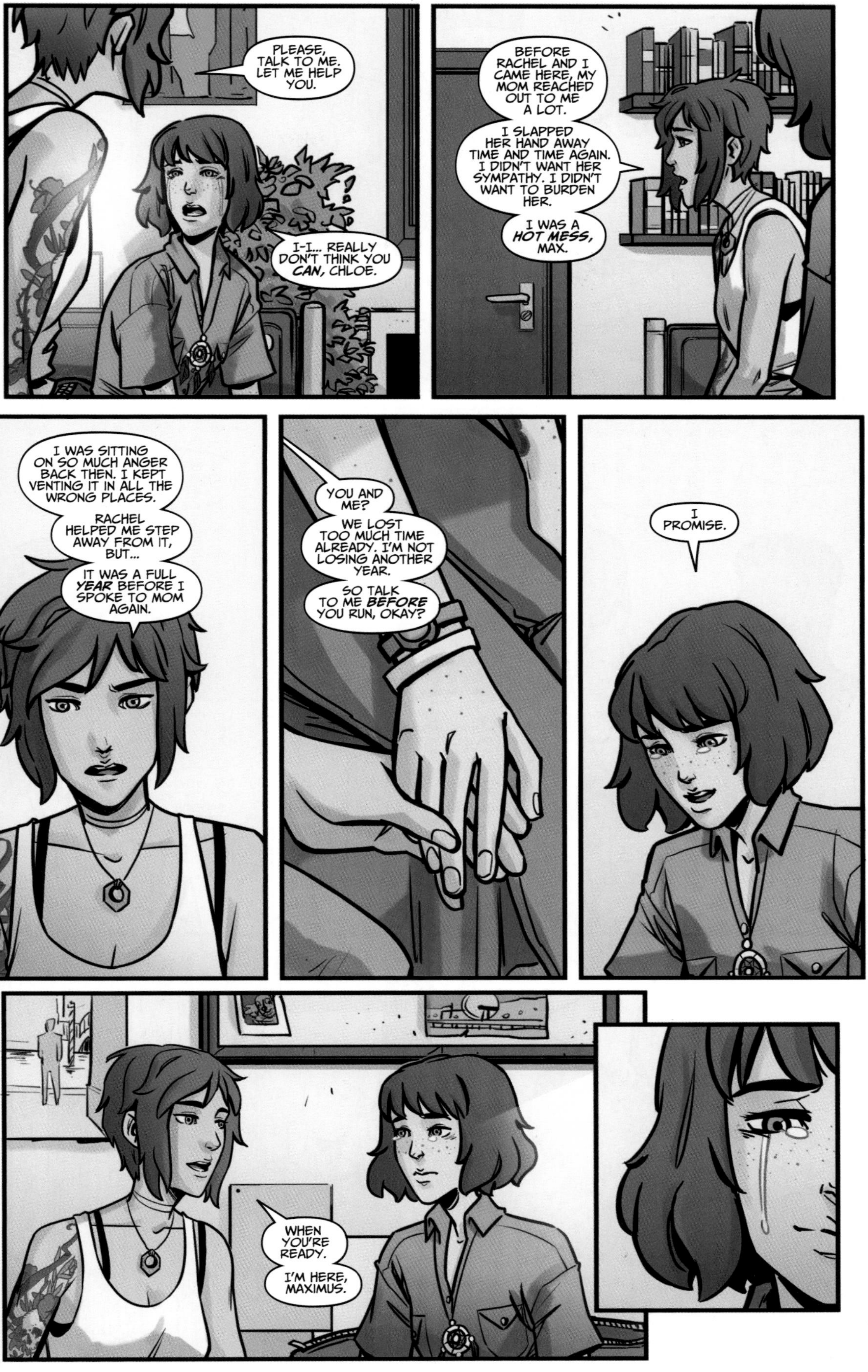
PLEASE, TALK TO ME. LET ME HELP YOU.
I-I... REALLY DON'T THINK YOU CAN, CHLOE.
BEFORE RACHEL AND I CAME HERE, MY MOM REACHED OUT TO ME A LOT.
I SLAPPED HER HAND AWAY TIME AND TIME AGAIN. I DIDN'T WANT HER SYMPATHY. I DIDN'T WANT TO BURDEN HER.
I WAS A HOT MESS, MAX.
I WAS SITTING ON SO MUCH ANGER BACK THEN. I KEPT VENTING IT IN ALL THE WRONG PLACES.
RACHEL HELPED ME STEP AWAY FROM IT, BUT...
IT WAS A FULL YEAR BEFORE I SPOKE TO MOM AGAIN.
YOU AND ME?
WE LOST TOO MUCH TIME ALREADY. I'M NOT LOSING ANOTHER YEAR.
SO TALK TO ME BEFORE YOU RUN, OKAY?
I PROMISE.
WHEN YOU'RE READY.
I'M HERE, MAXIMUS.

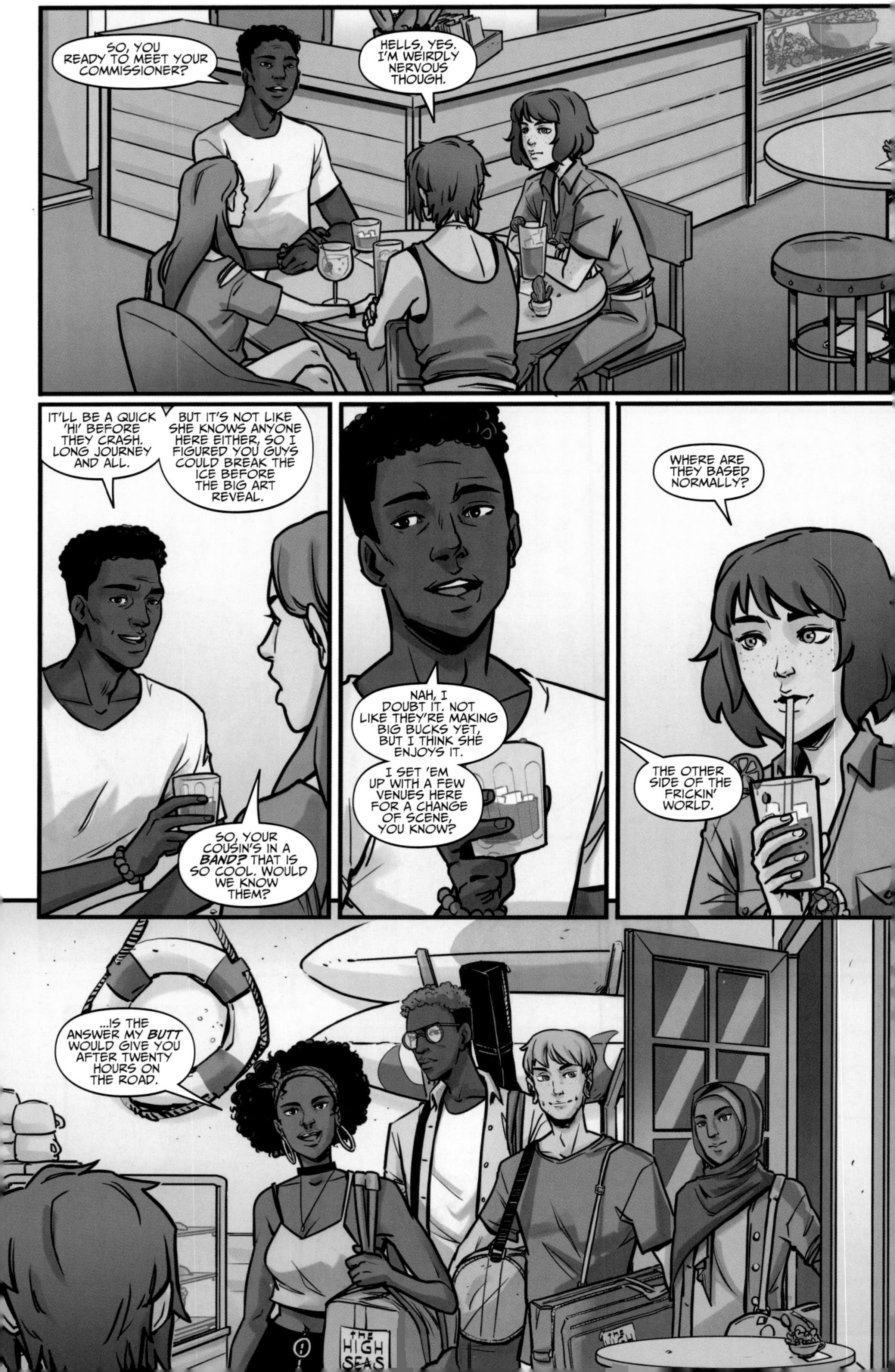
SO, YOU READY TO MEET YOUR COMMISSIONER?
HELLS, YES. I'M WEIRDLY NERVOUS THOUGH.
IT'LL BE A QUICK 'HI' BEFORE THEY CRASH. LONG JOURNEY AND ALL.
BUT IT'S NOT LIKE SHE KNOWS ANYONE HERE EITHER, SO I FIGURED YOU GUYS COULD BREAK THE ICE BEFORE THE BIG ART REVEAL.
SO, YOUR COUSIN'S IN A *BAND?* THAT IS SO COOL. WOULD WE KNOW THEM?
NAH, I DOUBT IT. NOT LIKE THEY'RE MAKING BIG BUCKS YET, BUT I THINK SHE ENJOYS IT.
I SET 'EM UP WITH A FEW VENUES HERE FOR A CHANGE OF SCENE, YOU KNOW?
WHERE ARE THEY BASED NORMALLY?
THE OTHER SIDE OF THE FRICKIN' WORLD.
...IS THE ANSWER MY *BUTT* WOULD GIVE YOU AFTER TWENTY HOURS ON THE ROAD.
THE HIGH SEAS

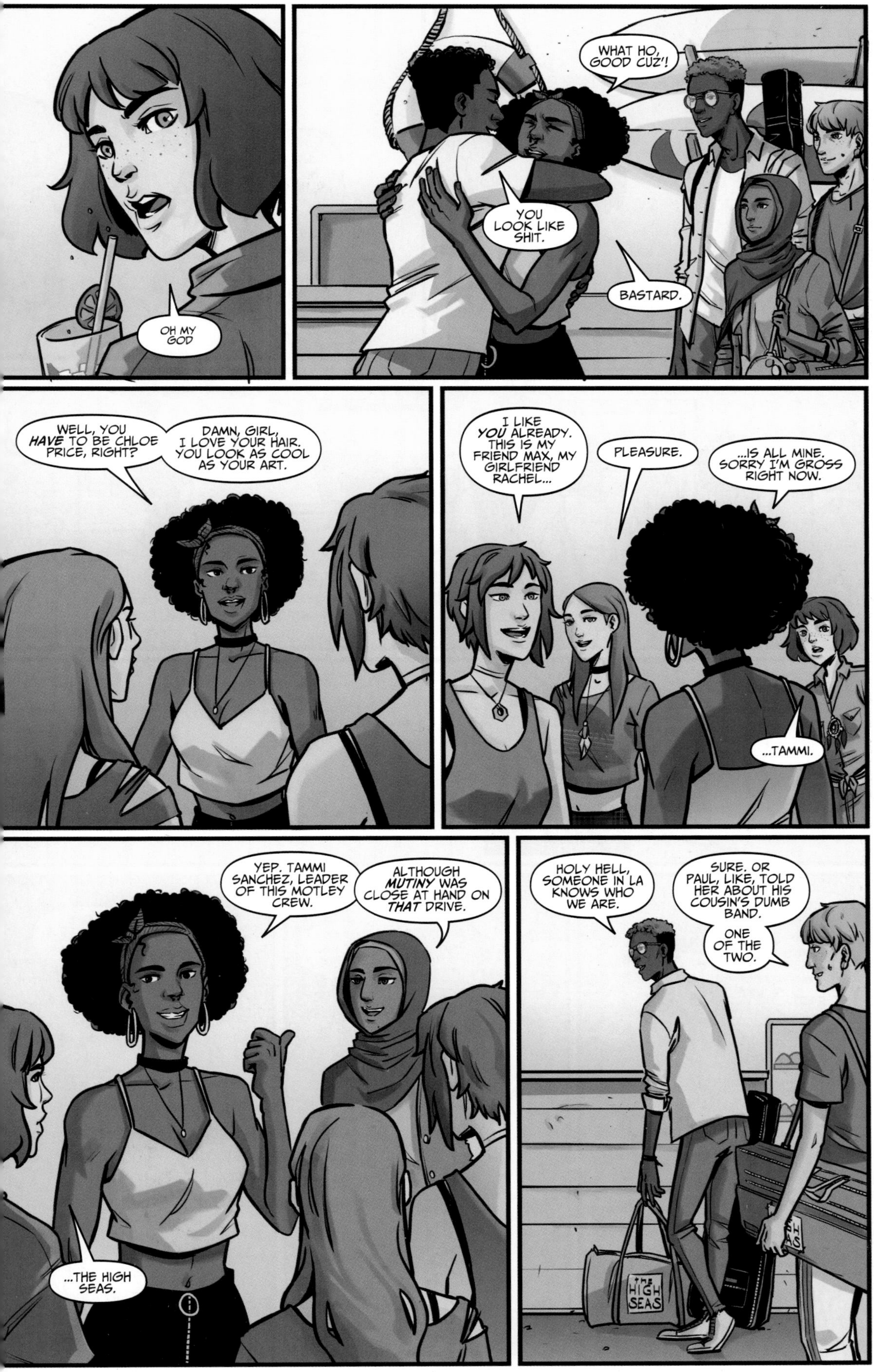
OH MY GOD
WHAT HO, GOOD CUZ'!
YOU LOOK LIKE SHIT.
BASTARD.
WELL, YOU HAVE TO BE CHLOE PRICE, RIGHT?
DAMN, GIRL, I LOVE YOUR HAIR. YOU LOOK AS COOL AS YOUR ART.
I LIKE YOU ALREADY. THIS IS MY FRIEND MAX, MY GIRLFRIEND RACHEL...
PLEASURE.
...IS ALL MINE. SORRY I'M GROSS RIGHT NOW.
...TAMMI.
YEP. TAMMI SANCHEZ, LEADER OF THIS MOTLEY CREW.
ALTHOUGH MUTINY WAS CLOSE AT HAND ON THAT DRIVE.
...THE HIGH SEAS.
HOLY HELL, SOMEONE IN LA KNOWS WHO WE ARE.
SURE. OR PAUL, LIKE, TOLD HER ABOUT HIS COUSIN'S DUMB BAND.
ONE OF THE TWO.
THE HIGH SEAS

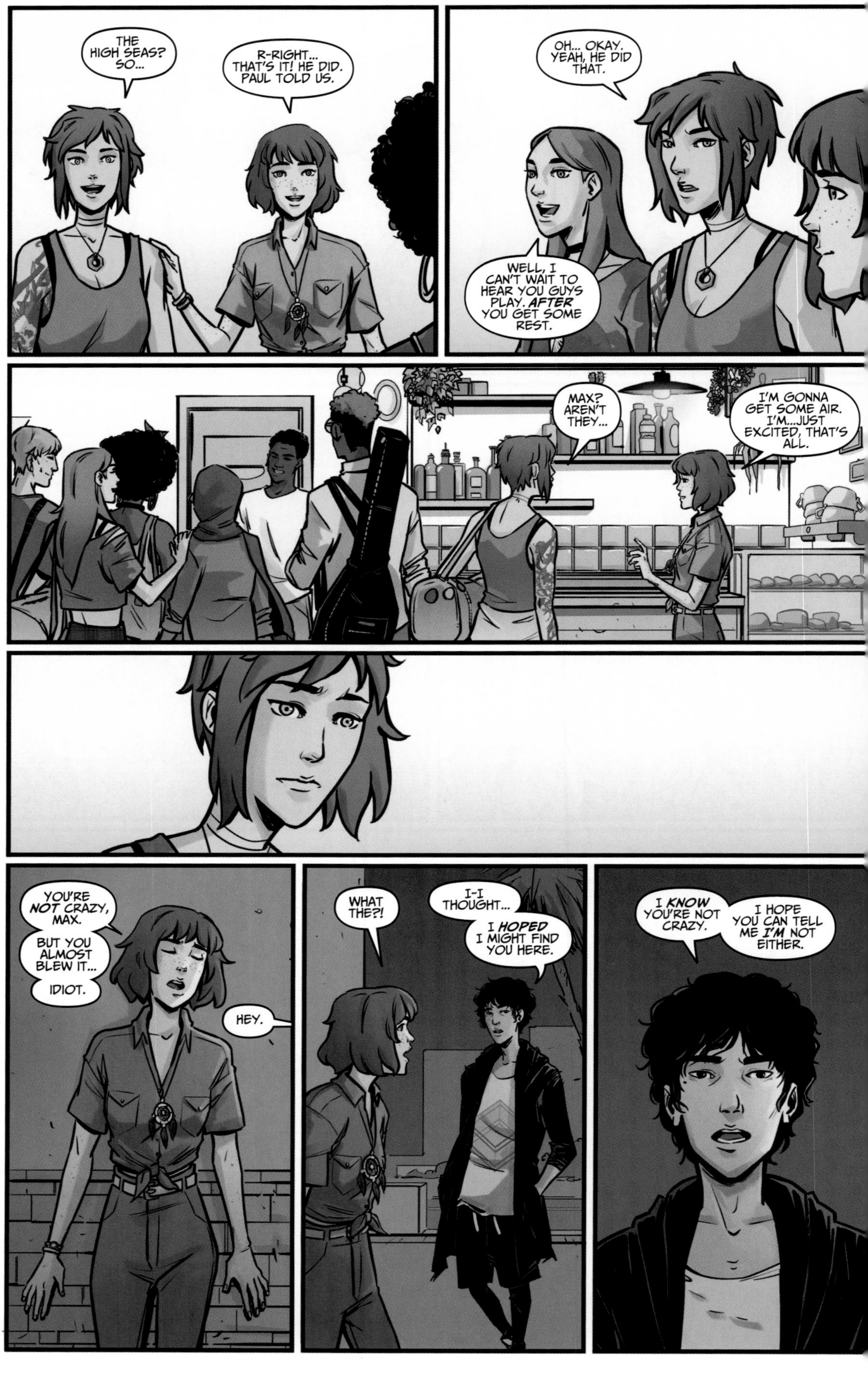
THE HIGH SEAS? SO...
R-RIGHT... THAT'S IT! HE DID. PAUL TOLD US.
OH... OKAY. YEAH, HE DID THAT.
WELL, I CAN'T WAIT TO HEAR YOU GUYS PLAY. AFTER YOU GET SOME REST.
MAX? AREN'T THEY...
I'M GONNA GET SOME AIR. I'M...JUST EXCITED, THAT'S ALL.
YOU'RE NOT CRAZY, MAX.
BUT YOU ALMOST BLEW IT...
IDIOT.
HEY.
WHAT THE?!
I-I THOUGHT...
I HOPED I MIGHT FIND YOU HERE.
I KNOW YOU'RE NOT CRAZY.
I HOPE YOU CAN TELL ME I'M NOT EITHER.

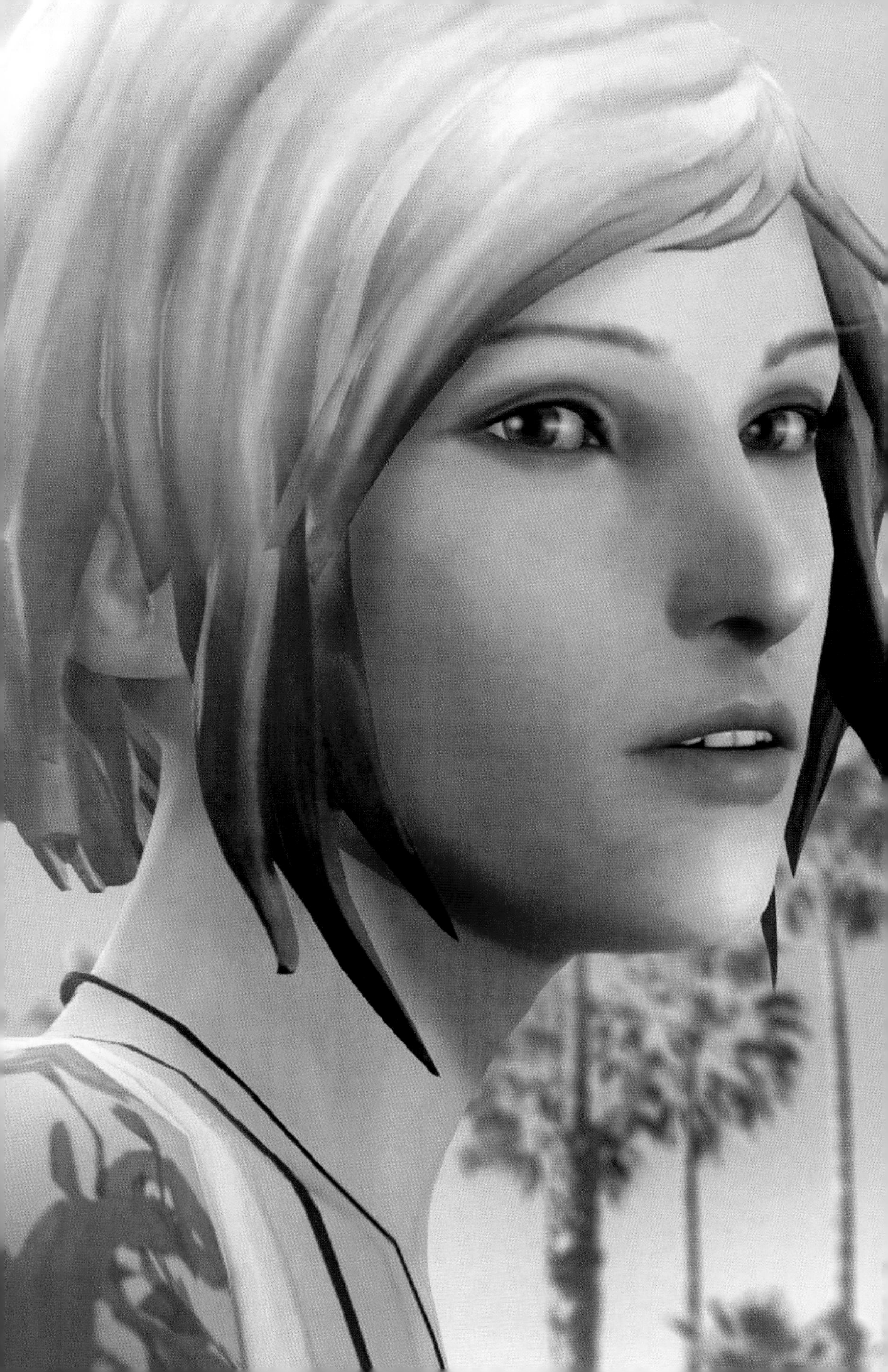

CHAPTER 3

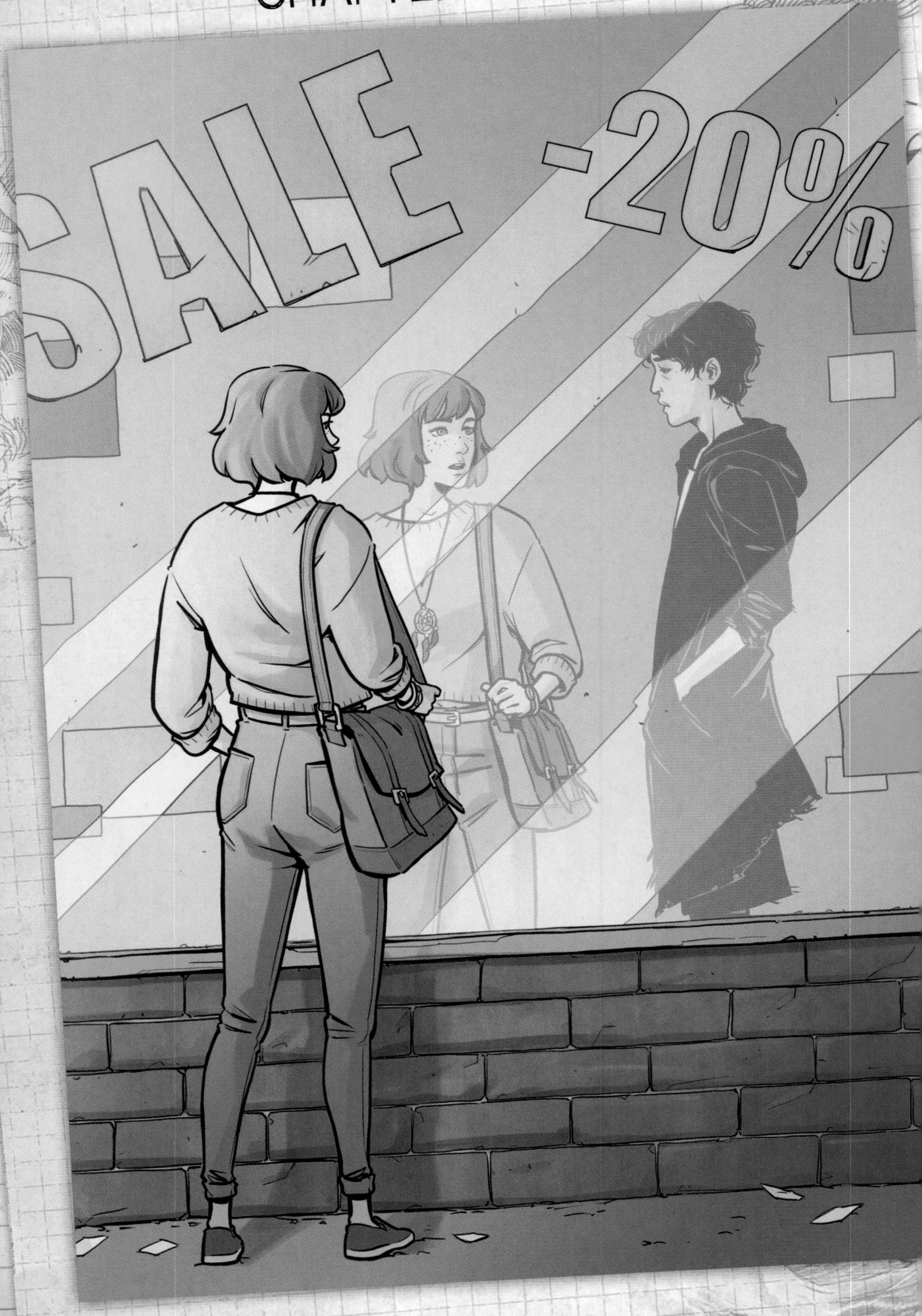

SALE -20%

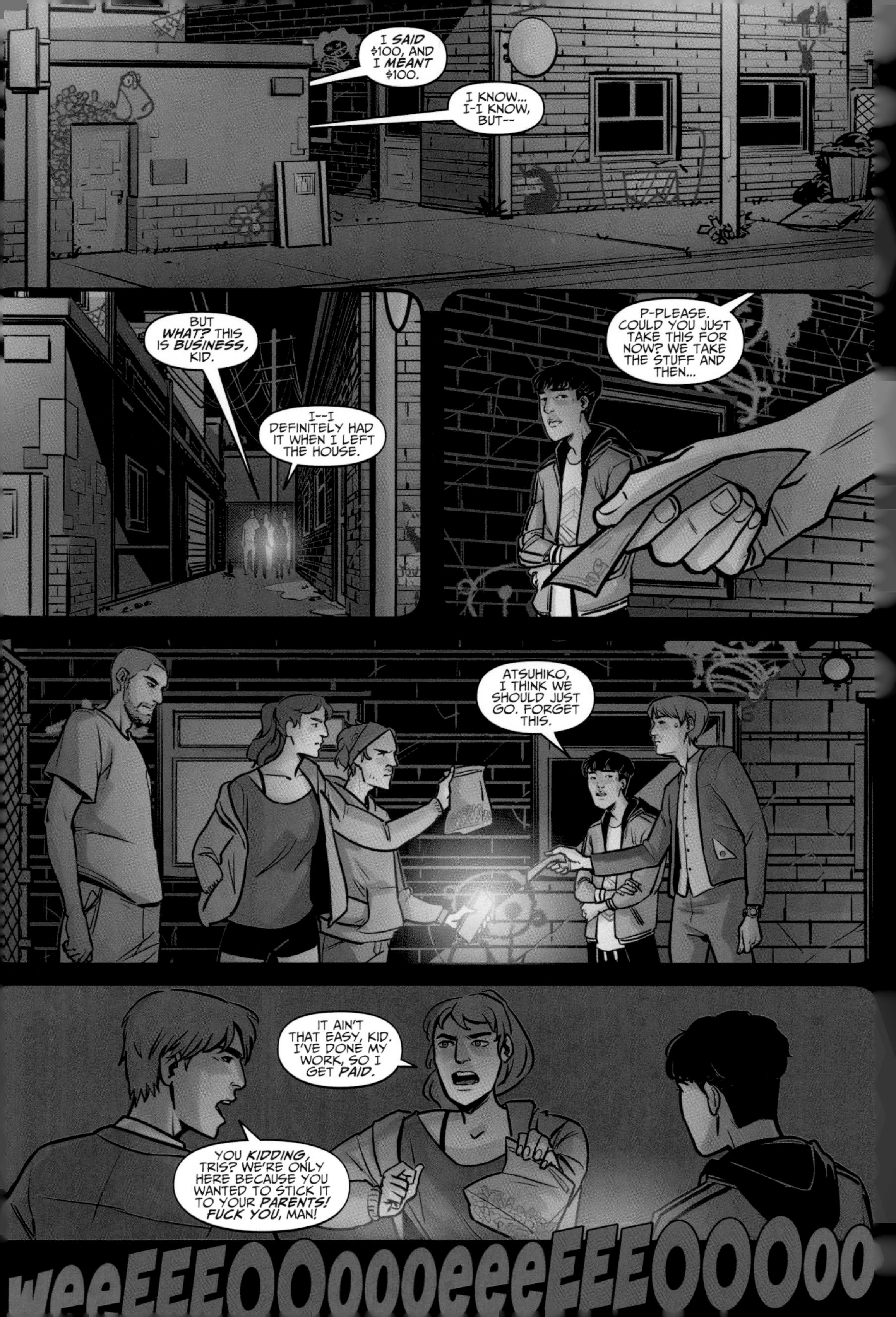
I SAID $100, AND I MEANT $100.
I KNOW... I-I KNOW, BUT--
BUT WHAT? THIS IS BUSINESS, KID.
I--I DEFINITELY HAD IT WHEN I LEFT THE HOUSE.
P-PLEASE. COULD YOU JUST TAKE THIS FOR NOW? WE TAKE THE STUFF AND THEN...
ATSUHIKO, I THINK WE SHOULD JUST GO. FORGET THIS.
IT AIN'T THAT EASY, KID. I'VE DONE MY WORK, SO I GET PAID.
YOU KIDDING, TRIS? WE'RE ONLY HERE BECAUSE YOU WANTED TO STICK IT TO YOUR PARENTS! FUCK YOU, MAN!
weeEEEOOooooeeeEEEOOOOO

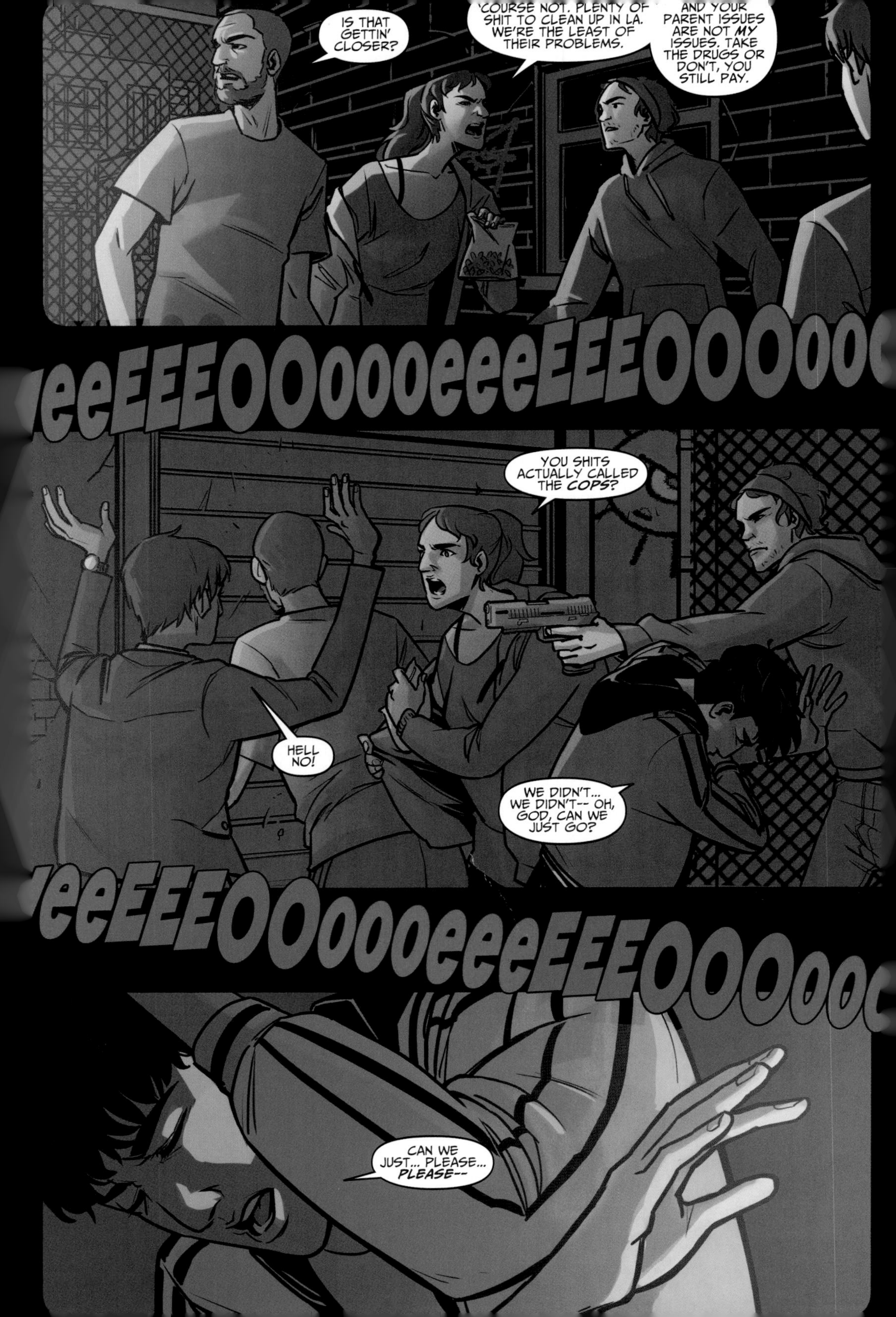
IS THAT GETTIN' CLOSER?
'COURSE NOT. PLENTY OF SHIT TO CLEAN UP IN LA. WE'RE THE LEAST OF THEIR PROBLEMS.
AND YOUR PARENT ISSUES ARE NOT *MY* ISSUES. TAKE THE DRUGS OR DON'T, YOU STILL PAY.
WEEEEOOOOOeeeEEEOOOOOO
YOU SHITS ACTUALLY CALLED THE *COPS*?
HELL NO!
WE DIDN'T... WE DIDN'T-- OH, GOD, CAN WE JUST GO?
WEEEEOOOOOeeeEEEOOOOOO
CAN WE JUST... PLEASE... *PLEASE--*

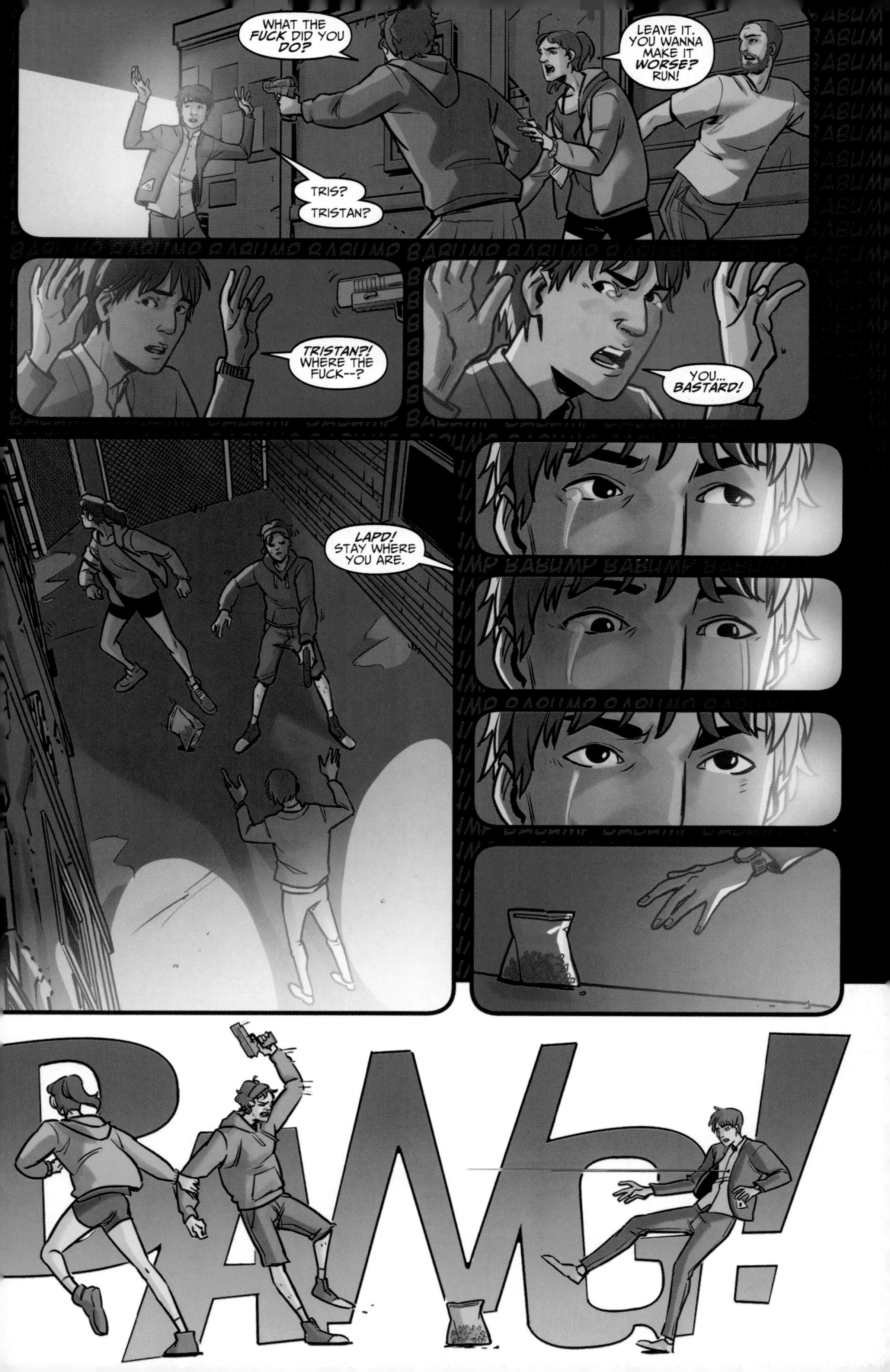

WHAT THE FUCK DID YOU DO?
LEAVE IT. YOU WANNA MAKE IT WORSE? RUN!
TRIS?
TRISTAN?
TRISTAN?! WHERE THE FUCK--?
YOU... BASTARD!
LAPD! STAY WHERE YOU ARE.
BAWG!

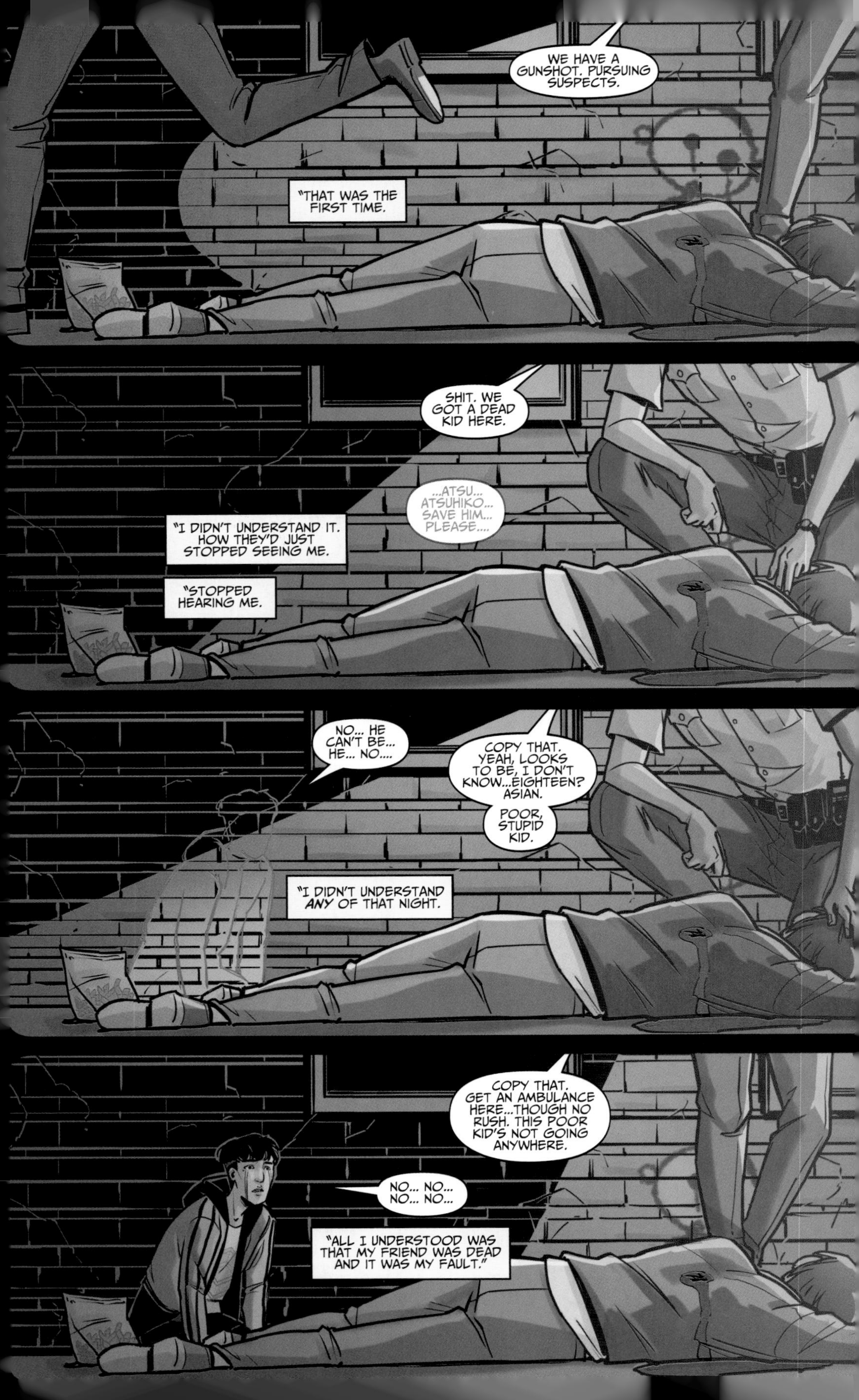
WE HAVE A GUNSHOT. PURSUING SUSPECTS.
"THAT WAS THE FIRST TIME.
SHIT. WE GOT A DEAD KID HERE.
...ATSU... ATSUHIKO... SAVE HIM... PLEASE....
"I DIDN'T UNDERSTAND IT. HOW THEY'D JUST STOPPED SEEING ME.
"STOPPED HEARING ME.
NO... HE CAN'T BE... HE... NO....
COPY THAT. YEAH, LOOKS TO BE, I DON'T KNOW...EIGHTEEN? ASIAN.
POOR, STUPID KID.
"I DIDN'T UNDERSTAND ANY OF THAT NIGHT.
COPY THAT. GET AN AMBULANCE HERE...THOUGH NO RUSH. THIS POOR KID'S NOT GOING ANYWHERE.
NO... NO... NO... NO...
"ALL I UNDERSTOOD WAS THAT MY FRIEND WAS DEAD AND IT WAS MY FAULT."

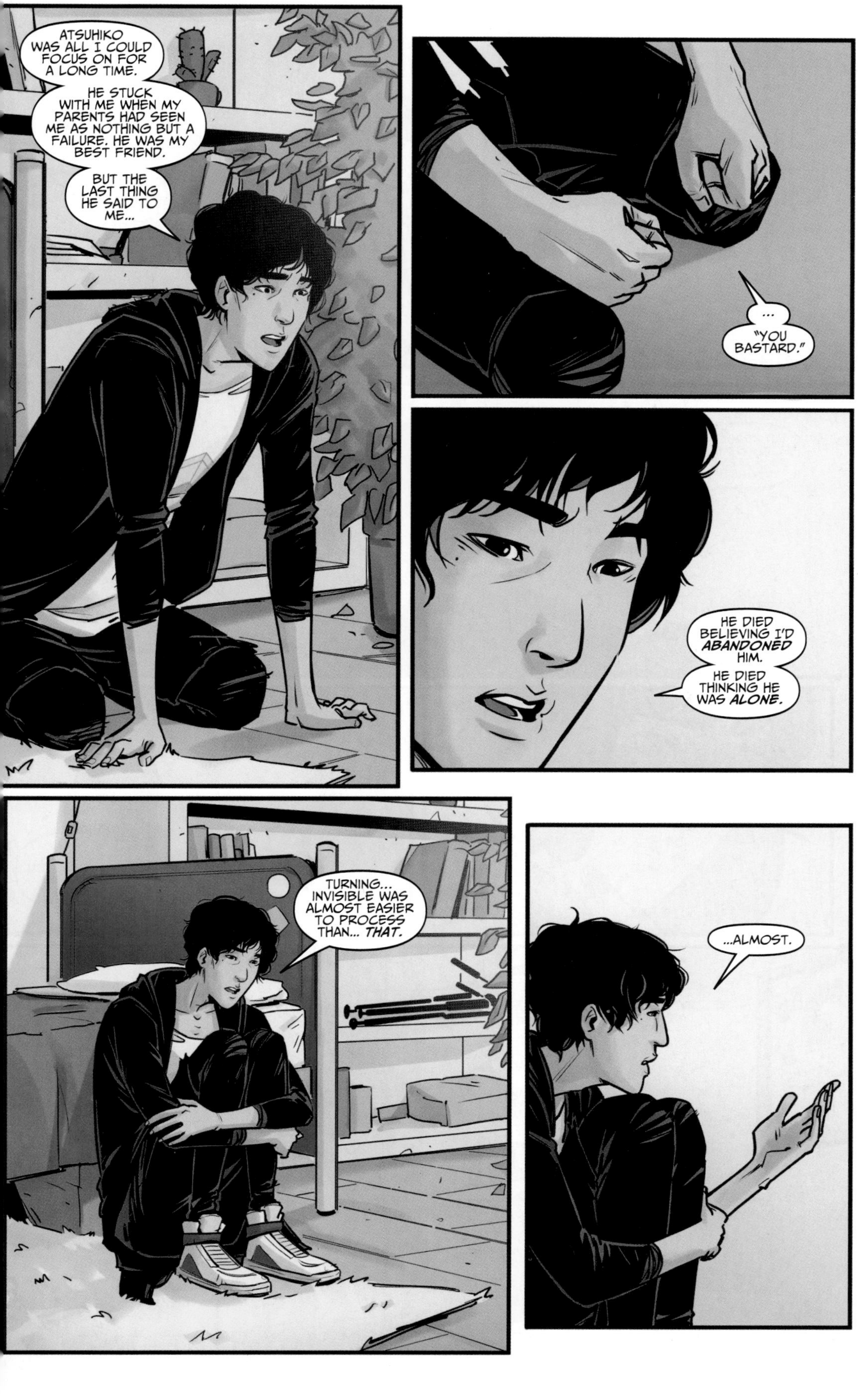

ATSUHIKO WAS ALL I COULD FOCUS ON FOR A LONG TIME.
HE STUCK WITH ME WHEN MY PARENTS HAD SEEN ME AS NOTHING BUT A FAILURE. HE WAS MY BEST FRIEND.
BUT THE LAST THING HE SAID TO ME...
... "YOU BASTARD."
HE DIED BELIEVING I'D *ABANDONED* HIM.
HE DIED THINKING HE WAS *ALONE.*
TURNING... INVISIBLE WAS ALMOST EASIER TO PROCESS THAN... *THAT.*
...ALMOST.

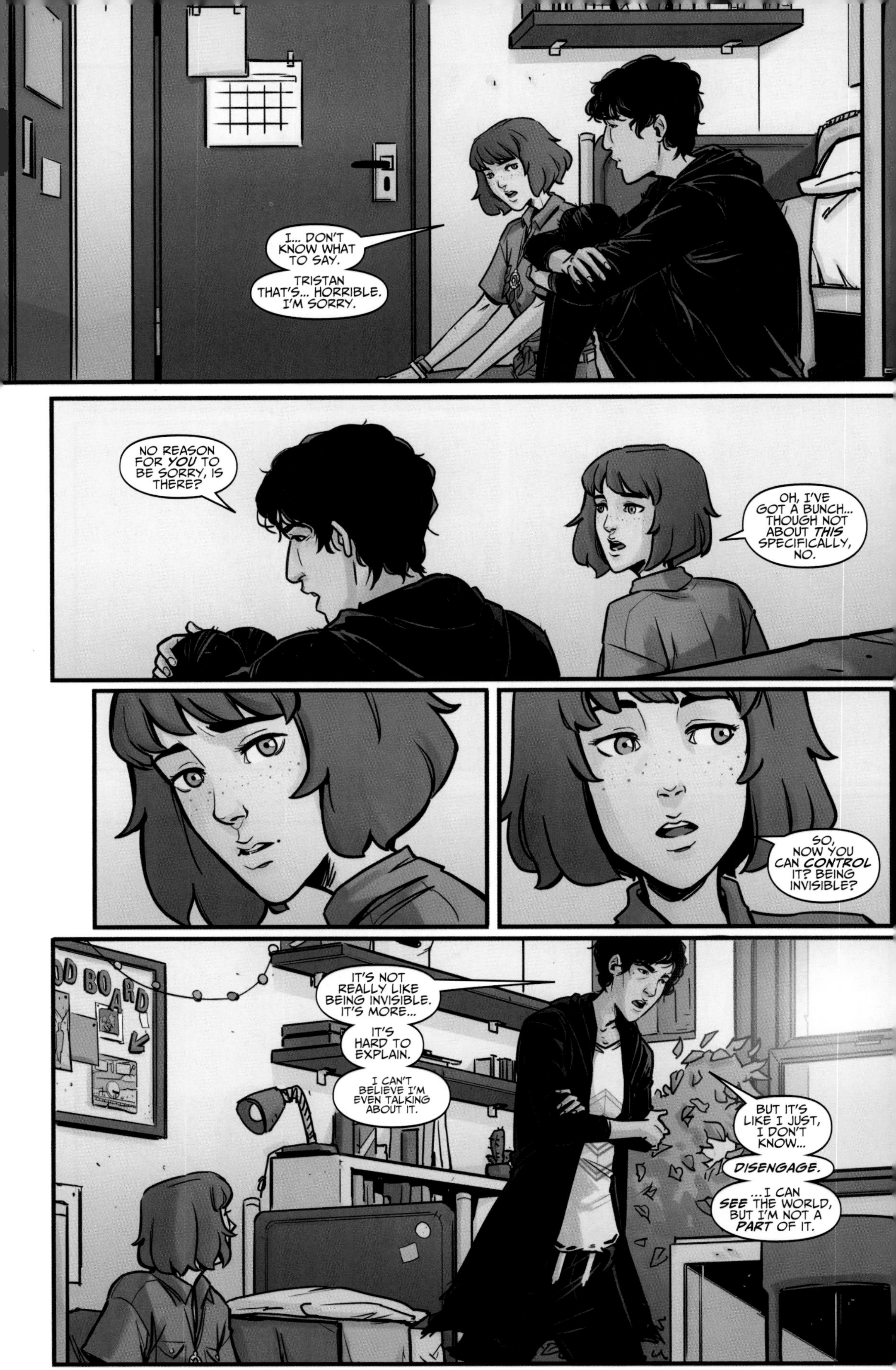
I... DON'T KNOW WHAT TO SAY.
TRISTAN THAT'S... HORRIBLE. I'M SORRY.
NO REASON FOR YOU TO BE SORRY, IS THERE?
OH, I'VE GOT A BUNCH... THOUGH NOT ABOUT THIS SPECIFICALLY, NO.
SO, NOW YOU CAN CONTROL IT? BEING INVISIBLE?
IT'S NOT REALLY LIKE BEING INVISIBLE. IT'S MORE...
IT'S HARD TO EXPLAIN.
I CAN'T BELIEVE I'M EVEN TALKING ABOUT IT.
BUT IT'S LIKE I JUST, I DON'T KNOW...
DISENGAGE.
...I CAN SEE THE WORLD, BUT I'M NOT A PART OF IT.

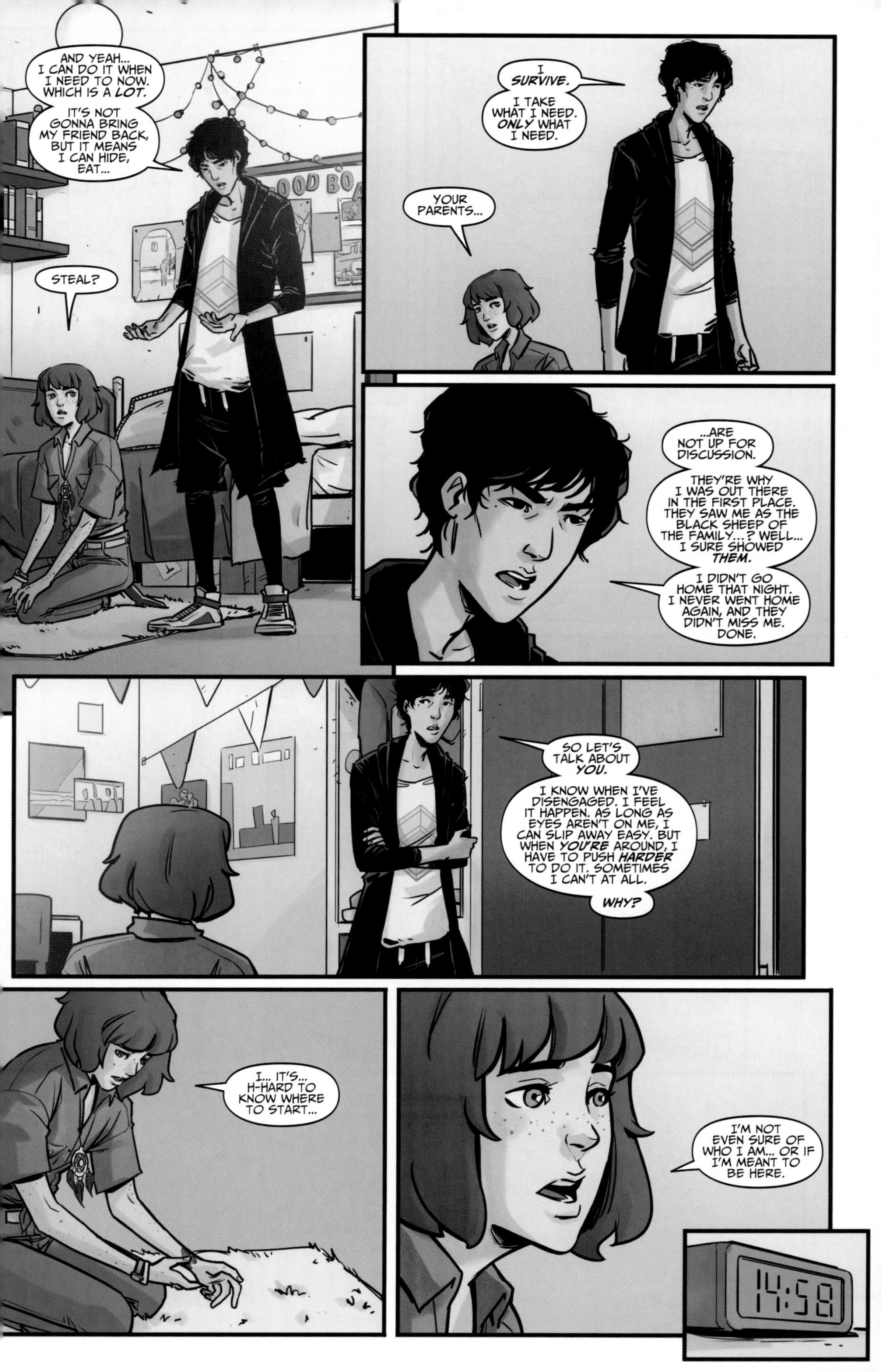
AND YEAH... I CAN DO IT WHEN I NEED TO NOW. WHICH IS A *LOT.*
IT'S NOT GONNA BRING MY FRIEND BACK, BUT IT MEANS I CAN HIDE, EAT...
STEAL?
I *SURVIVE.*
I TAKE WHAT I NEED. *ONLY* WHAT I NEED.
YOUR PARENTS...
...ARE NOT UP FOR DISCUSSION.
THEY'RE WHY I WAS OUT THERE IN THE FIRST PLACE. THEY SAW ME AS THE BLACK SHEEP OF THE FAMILY...? WELL... I SURE SHOWED *THEM.*
I DIDN'T GO HOME THAT NIGHT. I NEVER WENT HOME AGAIN, AND THEY DIDN'T MISS ME. DONE.
SO LET'S TALK ABOUT *YOU.*
I KNOW WHEN I'VE DISENGAGED. I FEEL IT HAPPEN. AS LONG AS EYES AREN'T ON ME, I CAN SLIP AWAY EASY. BUT WHEN *YOU'RE* AROUND, I HAVE TO PUSH *HARDER* TO DO IT. SOMETIMES I CAN'T AT ALL.
WHY?
I... IT'S... H-HARD TO KNOW WHERE TO START...
I'M NOT EVEN SURE OF WHO I AM... OR IF I'M MEANT TO BE HERE.
14:58

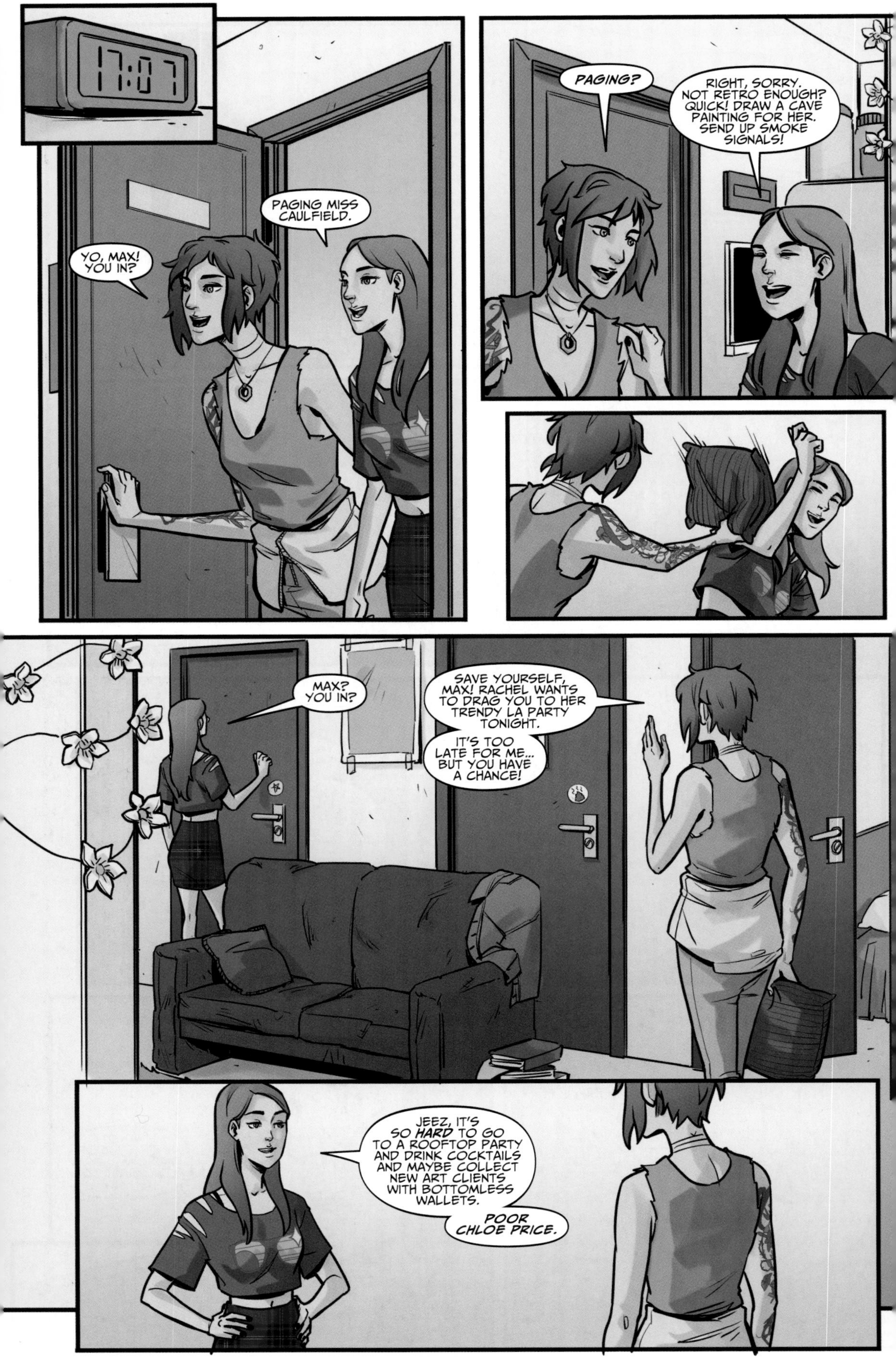
17:07
PAGING MISS CAULFIELD.
YO, MAX! YOU IN?
PAGING?
RIGHT, SORRY. NOT RETRO ENOUGH? QUICK! DRAW A CAVE PAINTING FOR HER. SEND UP SMOKE SIGNALS!
MAX? YOU IN?
SAVE YOURSELF, MAX! RACHEL WANTS TO DRAG YOU TO HER TRENDY LA PARTY TONIGHT.
IT'S TOO LATE FOR ME... BUT YOU HAVE A CHANCE!
JEEZ, IT'S SO **HARD** TO GO TO A ROOFTOP PARTY AND DRINK COCKTAILS AND MAYBE COLLECT NEW ART CLIENTS WITH BOTTOMLESS WALLETS.
POOR CHLOE PRICE.

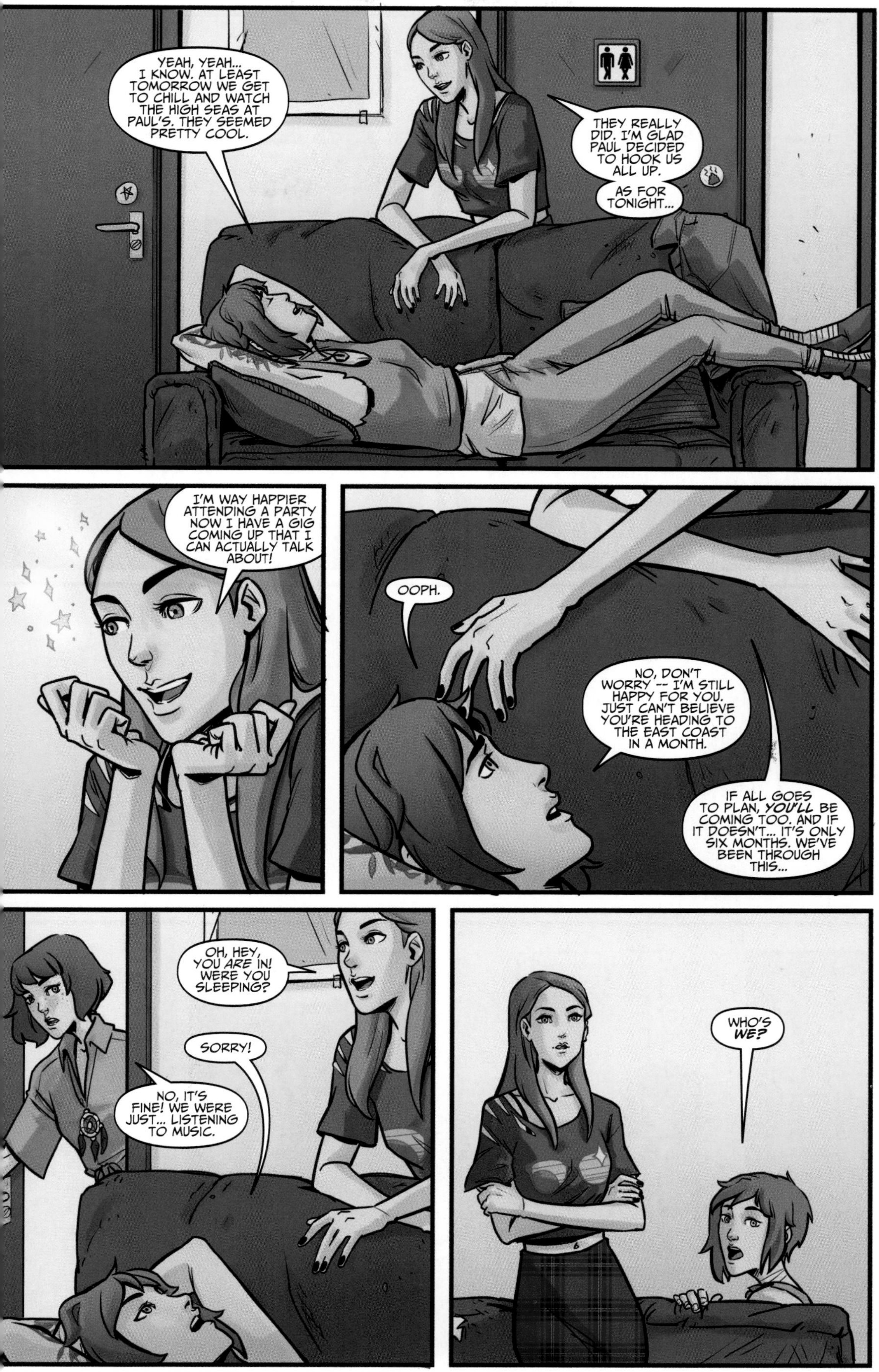
YEAH, YEAH... I KNOW. AT LEAST TOMORROW WE GET TO CHILL AND WATCH THE HIGH SEAS AT PAUL'S. THEY SEEMED PRETTY COOL.
THEY REALLY DID. I'M GLAD PAUL DECIDED TO HOOK US ALL UP.
AS FOR TONIGHT...
I'M WAY HAPPIER ATTENDING A PARTY NOW I HAVE A GIG COMING UP THAT I CAN ACTUALLY TALK ABOUT!
OOPH.
NO, DON'T WORRY -- I'M STILL HAPPY FOR YOU. JUST CAN'T BELIEVE YOU'RE HEADING TO THE EAST COAST IN A MONTH.
IF ALL GOES TO PLAN, *YOU'LL* BE COMING TOO. AND IF IT DOESN'T... IT'S ONLY SIX MONTHS. WE'VE BEEN THROUGH THIS...
OH, HEY, YOU *ARE* IN! WERE YOU SLEEPING?
SORRY!
NO, IT'S FINE! WE WERE JUST... LISTENING TO MUSIC.
WHO'S *WE?*

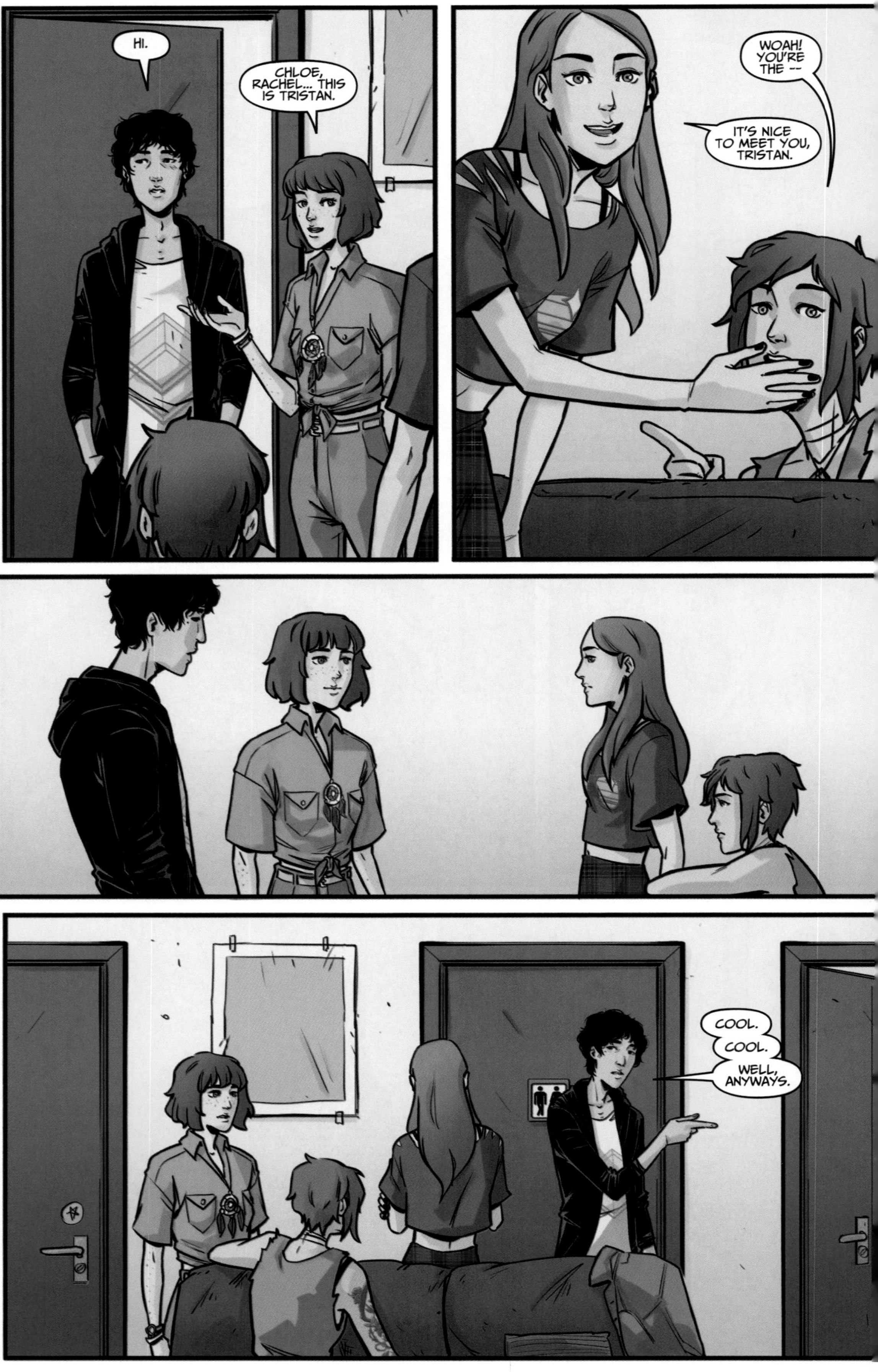
HI.
CHLOE, RACHEL... THIS IS TRISTAN.
WOAH! YOU'RE THE --
IT'S NICE TO MEET YOU, TRISTAN.
COOL.
COOL.
WELL, ANYWAYS.

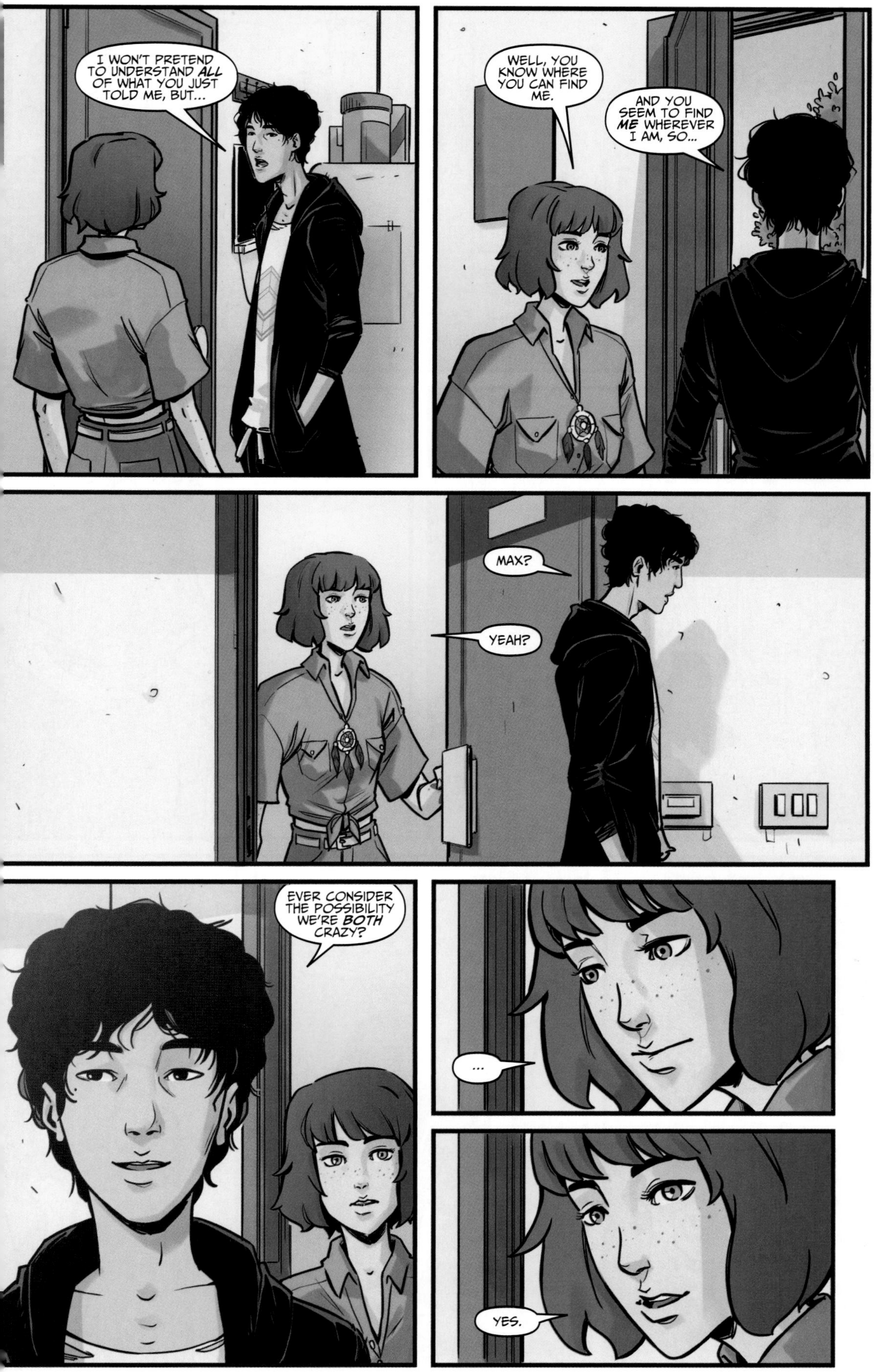

I WON'T PRETEND TO UNDERSTAND ALL OF WHAT YOU JUST TOLD ME, BUT...
WELL, YOU KNOW WHERE YOU CAN FIND ME.
AND YOU SEEM TO FIND ME WHEREVER I AM, SO...
MAX?
YEAH?
EVER CONSIDER THE POSSIBILITY WE'RE BOTH CRAZY?
...
YES.

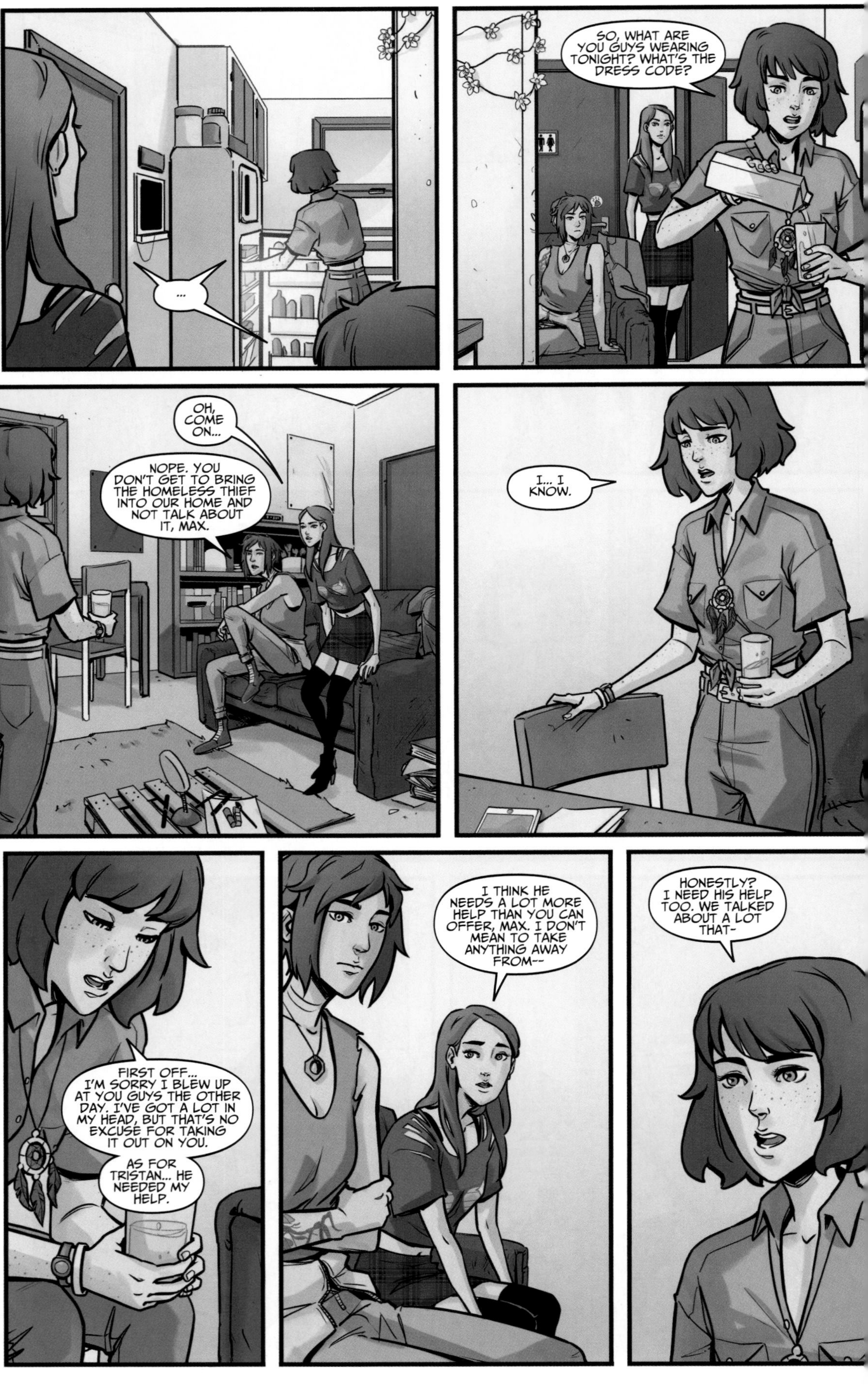
...
SO, WHAT ARE YOU GUYS WEARING TONIGHT? WHAT'S THE DRESS CODE?
OH, COME ON...
NOPE. YOU DON'T GET TO BRING THE HOMELESS THIEF INTO OUR HOME AND NOT TALK ABOUT IT, MAX.
I... I KNOW.
FIRST OFF... I'M SORRY I BLEW UP AT YOU GUYS THE OTHER DAY. I'VE GOT A LOT IN MY HEAD, BUT THAT'S NO EXCUSE FOR TAKING IT OUT ON YOU.
AS FOR TRISTAN... HE NEEDED MY HELP.
I THINK HE NEEDS A LOT MORE HELP THAN YOU CAN OFFER, MAX. I DON'T MEAN TO TAKE ANYTHING AWAY FROM--
HONESTLY? I NEED HIS HELP TOO. WE TALKED ABOUT A LOT THAT-

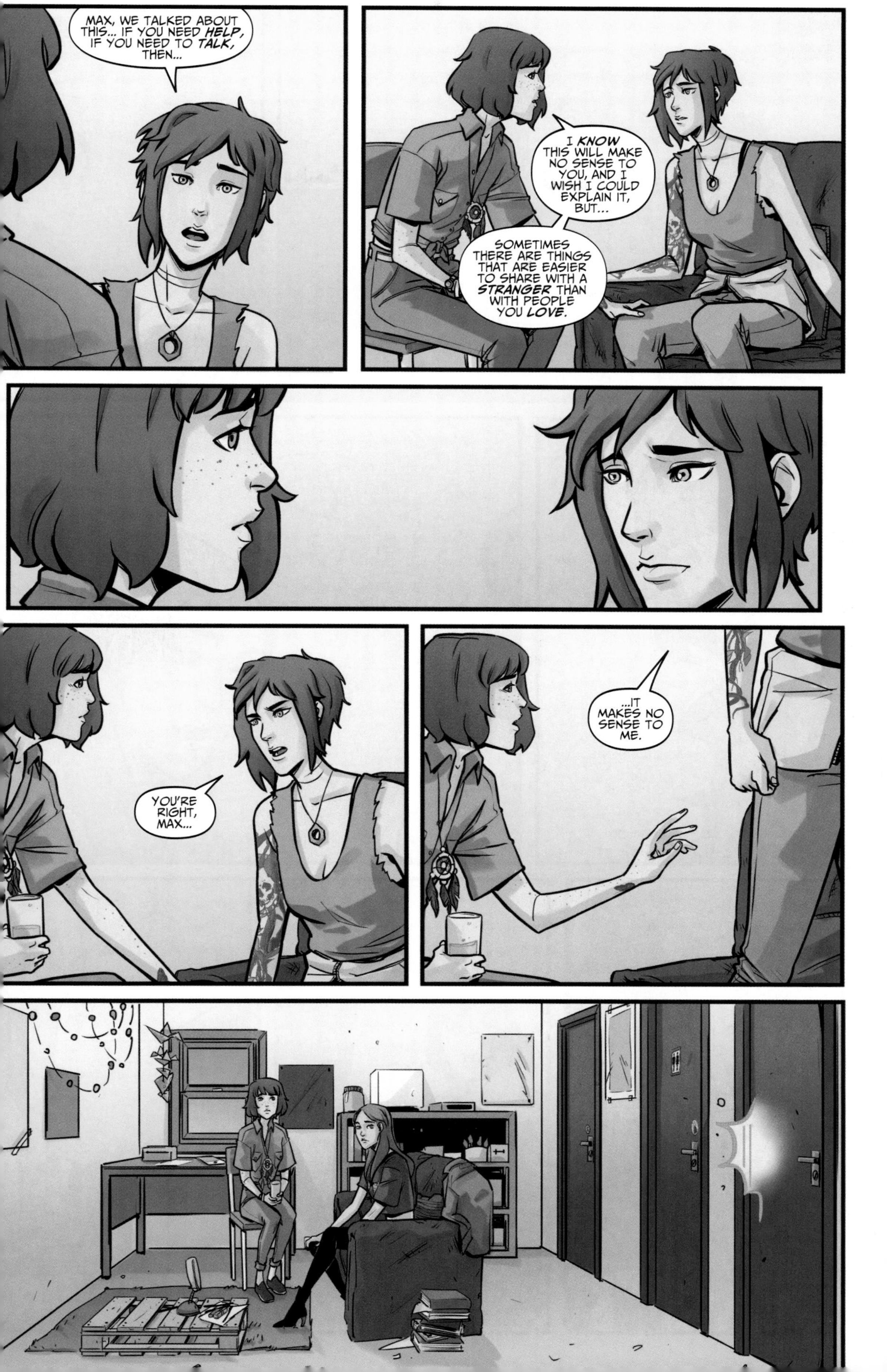
MAX, WE TALKED ABOUT THIS... IF YOU NEED *HELP*, IF YOU NEED TO *TALK*, THEN...
I *KNOW* THIS WILL MAKE NO SENSE TO YOU, AND I WISH I COULD EXPLAIN IT, BUT...
SOMETIMES THERE ARE THINGS THAT ARE EASIER TO SHARE WITH A *STRANGER* THAN WITH PEOPLE YOU *LOVE*.
YOU'RE RIGHT, MAX...
...IT MAKES NO SENSE TO ME.

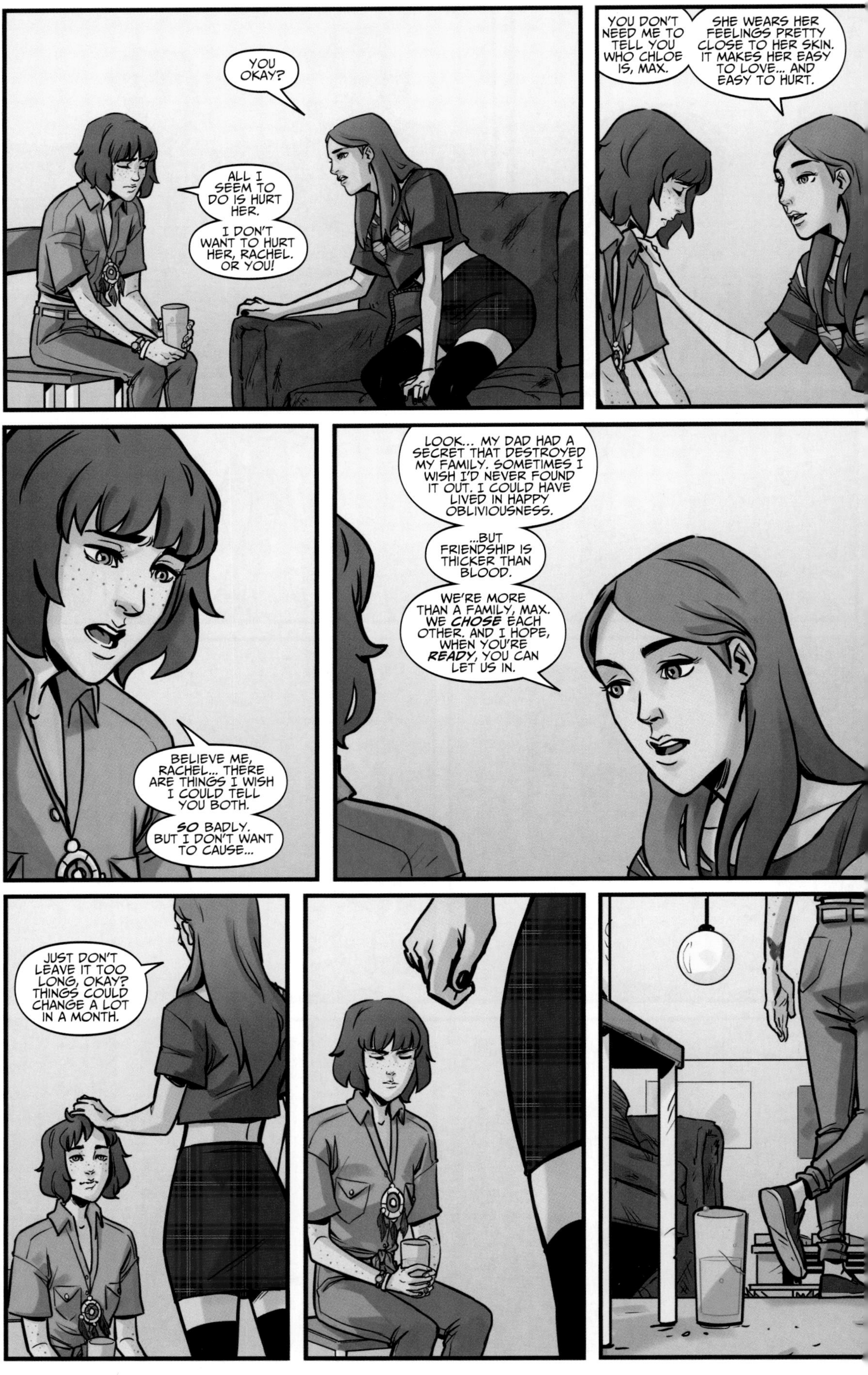
YOU OKAY?
ALL I SEEM TO DO IS HURT HER.
I DON'T WANT TO HURT HER, RACHEL. OR YOU!
YOU DON'T NEED ME TO TELL YOU WHO CHLOE IS, MAX.
SHE WEARS HER FEELINGS PRETTY CLOSE TO HER SKIN. IT MAKES HER EASY TO LOVE... AND EASY TO HURT.
BELIEVE ME, RACHEL... THERE ARE THINGS I WISH I COULD TELL YOU BOTH.
SO BADLY. BUT I DON'T WANT TO CAUSE...
LOOK... MY DAD HAD A SECRET THAT DESTROYED MY FAMILY. SOMETIMES I WISH I'D NEVER FOUND IT OUT. I COULD HAVE LIVED IN HAPPY OBLIVIOUSNESS.
...BUT FRIENDSHIP IS THICKER THAN BLOOD.
WE'RE MORE THAN A FAMILY, MAX. WE *CHOSE* EACH OTHER. AND I HOPE, WHEN YOU'RE *READY*, YOU CAN LET US IN.
JUST DON'T LEAVE IT TOO LONG, OKAY? THINGS COULD CHANGE A LOT IN A MONTH.

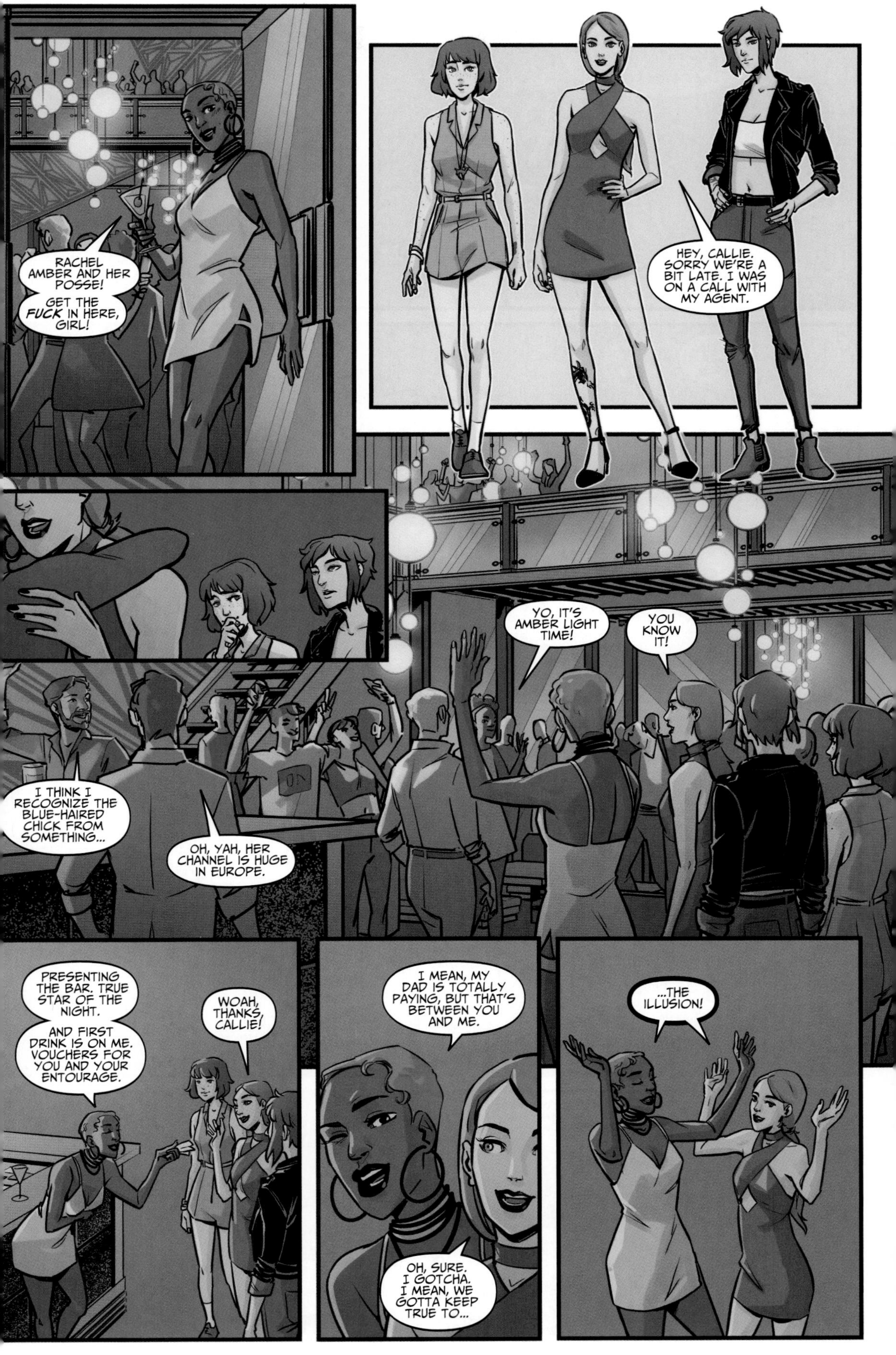
RACHEL AMBER AND HER POSSE!
GET THE *FUCK* IN HERE, GIRL!
HEY, CALLIE. SORRY WE'RE A BIT LATE. I WAS ON A CALL WITH MY AGENT.
YO, IT'S AMBER LIGHT TIME!
YOU KNOW IT!
I THINK I RECOGNIZE THE BLUE-HAIRED CHICK FROM SOMETHING...
OH, YAH, HER CHANNEL IS HUGE IN EUROPE.
PRESENTING THE BAR. TRUE STAR OF THE NIGHT.
AND FIRST DRINK IS ON ME. VOUCHERS FOR YOU AND YOUR ENTOURAGE.
WOAH, THANKS, CALLIE!
I MEAN, MY DAD IS TOTALLY PAYING, BUT THAT'S BETWEEN YOU AND ME.
OH, SURE. I GOTCHA. I MEAN, WE GOTTA KEEP TRUE TO...
...THE ILLUSION!

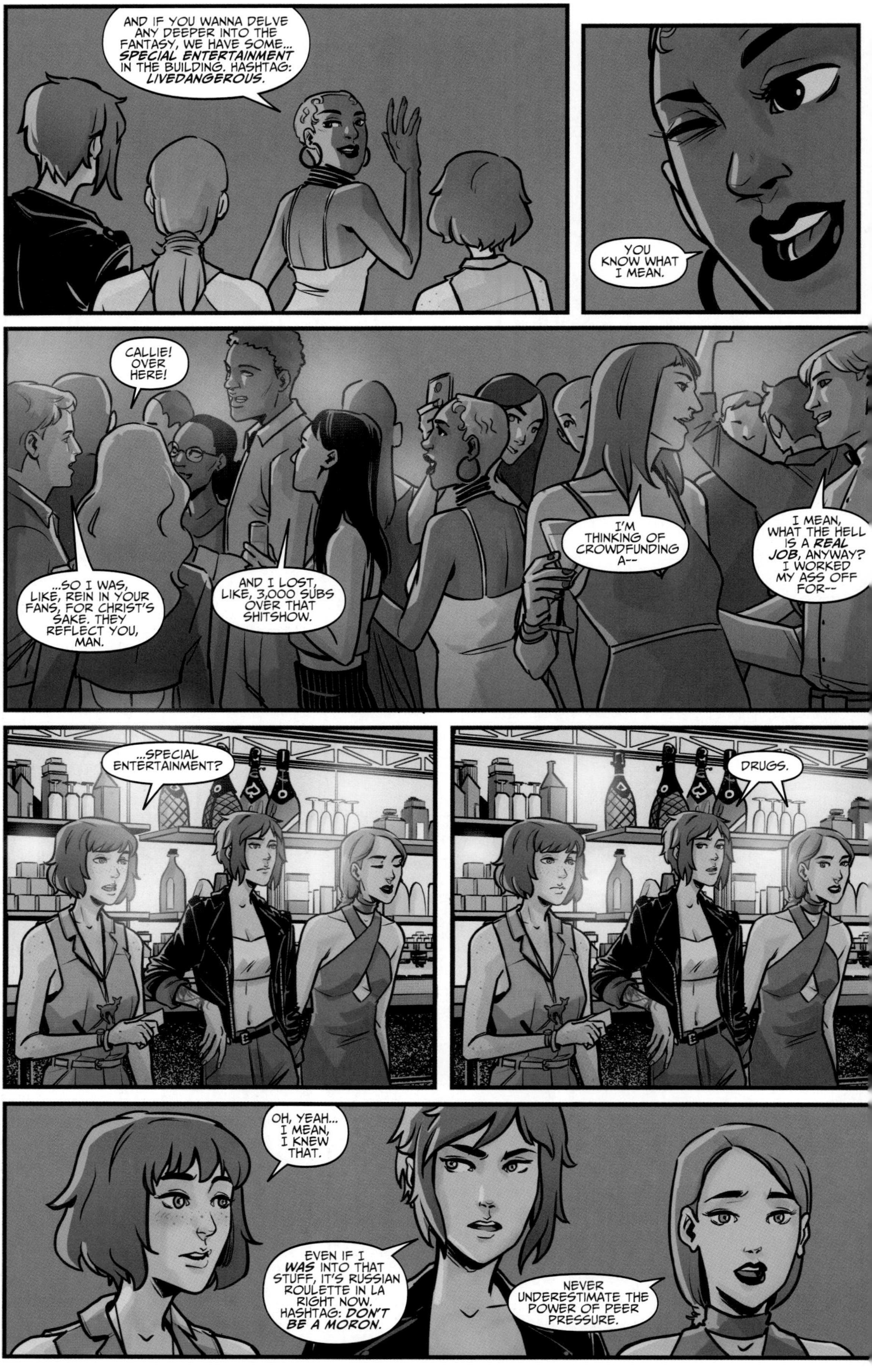

AND IF YOU WANNA DELVE ANY DEEPER INTO THE FANTASY, WE HAVE SOME... ***SPECIAL ENTERTAINMENT*** IN THE BUILDING. HASHTAG: ***LIVEDANGEROUS***.
YOU KNOW WHAT I MEAN.
CALLIE! OVER HERE!
...SO I WAS, LIKE, REIN IN YOUR FANS, FOR CHRIST'S SAKE. THEY REFLECT YOU, MAN.
AND I LOST, LIKE, 3,000 SUBS OVER THAT SHITSHOW.
I'M THINKING OF CROWDFUNDING A--
I MEAN, WHAT THE HELL IS A ***REAL JOB***, ANYWAY? I WORKED MY ASS OFF FOR--
...SPECIAL ENTERTAINMENT?
DRUGS.
OH, YEAH... I MEAN, I KNEW THAT.
EVEN IF I ***WAS*** INTO THAT STUFF, IT'S RUSSIAN ROULETTE IN LA RIGHT NOW. HASHTAG: ***DON'T BE A MORON***.
NEVER UNDERESTIMATE THE POWER OF PEER PRESSURE.

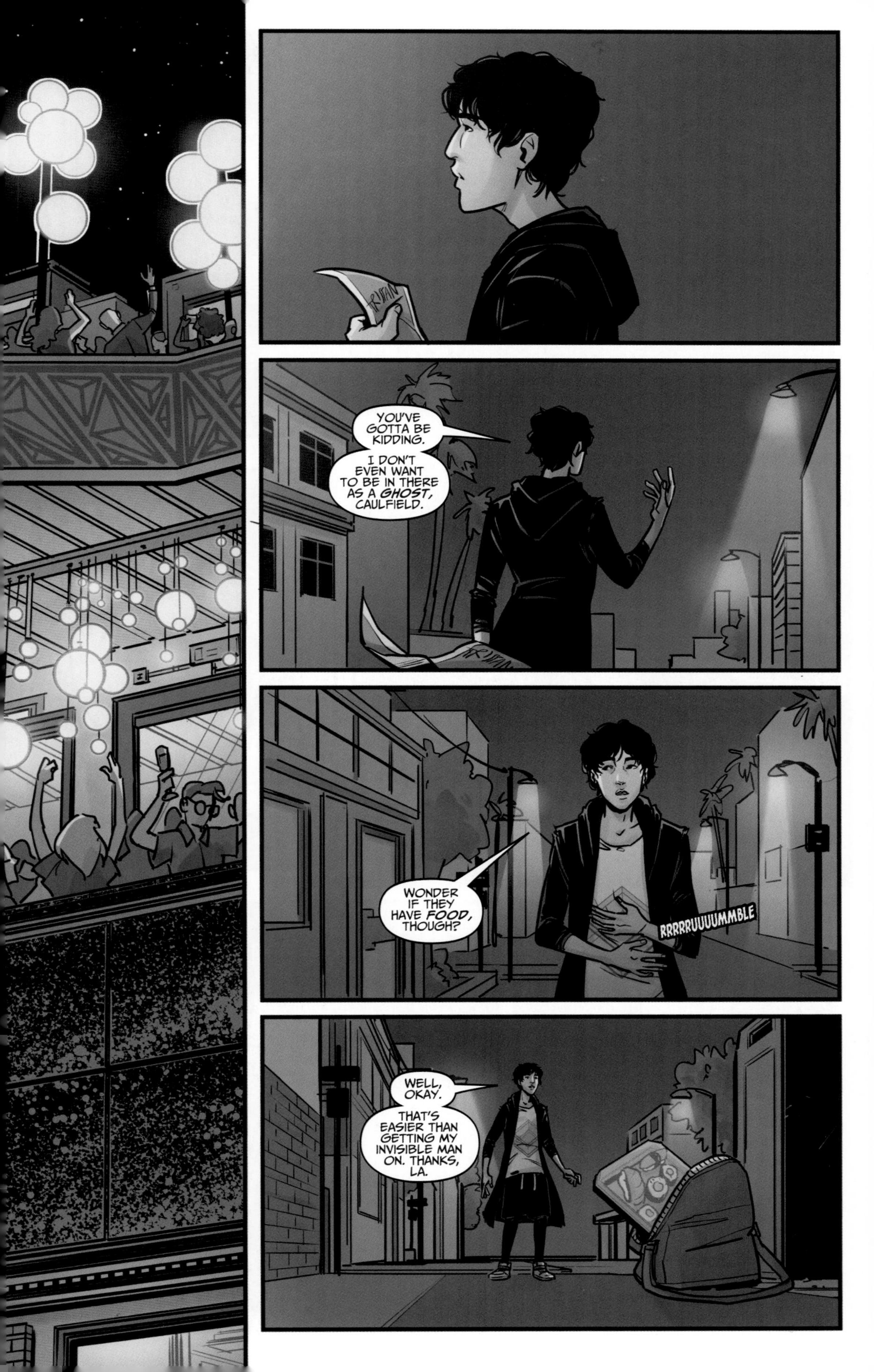

TRISTAN
YOU'VE GOTTA BE KIDDING.
I DON'T EVEN WANT TO BE IN THERE AS A *GHOST*, CAULFIELD.
WONDER IF THEY HAVE *FOOD*, THOUGH?
RRRRRUUUUMMBLE
WELL, OKAY.
THAT'S EASIER THAN GETTING MY INVISIBLE MAN ON. THANKS, LA.

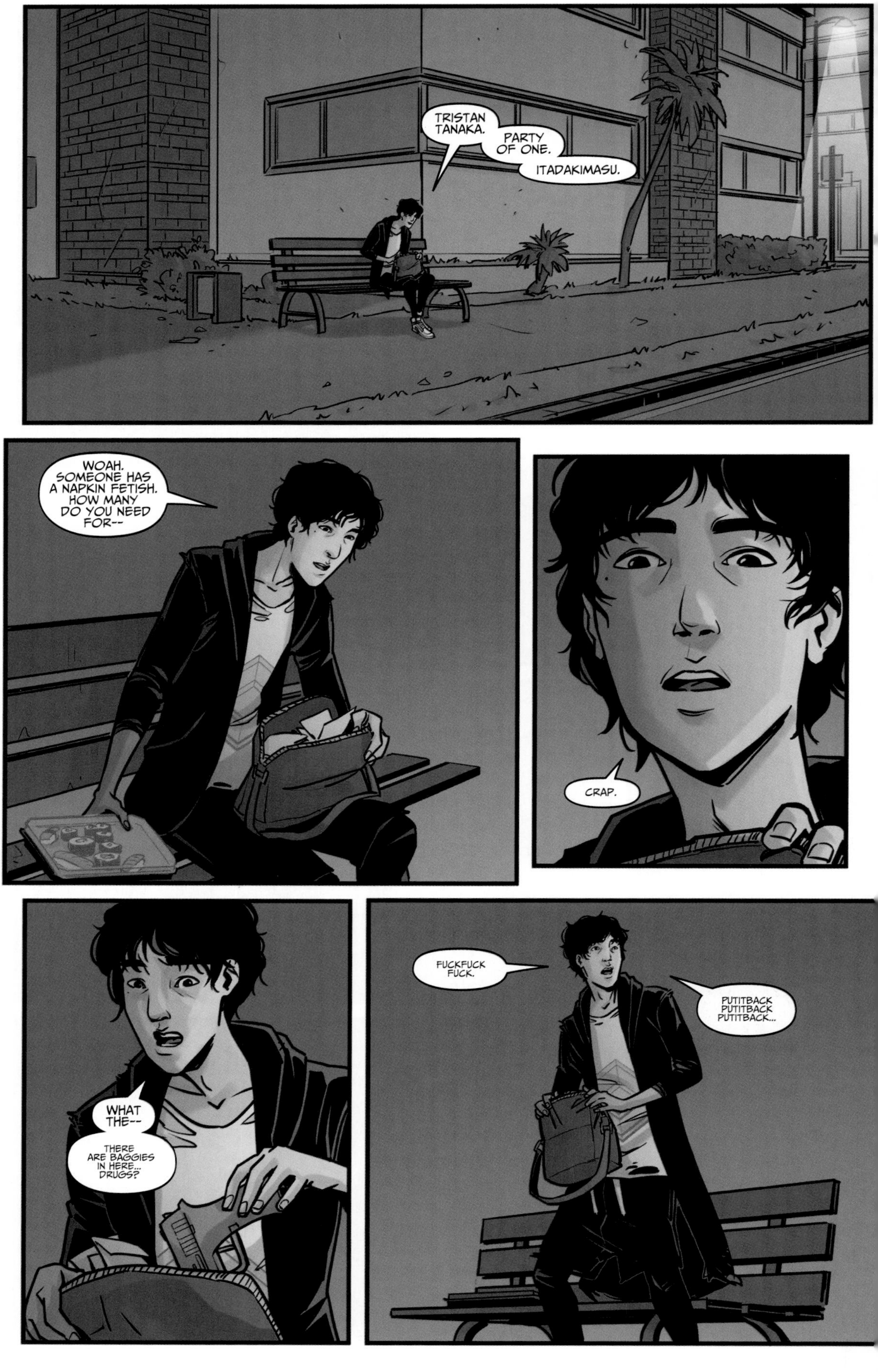
TRISTAN TANAKA.
PARTY OF ONE.
ITADAKIMASU.
WOAH. SOMEONE HAS A NAPKIN FETISH. HOW MANY DO YOU NEED FOR--
CRAP.
WHAT THE--
THERE ARE BAGGIES IN HERE... DRUGS?
FUCKFUCK FUCK.
PUTITBACK PUTITBACK PUTITBACK...

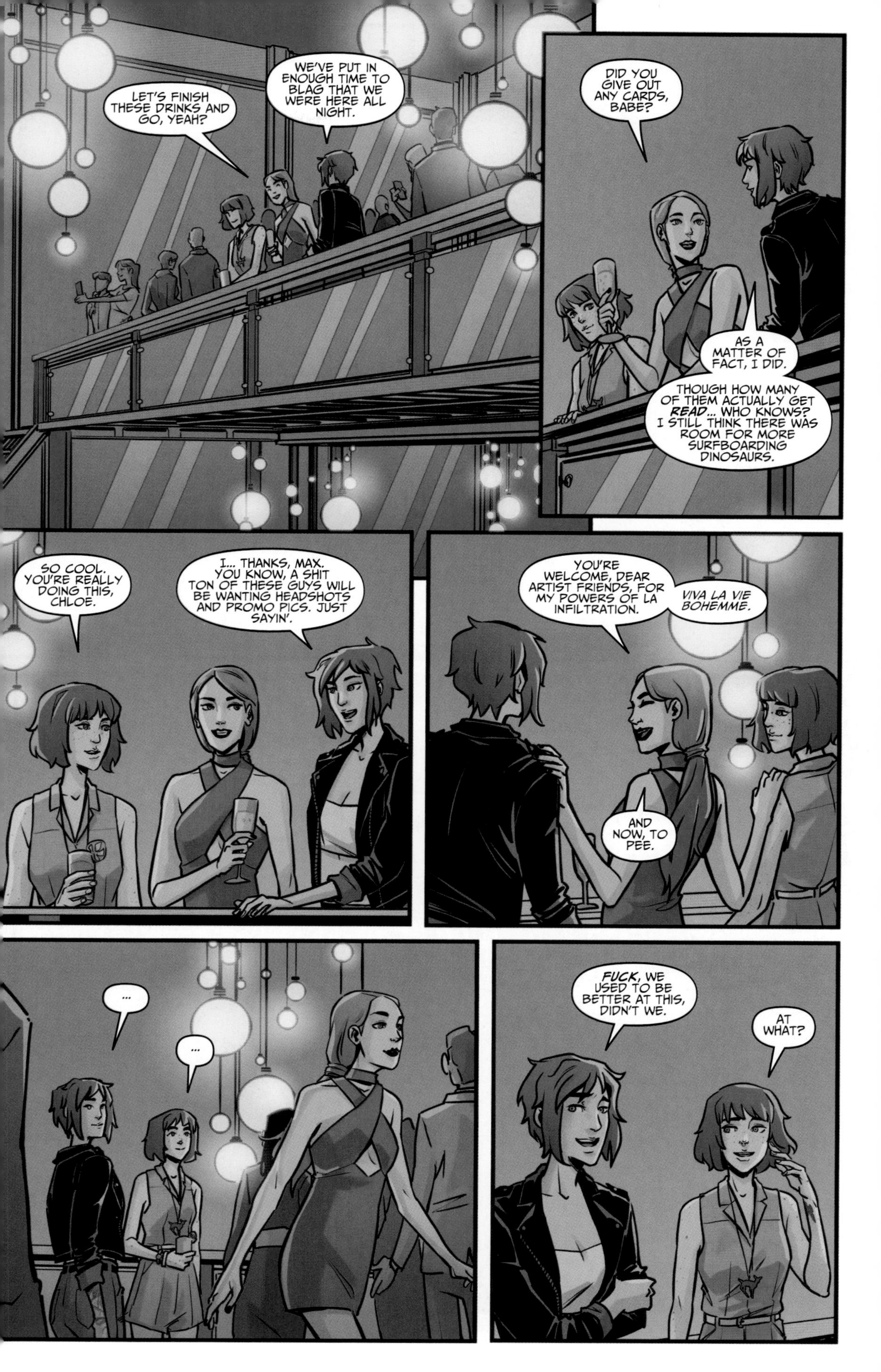
LET'S FINISH THESE DRINKS AND GO, YEAH?
WE'VE PUT IN ENOUGH TIME TO BLAG THAT WE WERE HERE ALL NIGHT.
DID YOU GIVE OUT ANY CARDS, BABE?
AS A MATTER OF FACT, I DID.
THOUGH HOW MANY OF THEM ACTUALLY GET READ... WHO KNOWS? I STILL THINK THERE WAS ROOM FOR MORE SURFBOARDING DINOSAURS.
SO COOL. YOU'RE REALLY DOING THIS, CHLOE.
I... THANKS, MAX. YOU KNOW, A SHIT TON OF THESE GUYS WILL BE WANTING HEADSHOTS AND PROMO PICS. JUST SAYIN'.
YOU'RE WELCOME, DEAR ARTIST FRIENDS, FOR MY POWERS OF LA INFILTRATION.
VIVA LA VIE BOHEMME.
AND NOW, TO PEE.
...
...
FUCK, WE USED TO BE BETTER AT THIS, DIDN'T WE.
AT WHAT?

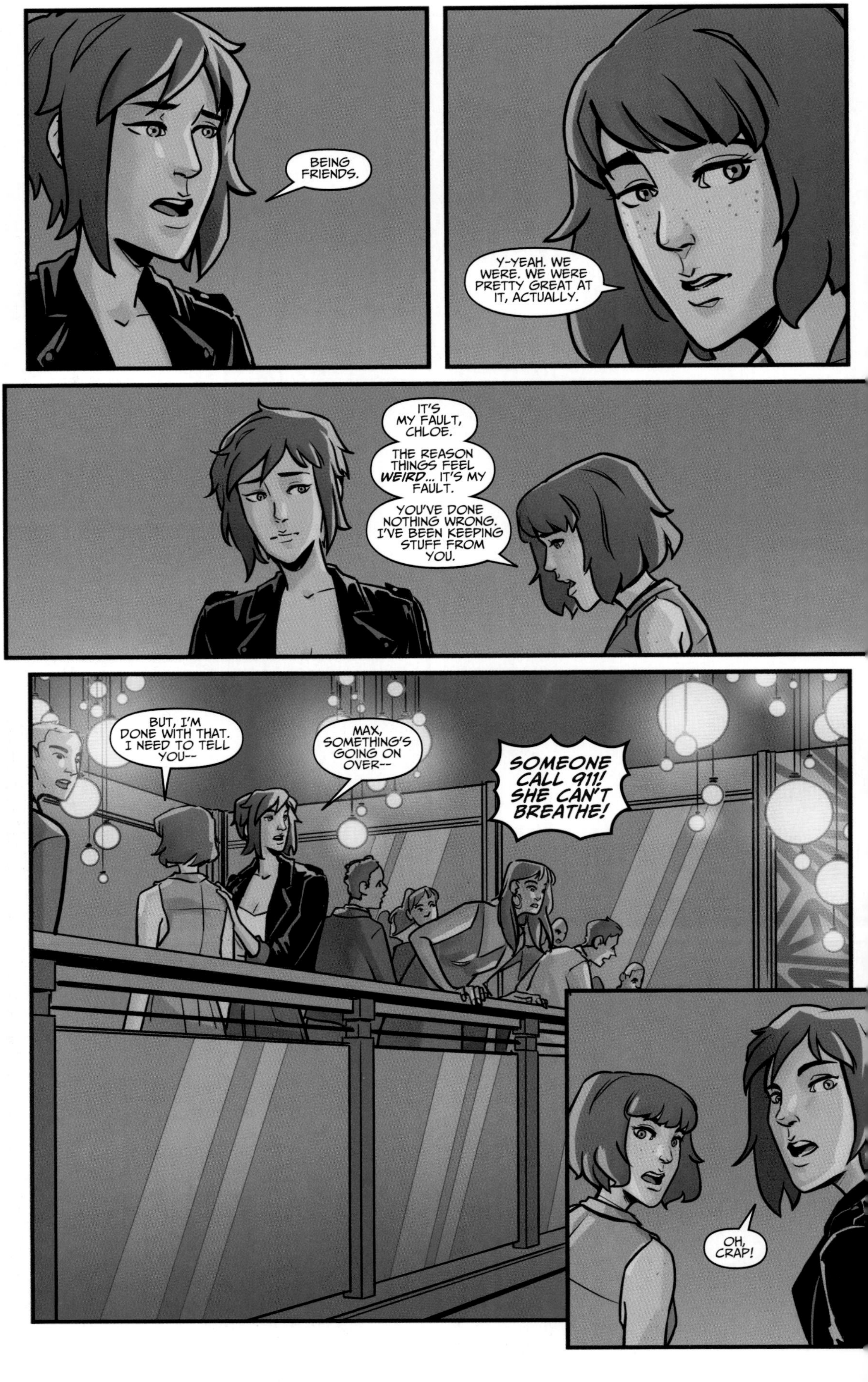
BEING FRIENDS.
Y-YEAH. WE WERE. WE WERE PRETTY GREAT AT IT, ACTUALLY.
IT'S MY FAULT, CHLOE.
THE REASON THINGS FEEL *WEIRD*... IT'S MY FAULT.
YOU'VE DONE NOTHING WRONG. I'VE BEEN KEEPING STUFF FROM YOU.
BUT, I'M DONE WITH THAT. I NEED TO TELL YOU--
MAX, SOMETHING'S GOING ON OVER--
SOMEONE CALL 911! SHE CAN'T BREATHE!
OH, CRAP!

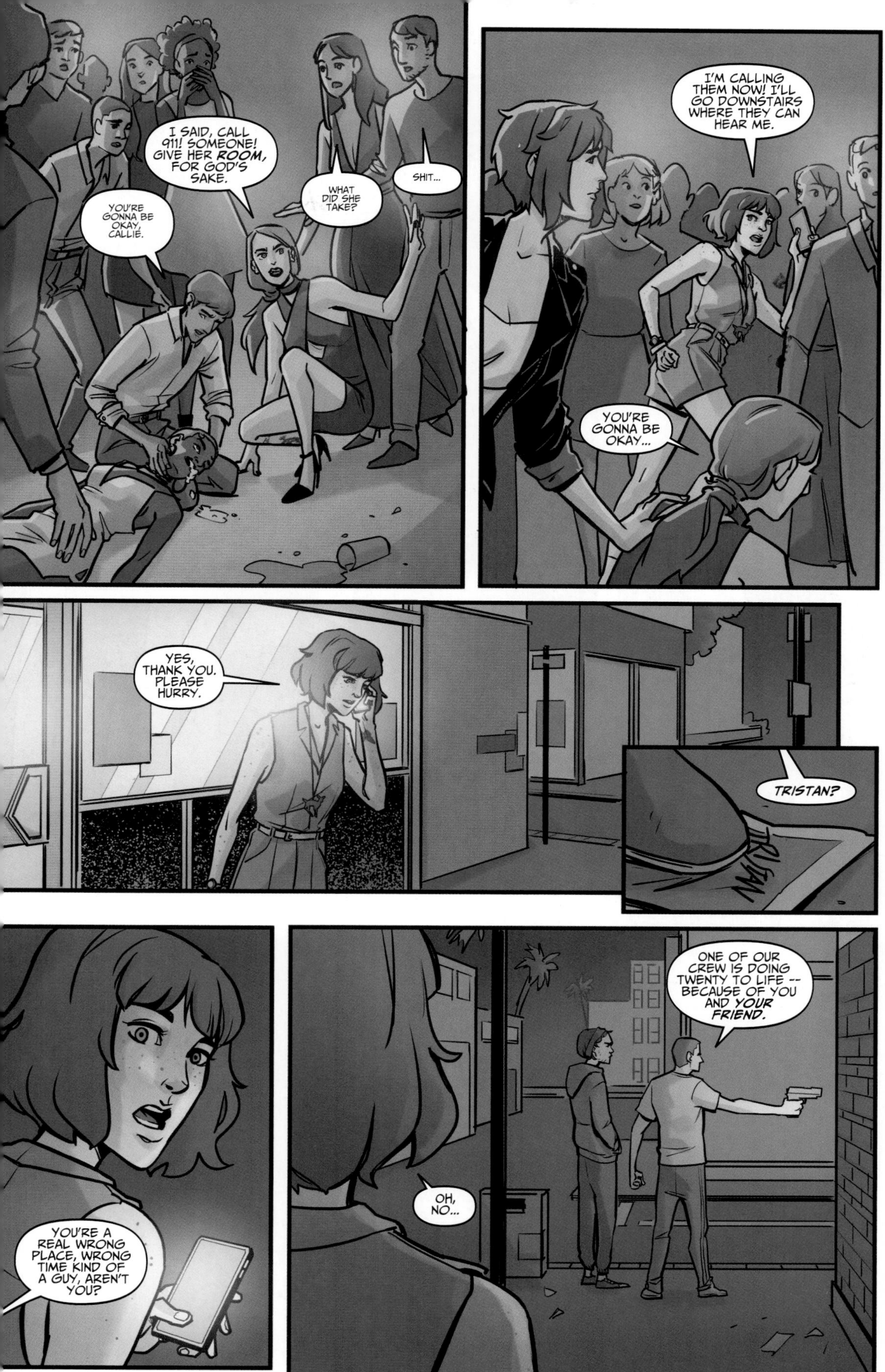
I SAID, CALL 911! SOMEONE! GIVE HER ROOM, FOR GOD'S SAKE.
YOU'RE GONNA BE OKAY, CALLIE.
WHAT DID SHE TAKE?
SHIT...
I'M CALLING THEM NOW! I'LL GO DOWNSTAIRS WHERE THEY CAN HEAR ME.
YOU'RE GONNA BE OKAY...
YES, THANK YOU. PLEASE HURRY.
TRISTAN?
YOU'RE A REAL WRONG PLACE, WRONG TIME KIND OF A GUY, AREN'T YOU?
OH, NO...
ONE OF OUR CREW IS DOING TWENTY TO LIFE -- BECAUSE OF YOU AND YOUR FRIEND.

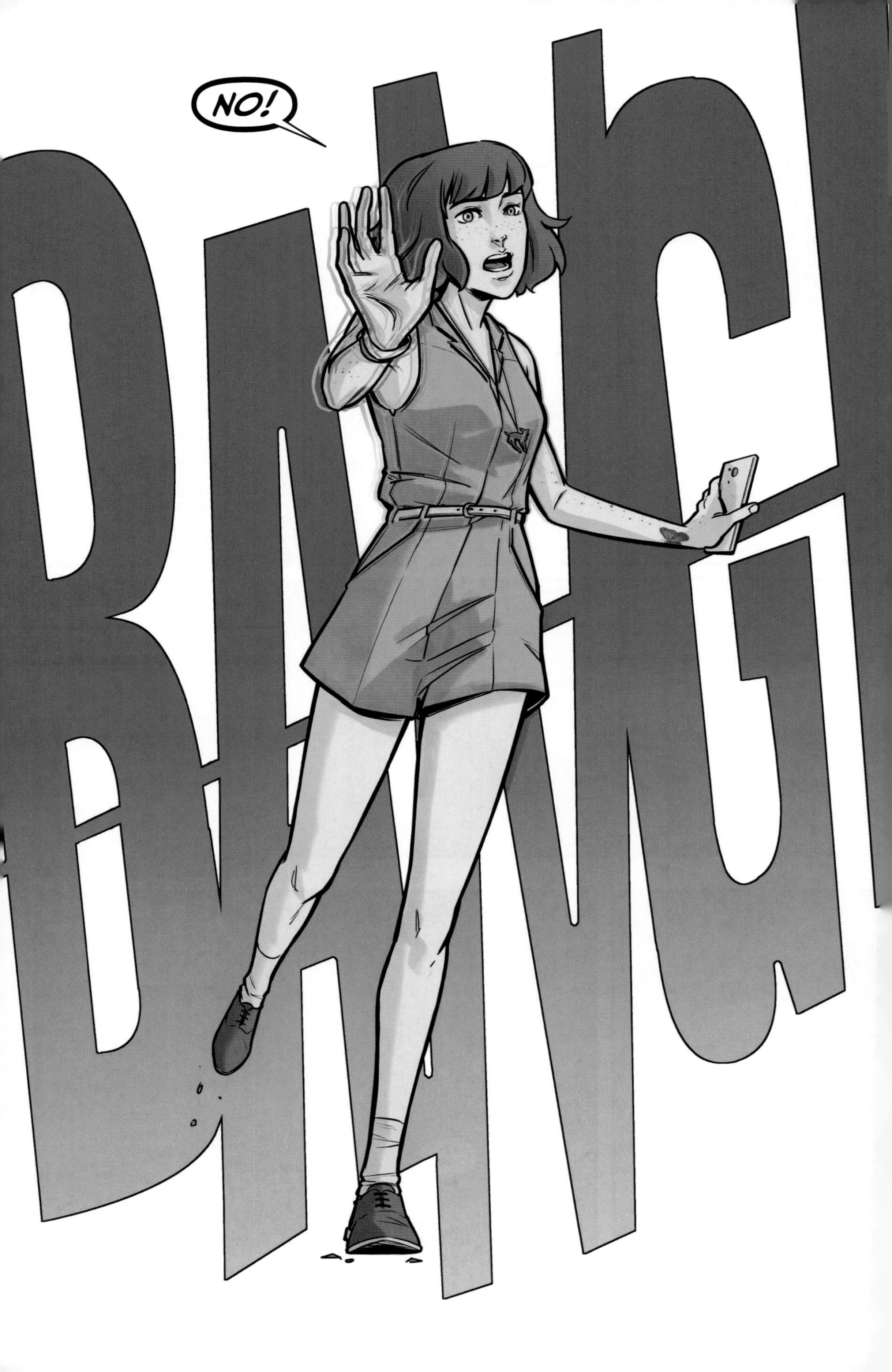
NO!
BANG

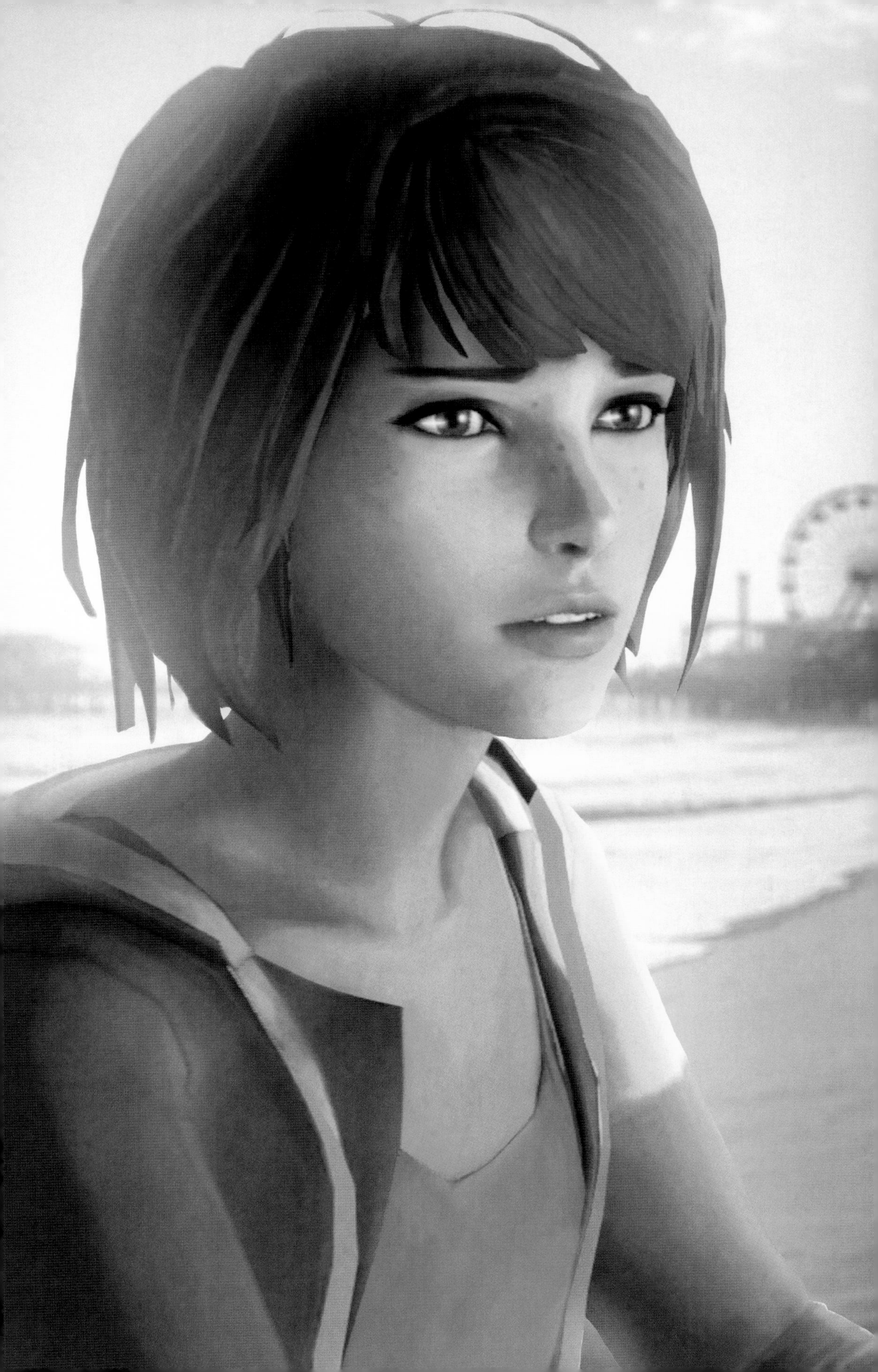

CHAPTER 4

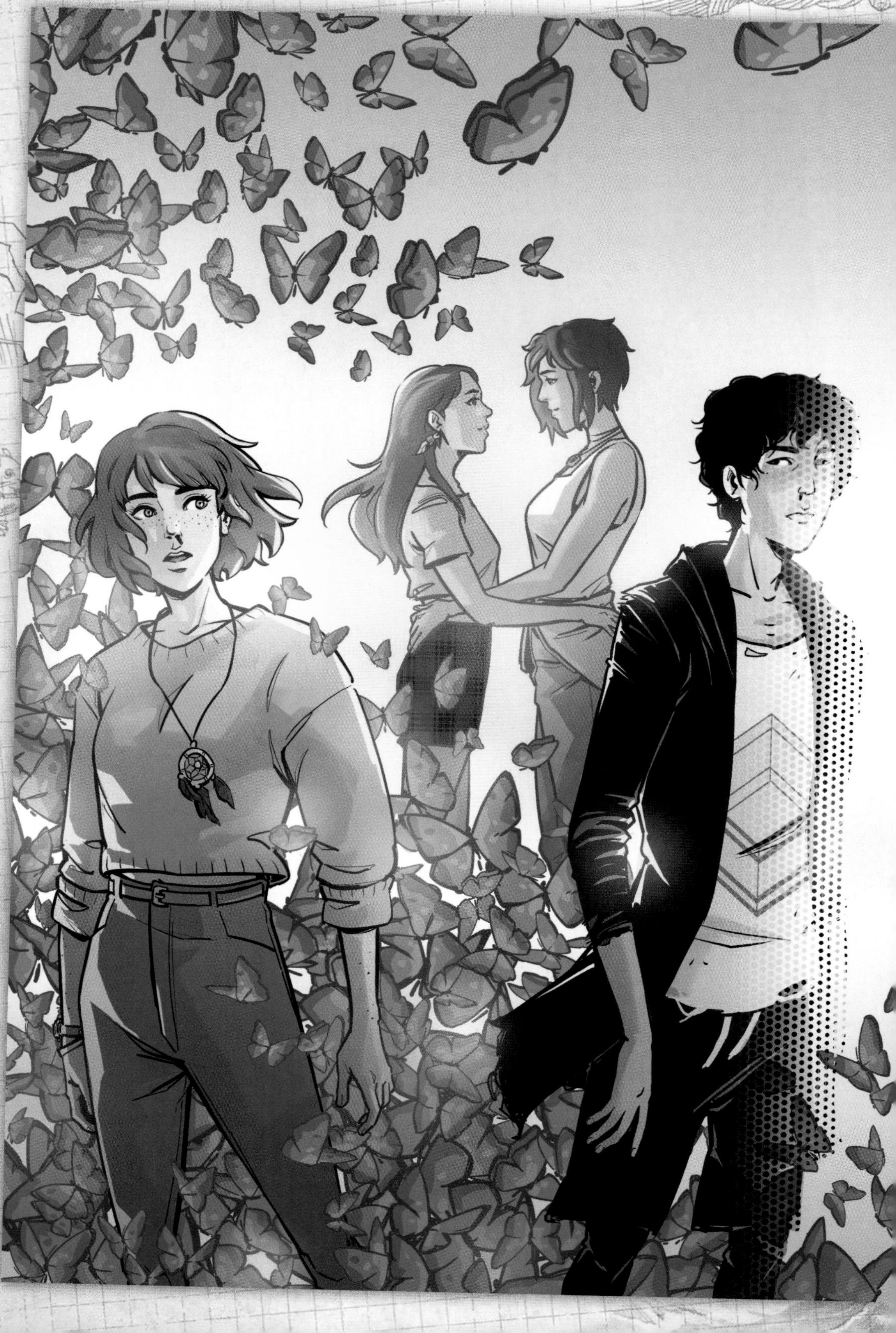

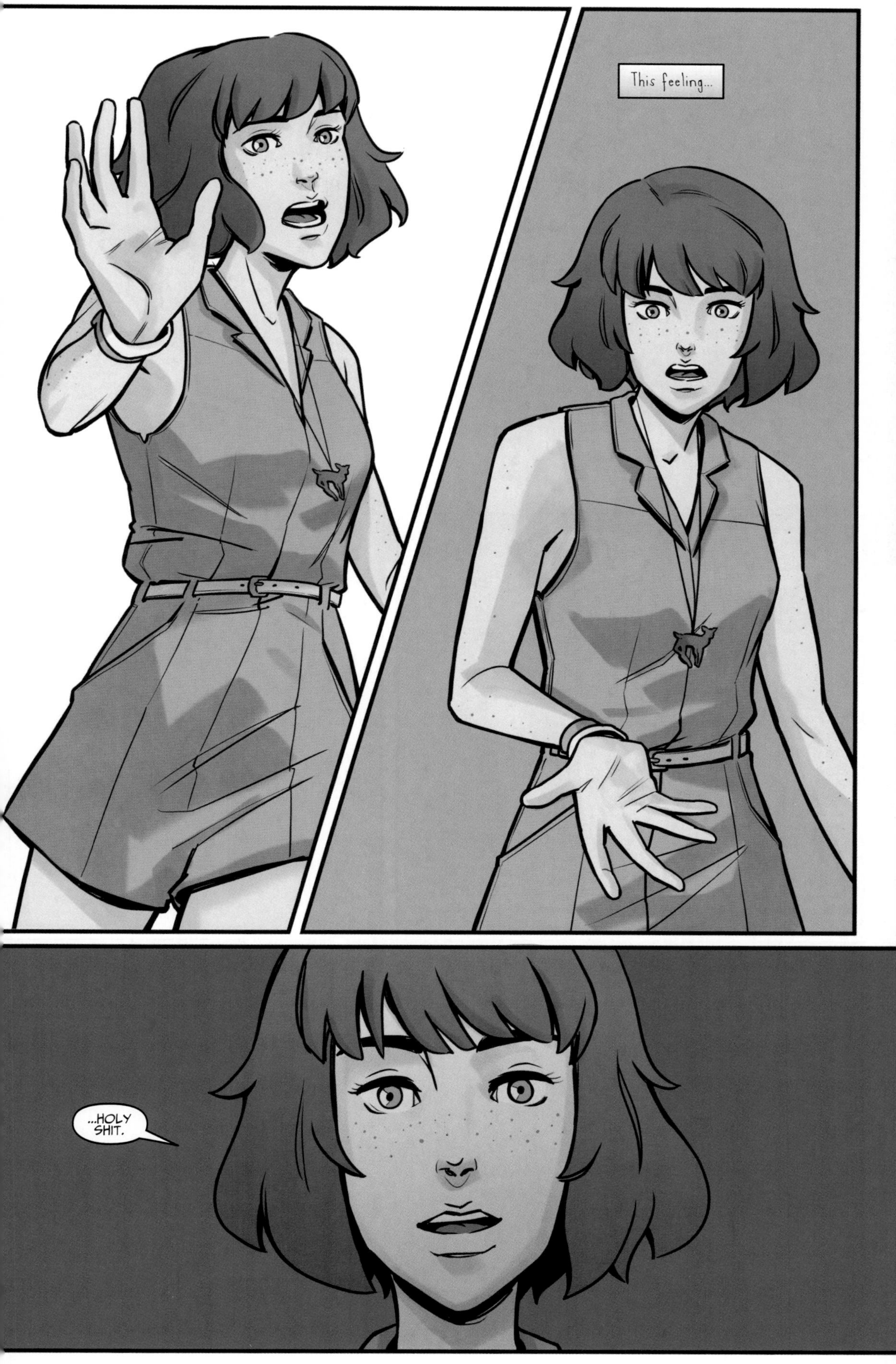
This feeling...
...HOLY SHIT.

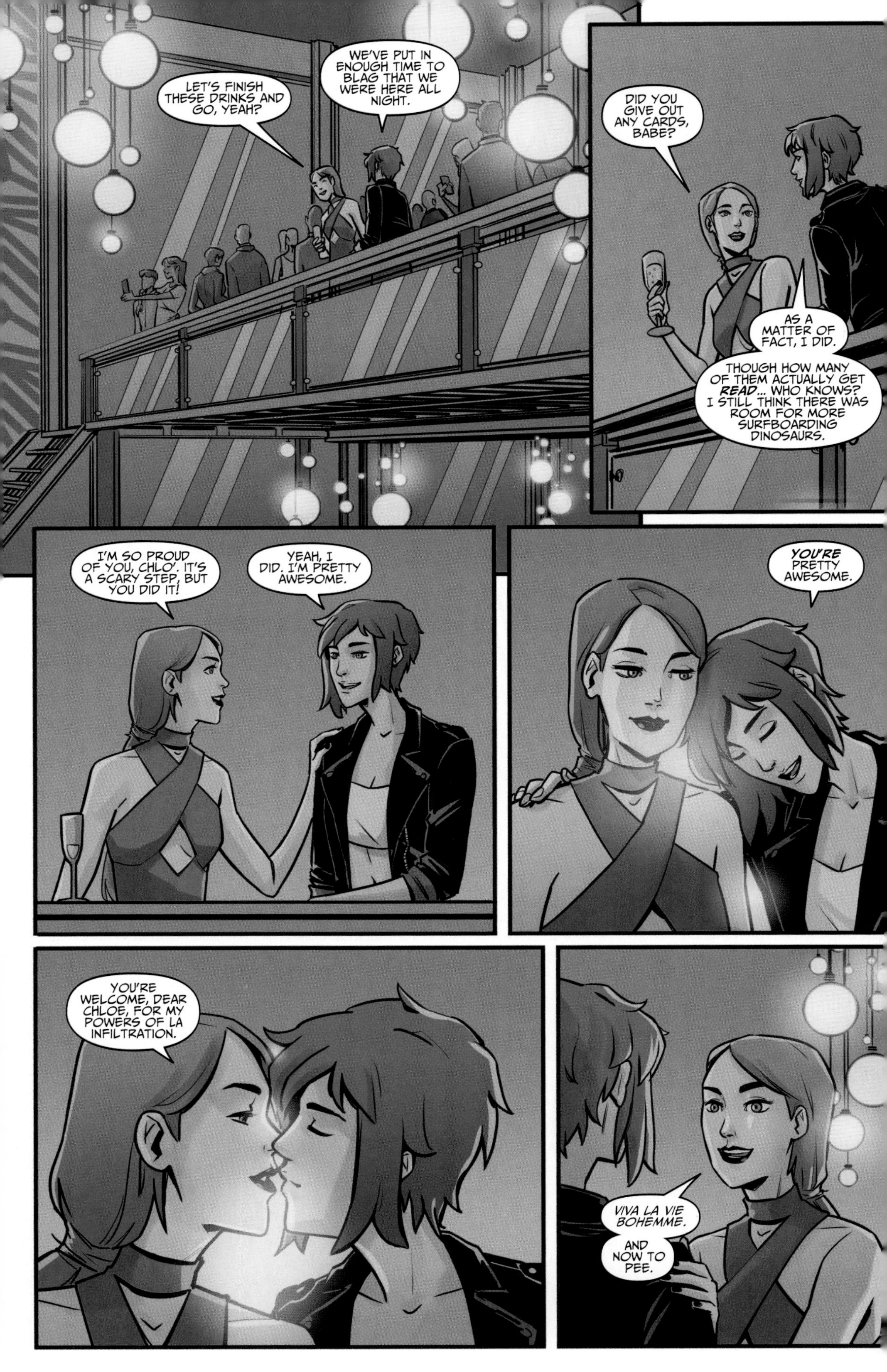
LET'S FINISH THESE DRINKS AND GO, YEAH?
WE'VE PUT IN ENOUGH TIME TO BLAG THAT WE WERE HERE ALL NIGHT.
DID YOU GIVE OUT ANY CARDS, BABE?
AS A MATTER OF FACT, I DID.
THOUGH HOW MANY OF THEM ACTUALLY GET READ... WHO KNOWS? I STILL THINK THERE WAS ROOM FOR MORE SURFBOARDING DINOSAURS.
I'M SO PROUD OF YOU, CHLO'. IT'S A SCARY STEP, BUT YOU DID IT!
YEAH, I DID. I'M PRETTY AWESOME.
YOU'RE PRETTY AWESOME.
YOU'RE WELCOME, DEAR CHLOE, FOR MY POWERS OF LA INFILTRATION.
VIVA LA VIE BOHEMME.
AND NOW TO PEE.

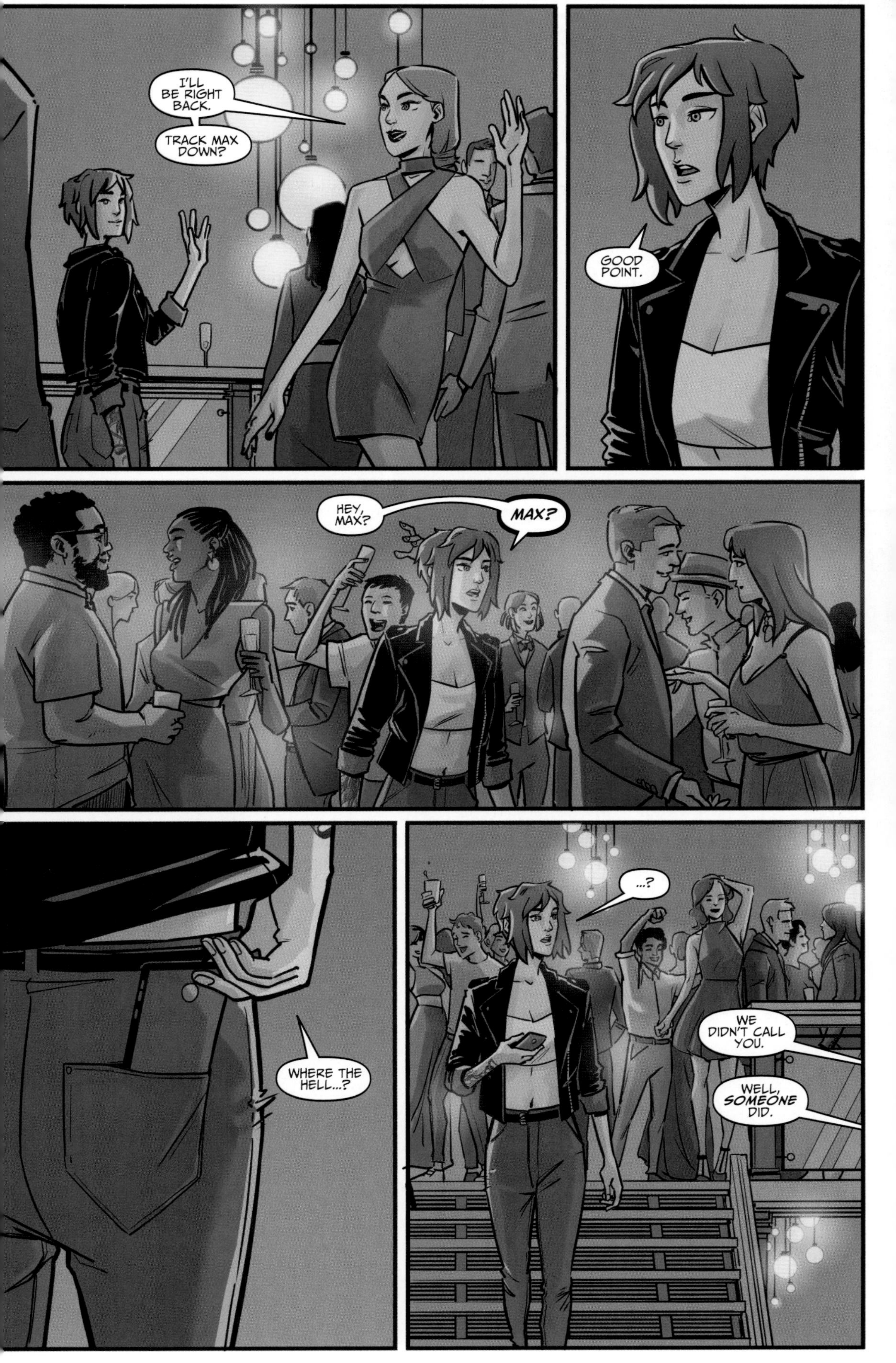
I'LL BE RIGHT BACK.
TRACK MAX DOWN?
GOOD POINT.
HEY, MAX?
MAX?
WHERE THE HELL...?
...?
WE DIDN'T CALL YOU.
WELL, SOMEONE DID.

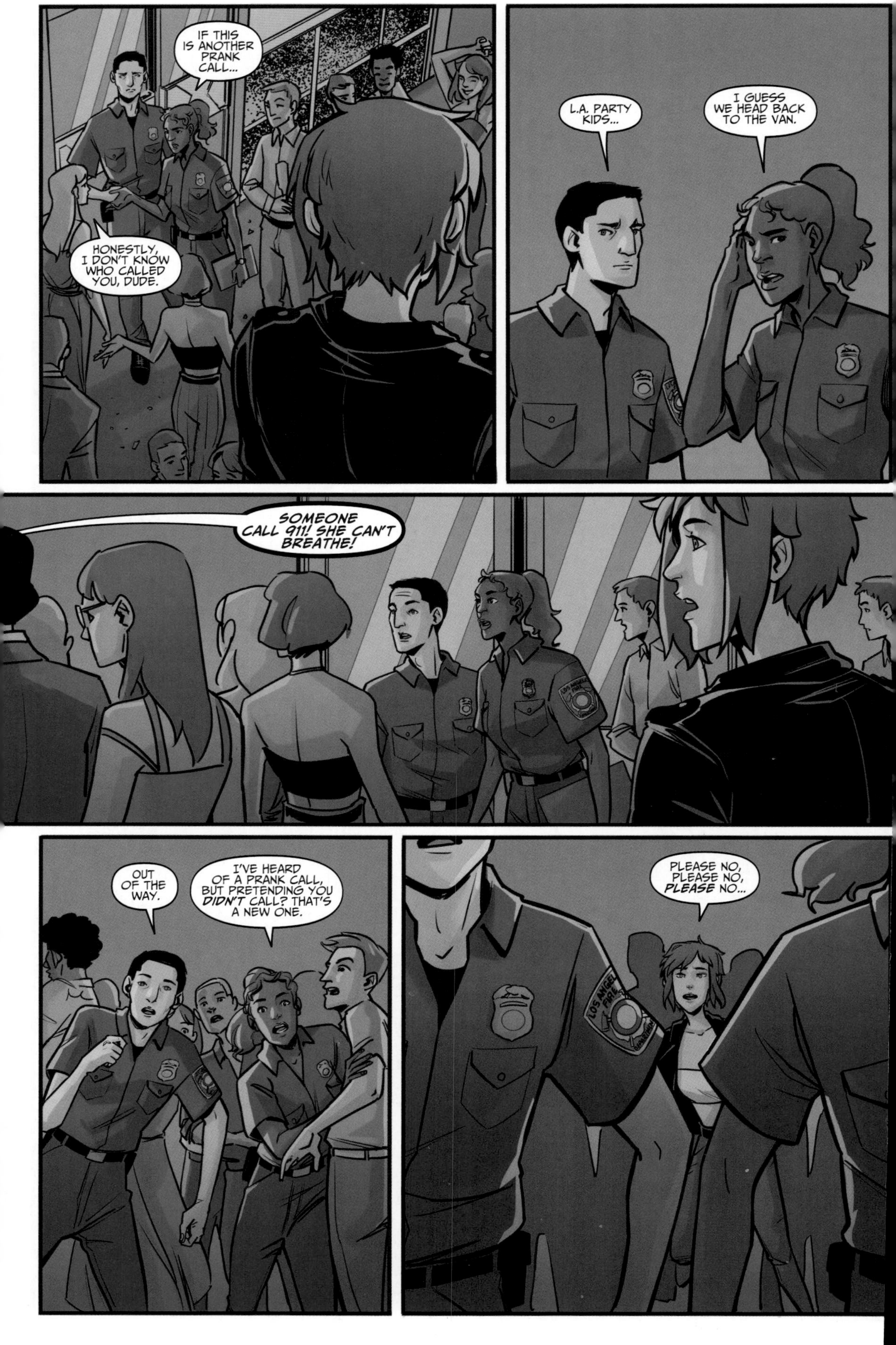
IF THIS IS ANOTHER PRANK CALL...
HONESTLY, I DON'T KNOW WHO CALLED YOU, DUDE.
L.A. PARTY KIDS...
I GUESS WE HEAD BACK TO THE VAN.
SOMEONE CALL 911! SHE CAN'T BREATHE!
OUT OF THE WAY.
I'VE HEARD OF A PRANK CALL, BUT PRETENDING YOU DIDN'T CALL? THAT'S A NEW ONE.
PLEASE NO, PLEASE NO, PLEASE NO...

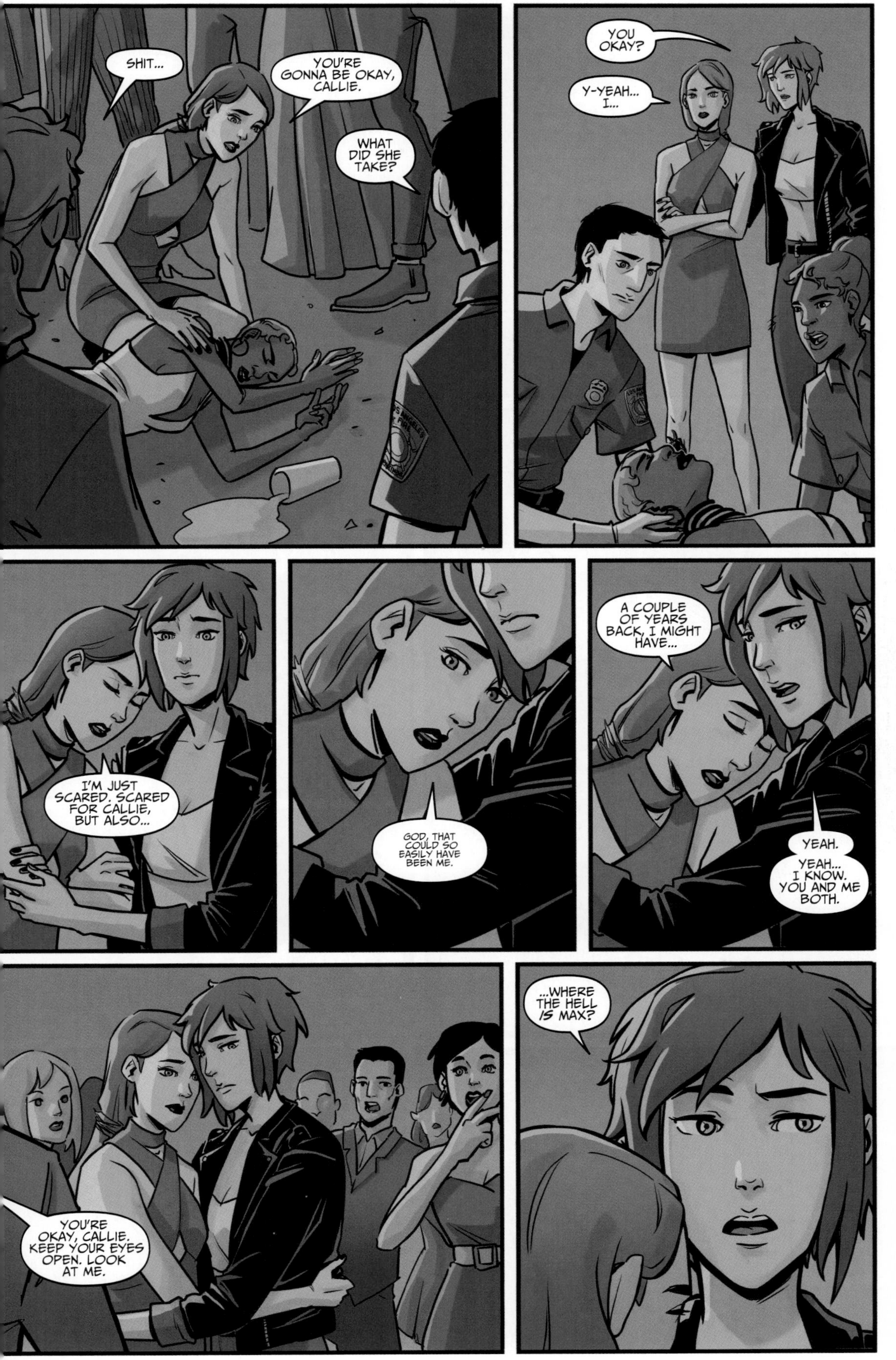
SHIT...
YOU'RE GONNA BE OKAY, CALLIE.
WHAT DID SHE TAKE?
YOU OKAY?
Y-YEAH... I...
I'M JUST SCARED. SCARED FOR CALLIE, BUT ALSO...
GOD, THAT COULD SO EASILY HAVE BEEN ME.
A COUPLE OF YEARS BACK, I MIGHT HAVE...
YEAH.
YEAH... I KNOW. YOU AND ME BOTH.
YOU'RE OKAY, CALLIE. KEEP YOUR EYES OPEN. LOOK AT ME.
...WHERE THE HELL *IS* MAX?

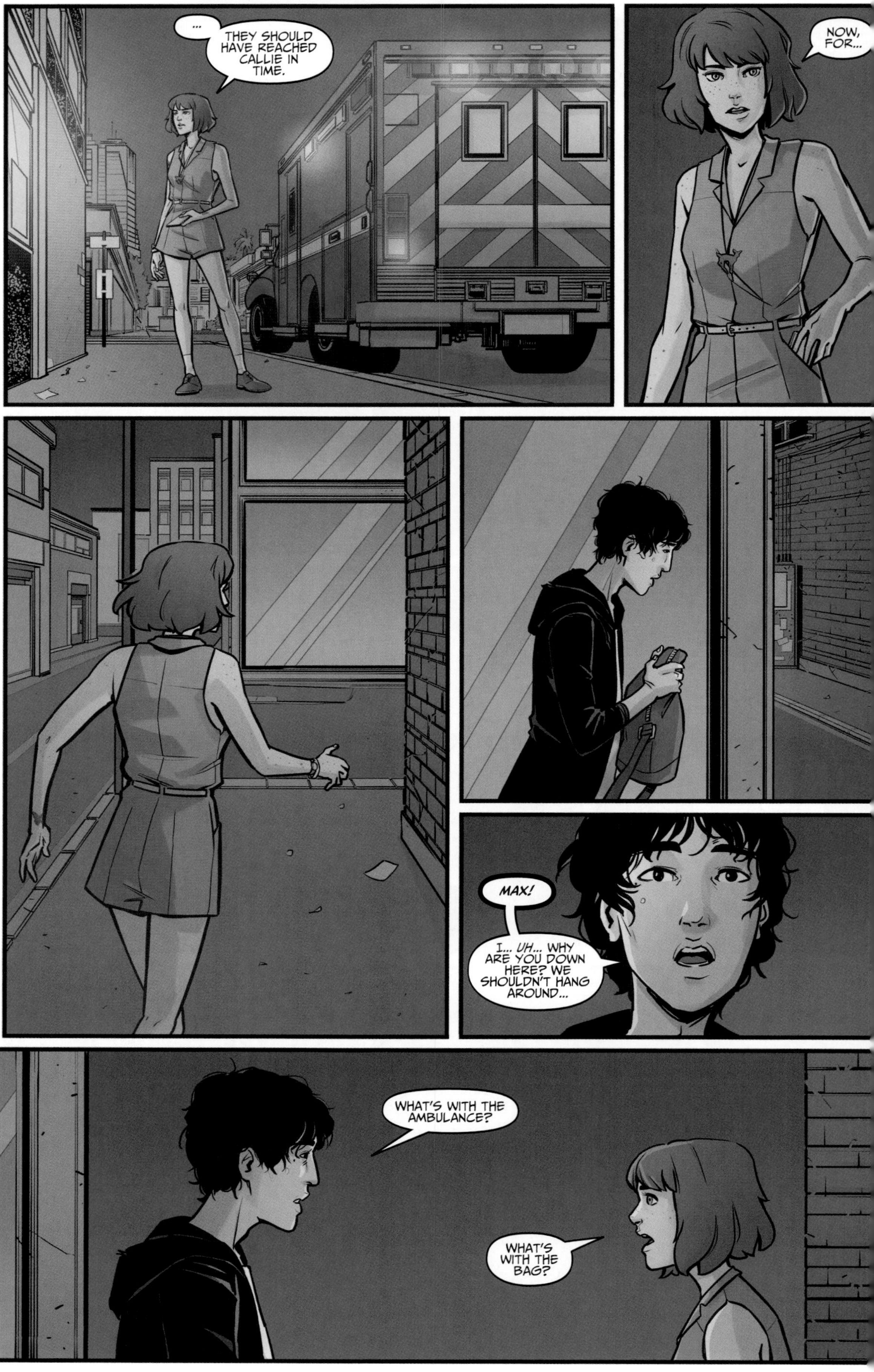
...
THEY SHOULD HAVE REACHED CALLIE IN TIME.
NOW, FOR...
MAX!
I... UH... WHY ARE YOU DOWN HERE? WE SHOULDN'T HANG AROUND...
WHAT'S WITH THE AMBULANCE?
WHAT'S WITH THE BAG?

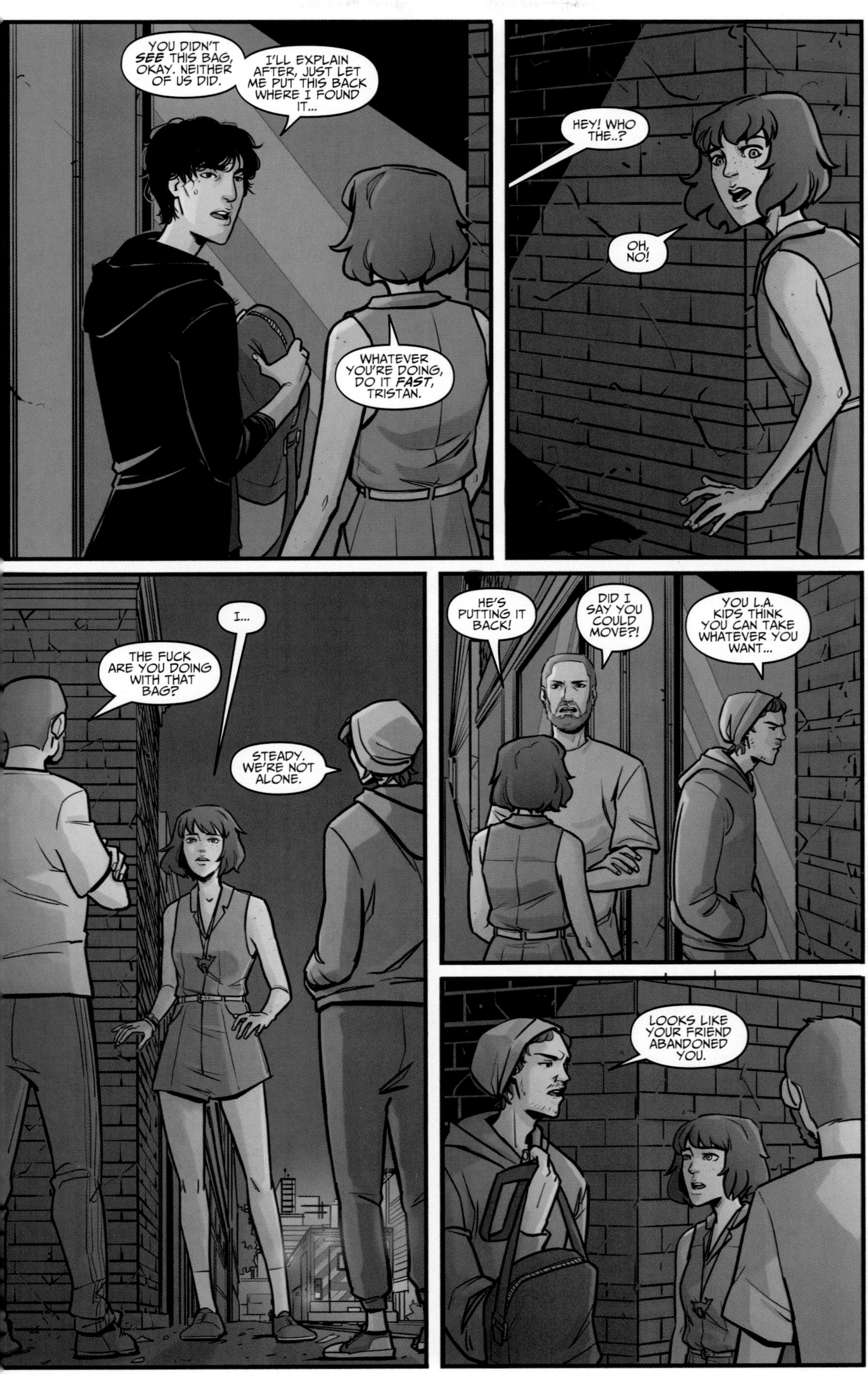
YOU DIDN'T SEE THIS BAG, OKAY. NEITHER OF US DID.
I'LL EXPLAIN AFTER, JUST LET ME PUT THIS BACK WHERE I FOUND IT...
WHATEVER YOU'RE DOING, DO IT FAST, TRISTAN.
HEY! WHO THE..?
OH, NO!
THE FUCK ARE YOU DOING WITH THAT BAG?
I...
STEADY. WE'RE NOT ALONE.
HE'S PUTTING IT BACK!
DID I SAY YOU COULD MOVE?!
YOU L.A. KIDS THINK YOU CAN TAKE WHATEVER YOU WANT...
LOOKS LIKE YOUR FRIEND ABANDONED YOU.

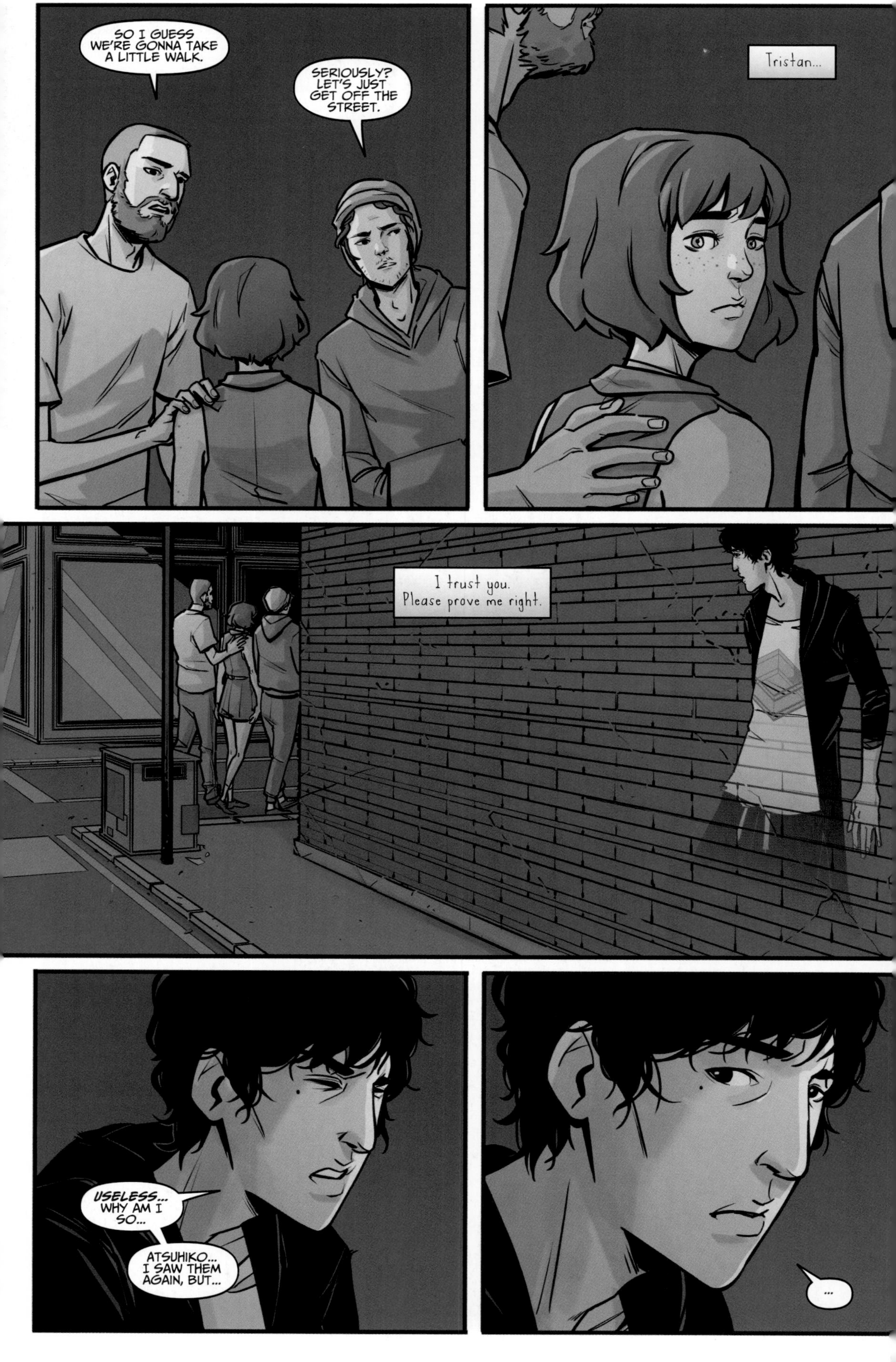
SO I GUESS WE'RE GONNA TAKE A LITTLE WALK.
SERIOUSLY? LET'S JUST GET OFF THE STREET.
Tristan...
I trust you. Please prove me right.
USELESS... WHY AM I SO...
ATSUHIKO... I SAW THEM AGAIN, BUT...
...

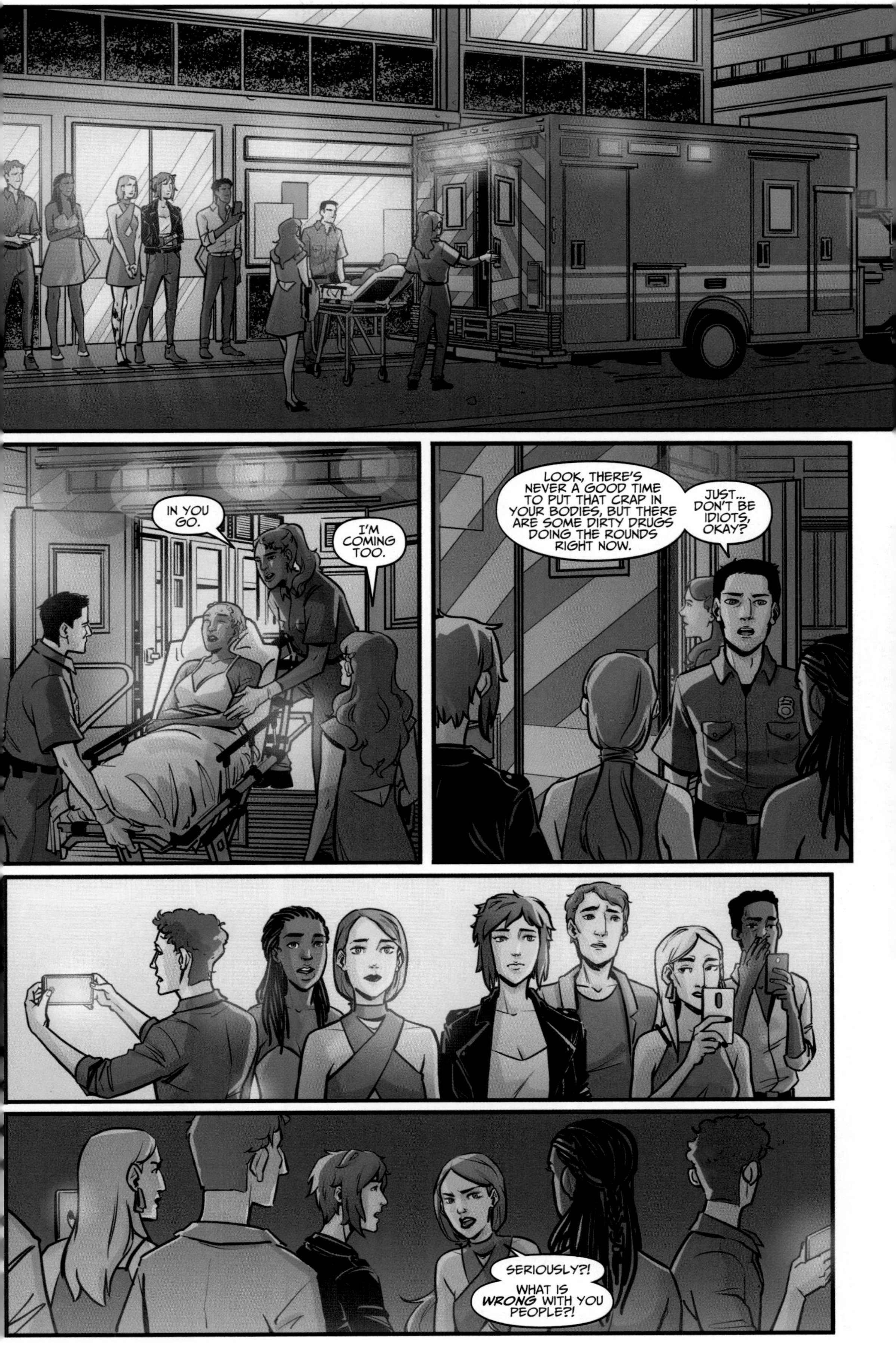
IN YOU GO.
I'M COMING TOO.
LOOK, THERE'S NEVER A GOOD TIME TO PUT THAT CRAP IN YOUR BODIES, BUT THERE ARE SOME DIRTY DRUGS DOING THE ROUNDS RIGHT NOW.
JUST... DON'T BE IDIOTS, OKAY?
SERIOUSLY?!
WHAT IS *WRONG* WITH YOU PEOPLE?!

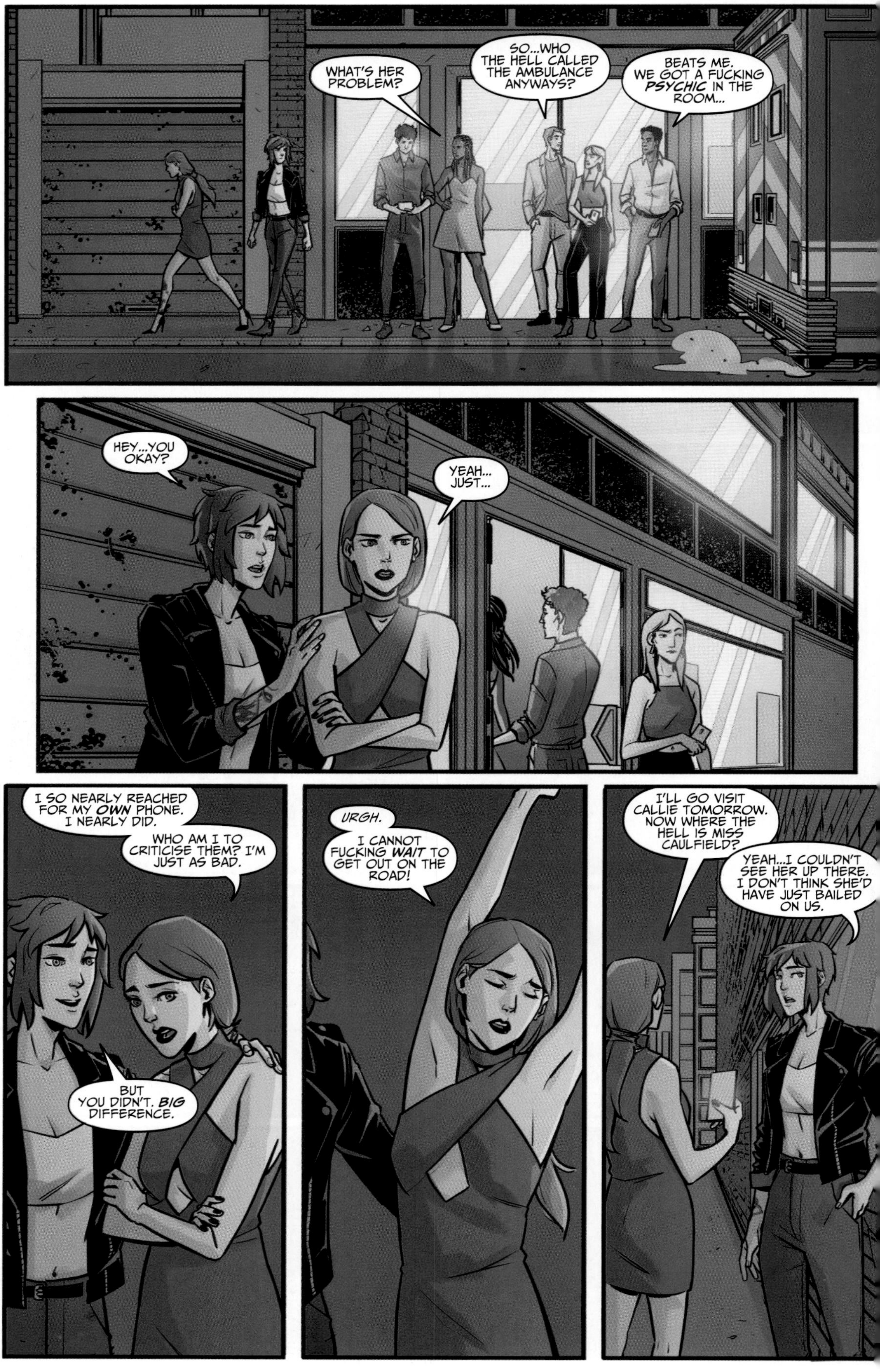
WHAT'S HER PROBLEM?
SO...WHO THE HELL CALLED THE AMBULANCE ANYWAYS?
BEATS ME. WE GOT A FUCKING PSYCHIC IN THE ROOM...
HEY...YOU OKAY?
YEAH... JUST...
I SO NEARLY REACHED FOR MY OWN PHONE. I NEARLY DID.
WHO AM I TO CRITICISE THEM? I'M JUST AS BAD.
BUT YOU DIDN'T. BIG DIFFERENCE.
URGH.
I CANNOT FUCKING WAIT TO GET OUT ON THE ROAD!
I'LL GO VISIT CALLIE TOMORROW. NOW WHERE THE HELL IS MISS CAULFIELD?
YEAH...I COULDN'T SEE HER UP THERE. I DON'T THINK SHE'D HAVE JUST BAILED ON US.

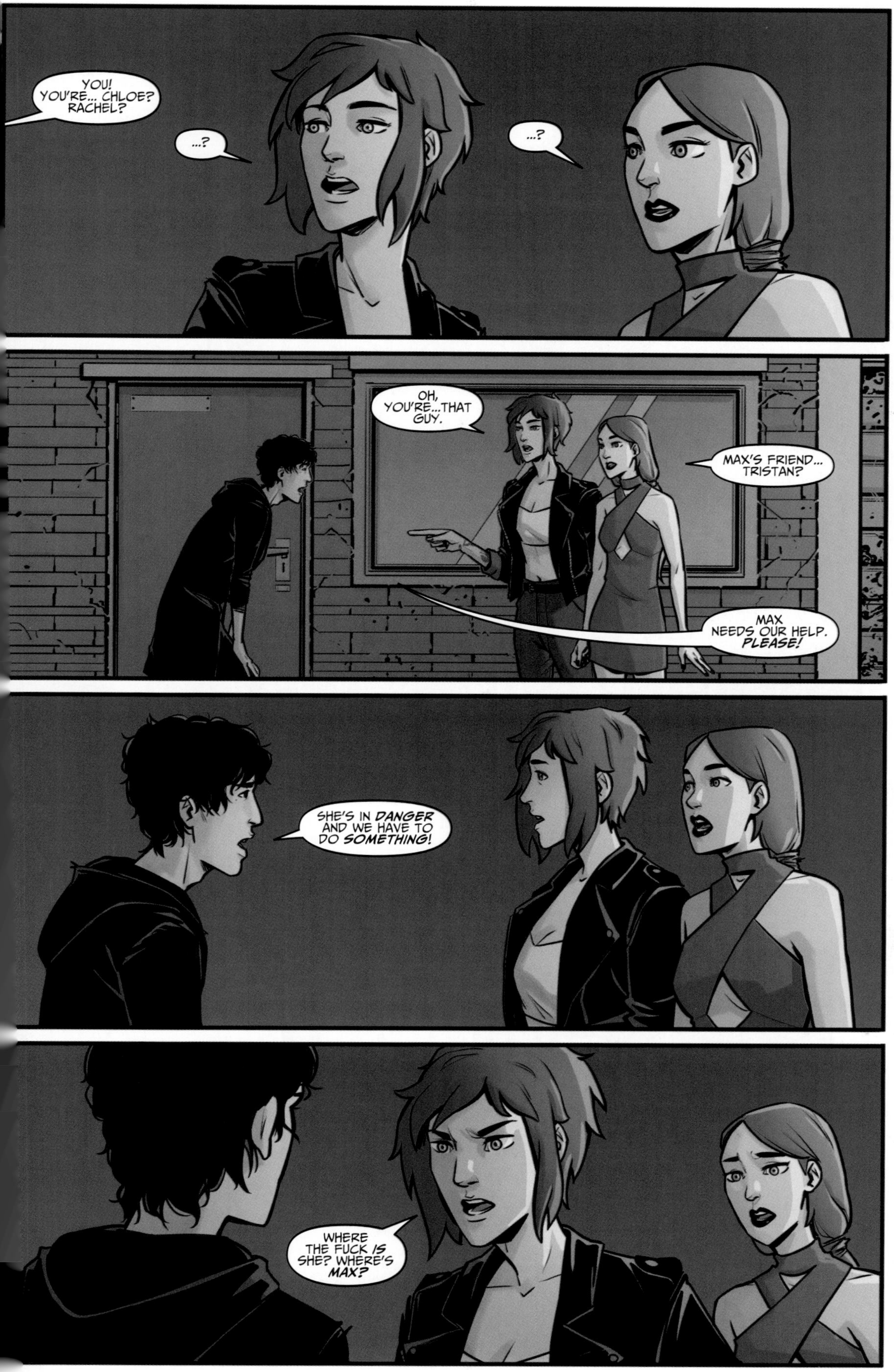
YOU! YOU'RE... CHLOE? RACHEL?
...?
...?
OH, YOU'RE...THAT GUY.
MAX'S FRIEND... TRISTAN?
MAX NEEDS OUR HELP. PLEASE!
SHE'S IN DANGER AND WE HAVE TO DO SOMETHING!
WHERE THE FUCK IS SHE? WHERE'S MAX?

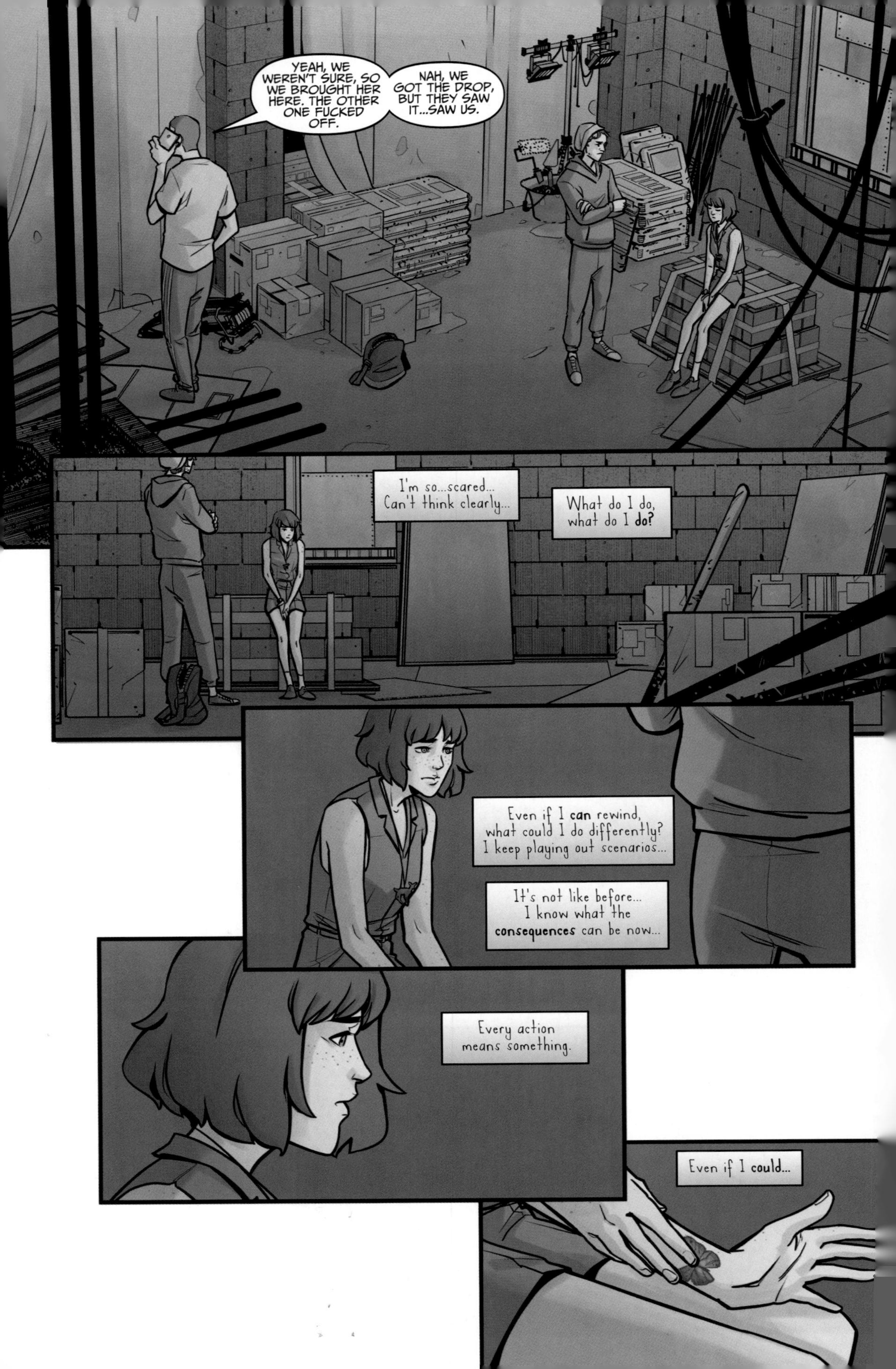
YEAH, WE WEREN'T SURE, SO WE BROUGHT HER HERE. THE OTHER ONE FUCKED OFF.
NAH, WE GOT THE DROP, BUT THEY SAW IT...SAW US.
I'm so...scared... Can't think clearly...
What do I do, what do I **do?**
Even if I **can** rewind, what could I do differently? I keep playing out scenarios...
It's not like before... I know what the **consequences** can be now...
Every action means something.
Even if I **could...**

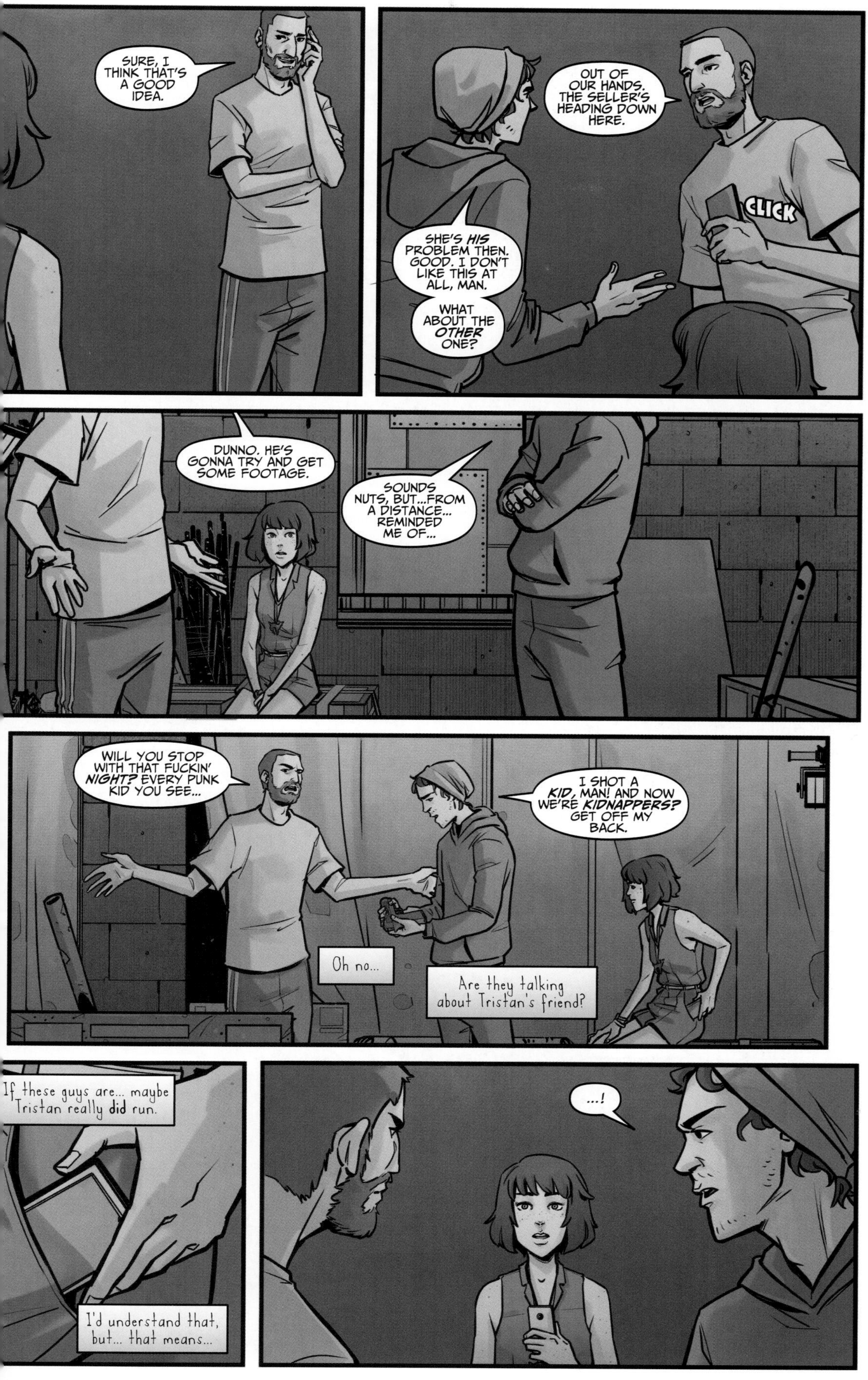
SURE, I THINK THAT'S A GOOD IDEA.
OUT OF OUR HANDS. THE SELLER'S HEADING DOWN HERE.
CLICK
SHE'S HIS PROBLEM THEN. GOOD. I DON'T LIKE THIS AT ALL, MAN.
WHAT ABOUT THE OTHER ONE?
DUNNO. HE'S GONNA TRY AND GET SOME FOOTAGE.
SOUNDS NUTS, BUT...FROM A DISTANCE... REMINDED ME OF...
WILL YOU STOP WITH THAT FUCKIN' NIGHT? EVERY PUNK KID YOU SEE...
I SHOT A KID, MAN! AND NOW WE'RE KIDNAPPERS? GET OFF MY BACK.
Oh no...
Are they talking about Tristan's friend?
If these guys are... maybe Tristan really did run.
I'd understand that, but... that means...
...!

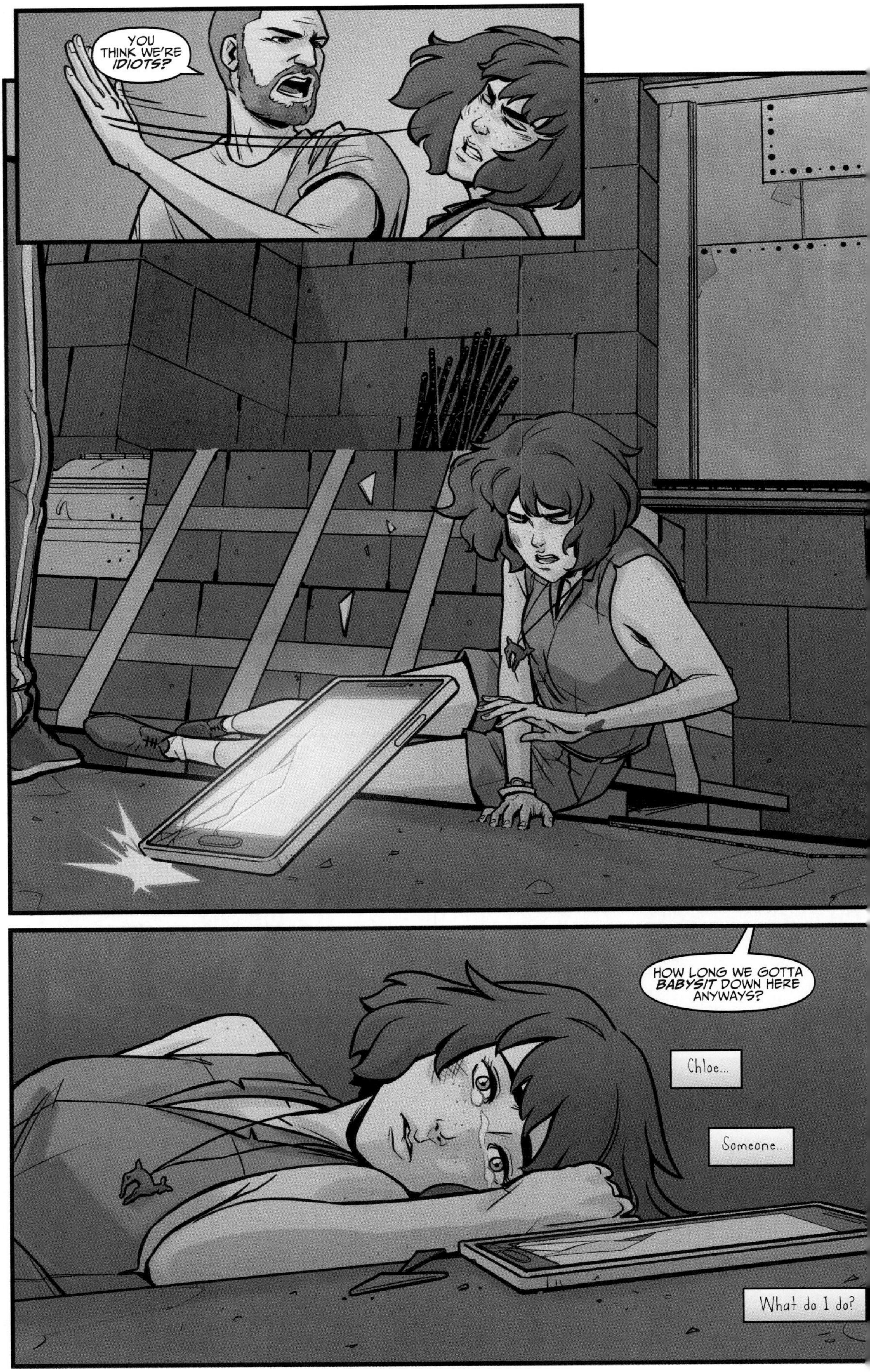
YOU THINK WE'RE *IDIOTS?*
HOW LONG WE GOTTA *BABYSIT* DOWN HERE ANYWAYS?
Chloe...
Someone...
What do I do?

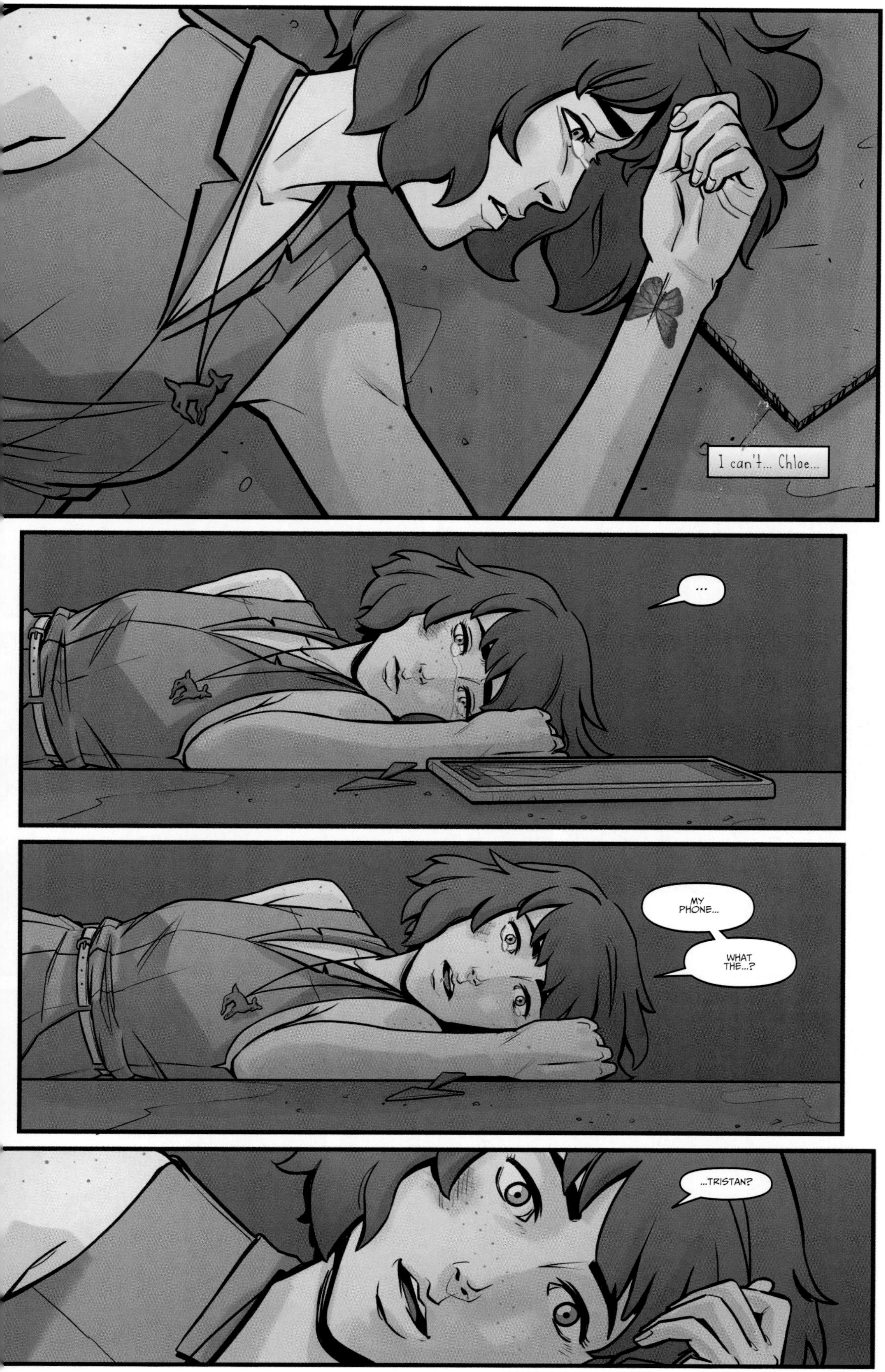
I can't... Chloe...
...
MY PHONE...
WHAT THE...?
...TRISTAN?

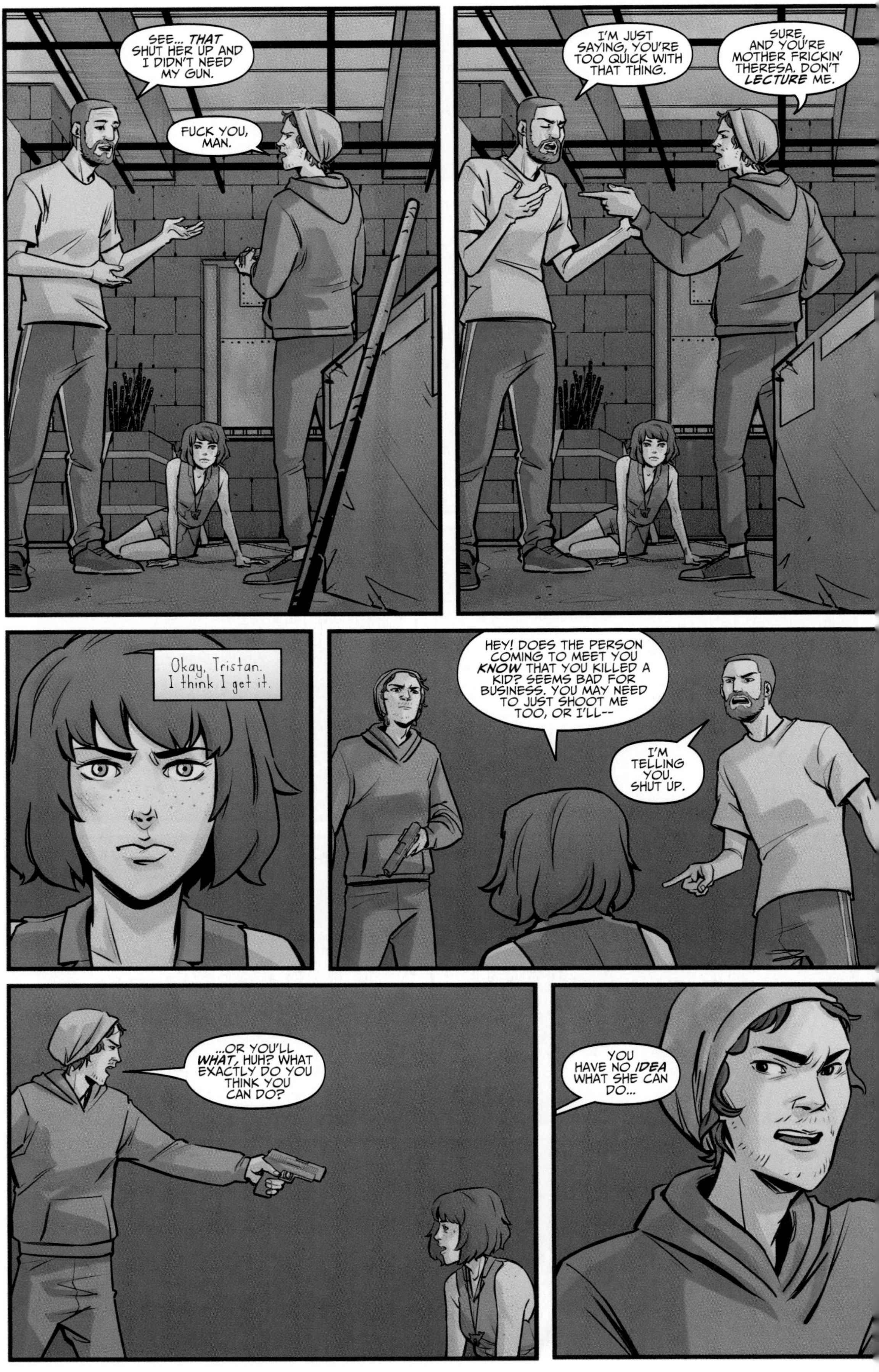

SEE... THAT SHUT HER UP AND I DIDN'T NEED MY GUN.
FUCK YOU, MAN.
I'M JUST SAYING, YOU'RE TOO QUICK WITH THAT THING.
SURE, AND YOU'RE MOTHER FRICKIN' THERESA. DON'T LECTURE ME.
Okay, Tristan. I think I get it.
HEY! DOES THE PERSON COMING TO MEET YOU KNOW THAT YOU KILLED A KID? SEEMS BAD FOR BUSINESS. YOU MAY NEED TO JUST SHOOT ME TOO, OR I'LL--
I'M TELLING YOU. SHUT UP.
...OR YOU'LL WHAT, HUH? WHAT EXACTLY DO YOU THINK YOU CAN DO?
YOU HAVE NO IDEA WHAT SHE CAN DO...

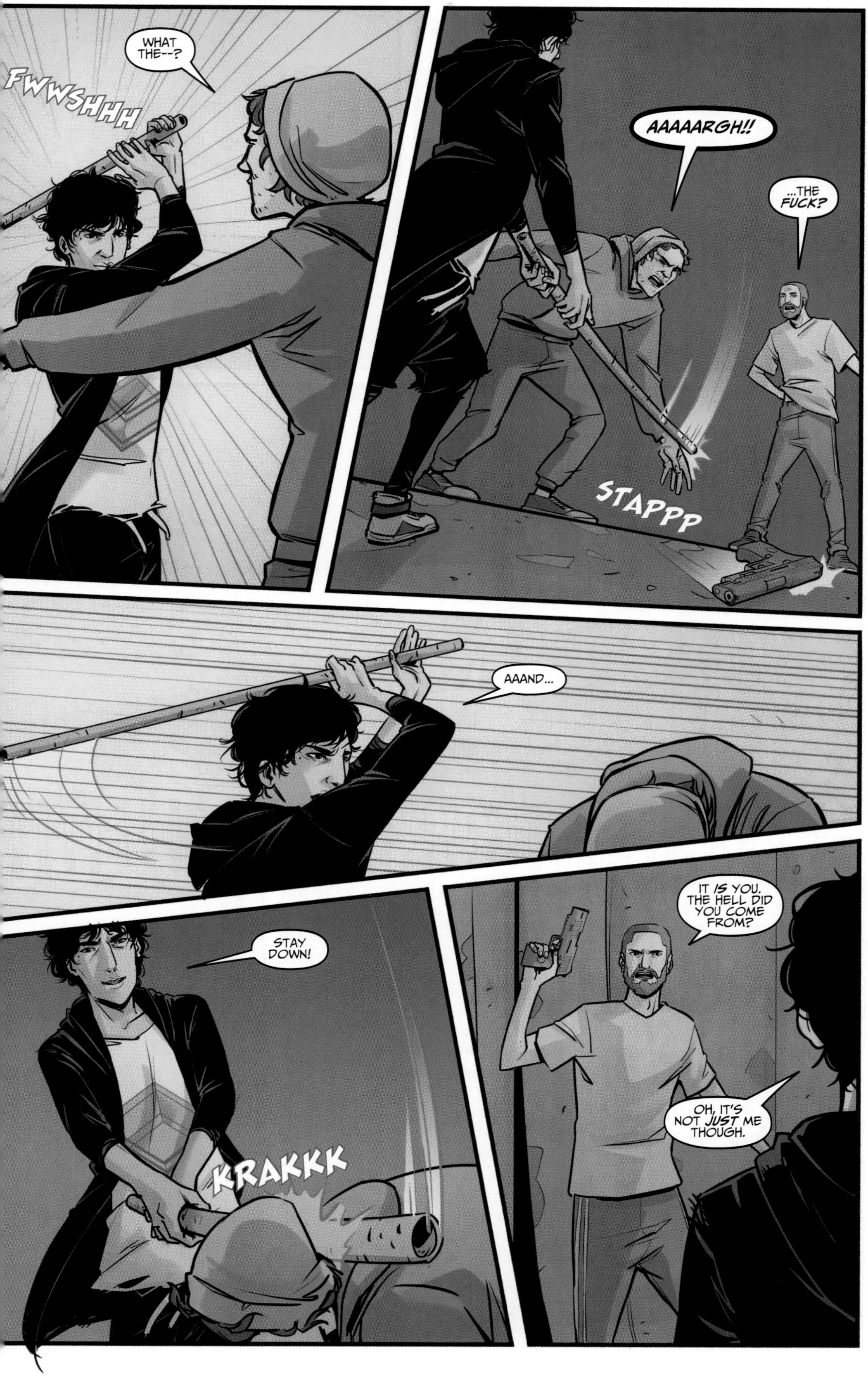
WHAT THE--?
FWWSHHH
AAAAARGH!!
...THE FUCK?
STAPPP
AAAND...
STAY DOWN!
KRAKKK
IT IS YOU. THE HELL DID YOU COME FROM?
OH, IT'S NOT JUST ME THOUGH.

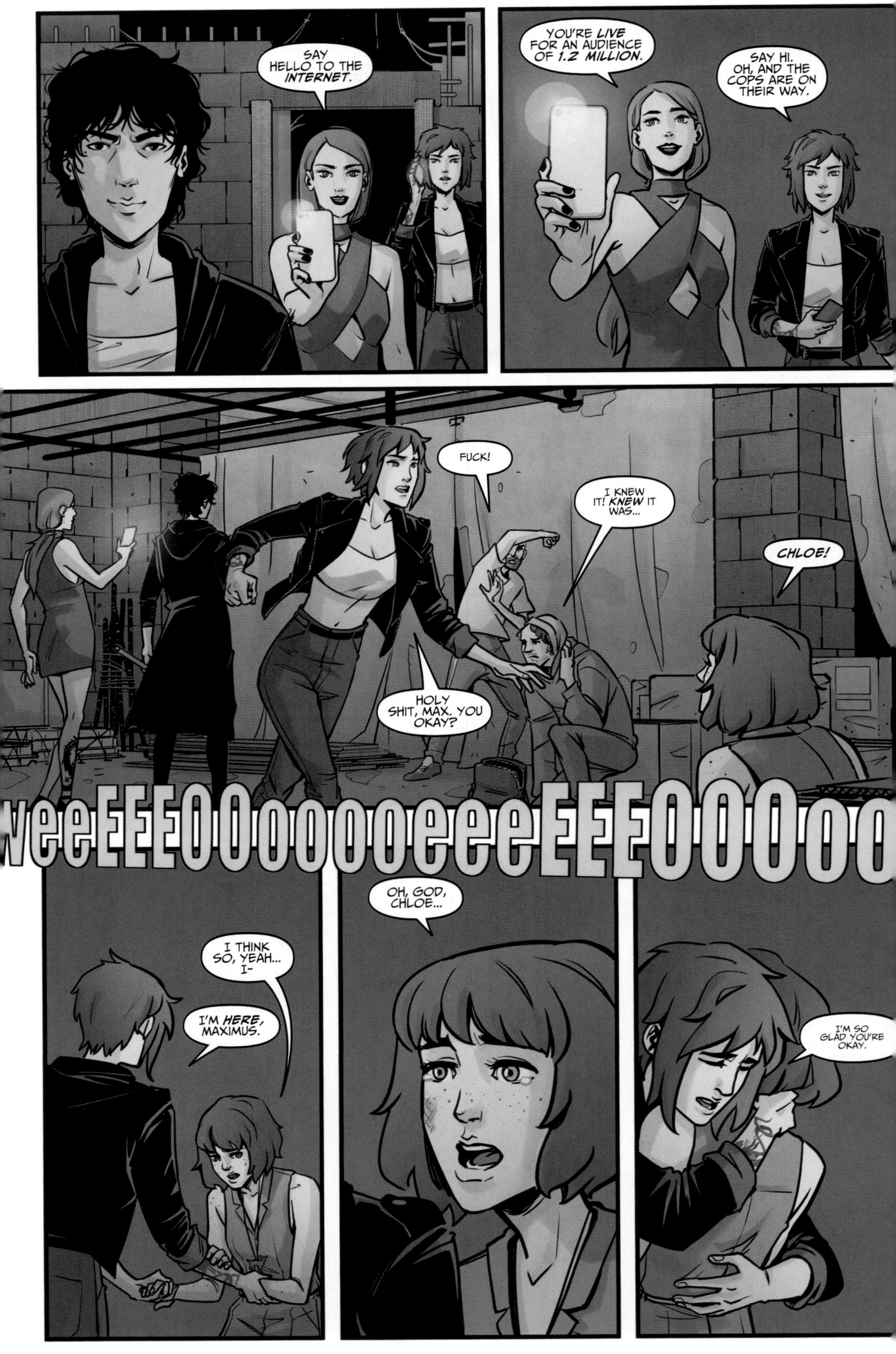
SAY HELLO TO THE *INTERNET*.
YOU'RE *LIVE* FOR AN AUDIENCE OF *1.2 MILLION*.
SAY HI. OH, AND THE COPS ARE ON THEIR WAY.
FUCK!
I KNEW IT! *KNEW* IT WAS...
CHLOE!
HOLY SHIT, MAX. YOU OKAY?
WeeEEEOOooooeeeEEEOOOoo
I THINK SO, YEAH... I-
I'M *HERE*, MAXIMUS.
OH, GOD, CHLOE...
I'M SO GLAD YOU'RE OKAY.

...I... I AM. ...THANKS TO YOU GUYS.

THANKS TO *THAT* GUY. *WHATEVER* THE HELL HE IS. DOES HE COME IN AN *ACTION FIGURE?*

EEEOOooooooeeeEEEOOO

THE BAG...

YOU *REALLY* WANT TO BE FILMED TAKING THAT BAG FULL OF *DRUGS* WITH YOU, SIR?

THE BITCH IS RIGHT. JUST *RUN!*

AmberLight   LIVE

DrowneDrone
♥♥♥

ScienceBoi01
be careful...

P.Nate5
our queen of justice!!

starSteven
you slay girl!

leftbehind2
Love you!

THANKS FOR WATCHING AMBER LIGHT, GUYS.

TOGETHER, WE ARE POWERFUL.

Comment   ...

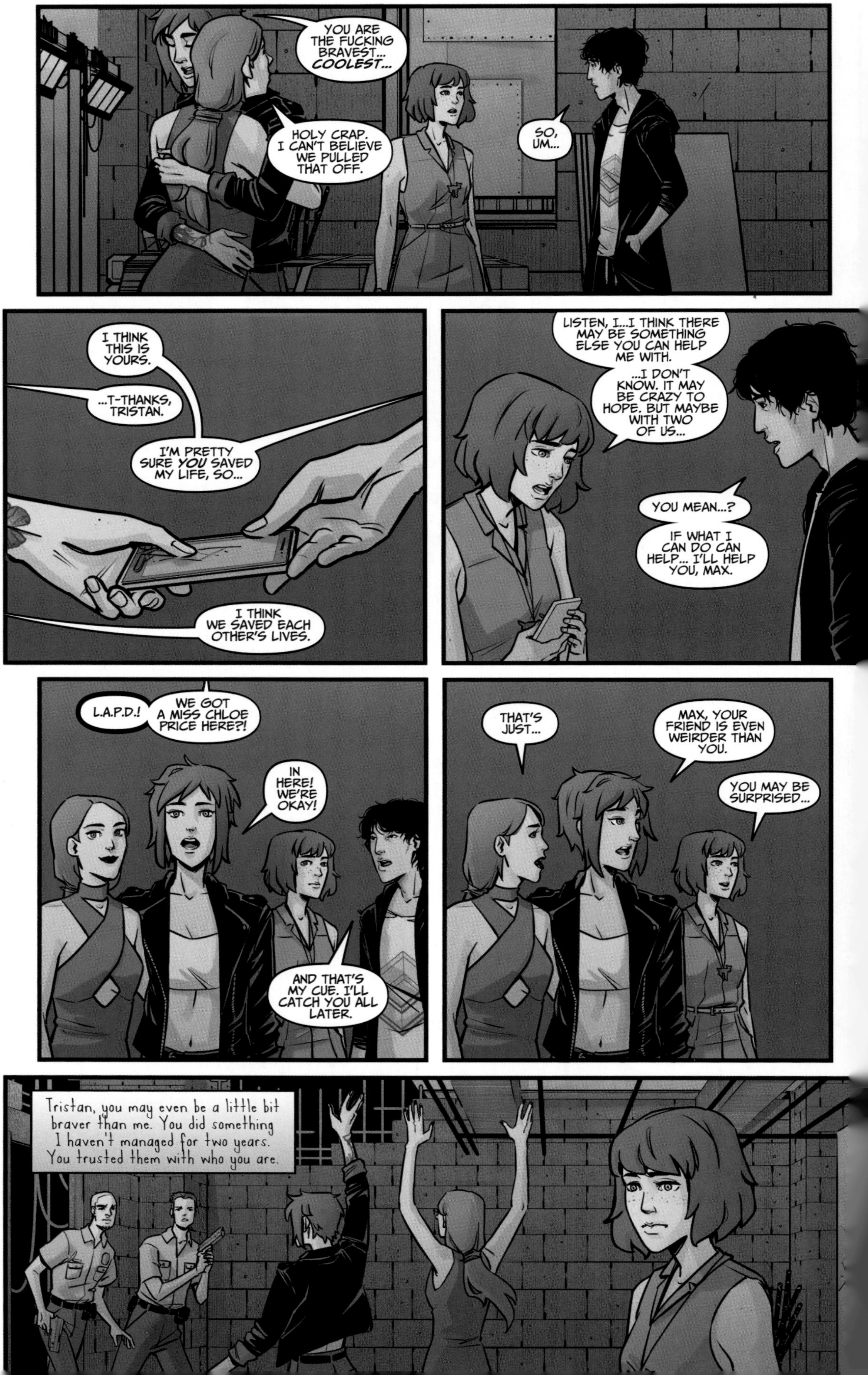
YOU ARE THE FUCKING BRAVEST... COOLEST...
HOLY CRAP. I CAN'T BELIEVE WE PULLED THAT OFF.
SO, UM...
I THINK THIS IS YOURS.
...T-THANKS, TRISTAN.
I'M PRETTY SURE YOU SAVED MY LIFE, SO...
I THINK WE SAVED EACH OTHER'S LIVES.
LISTEN, I...I THINK THERE MAY BE SOMETHING ELSE YOU CAN HELP ME WITH.
...I DON'T KNOW. IT MAY BE CRAZY TO HOPE. BUT MAYBE WITH TWO OF US...
YOU MEAN...?
IF WHAT I CAN DO CAN HELP... I'LL HELP YOU, MAX.
L.A.P.D.!
WE GOT A MISS CHLOE PRICE HERE?!
IN HERE! WE'RE OKAY!
AND THAT'S MY CUE. I'LL CATCH YOU ALL LATER.
THAT'S JUST...
MAX, YOUR FRIEND IS EVEN WEIRDER THAN YOU.
YOU MAY BE SURPRISED...
Tristan, you may even be a little bit braver than me. You did something I haven't managed for two years. You trusted them with who you are.

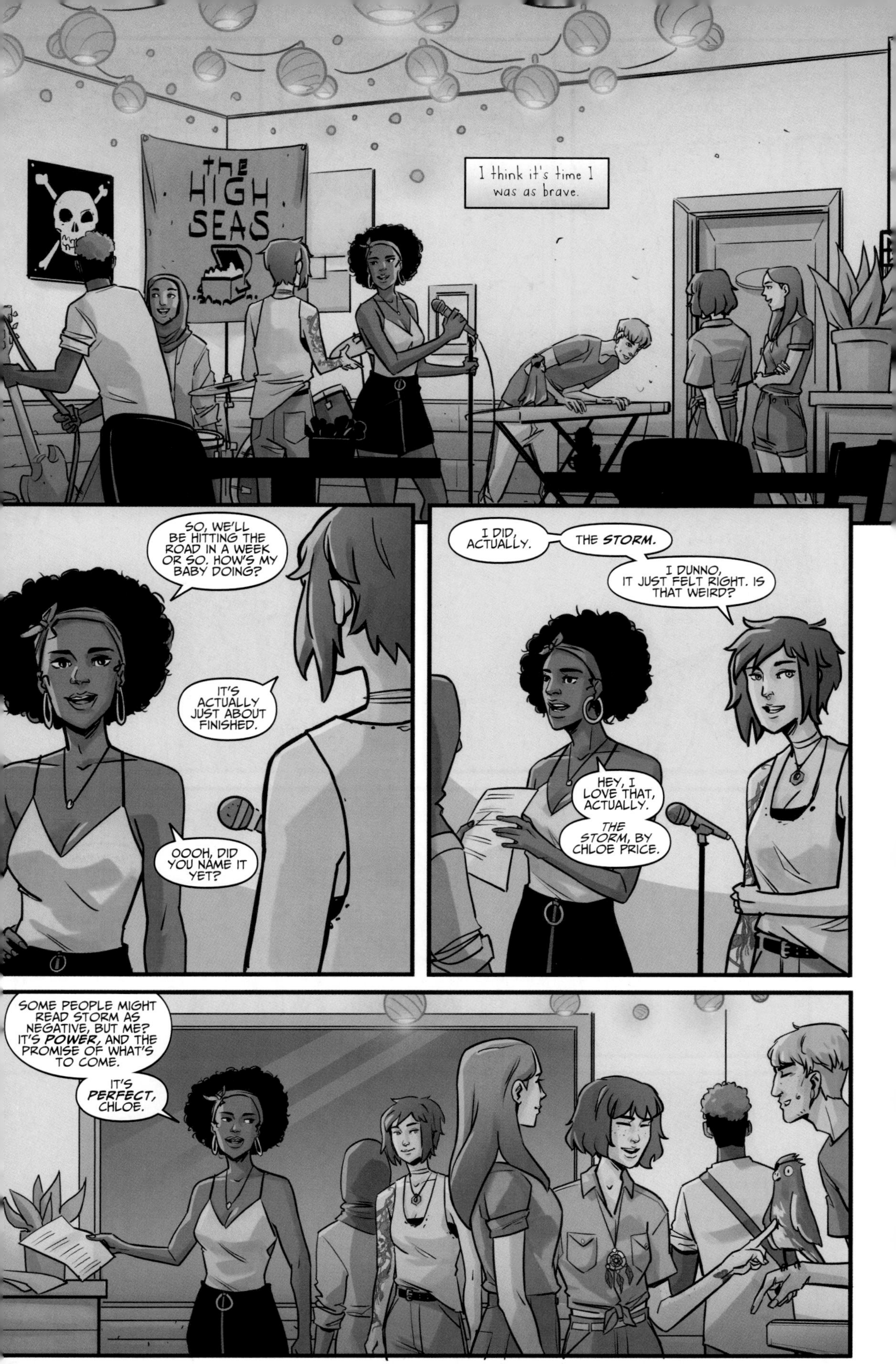

the HIGH SEAS
I think it's time I was as brave.
SO, WE'LL BE HITTING THE ROAD IN A WEEK OR SO. HOW'S MY BABY DOING?
IT'S ACTUALLY JUST ABOUT FINISHED.
OOOH, DID YOU NAME IT YET?
I DID, ACTUALLY.
THE *STORM.*
I DUNNO, IT JUST FELT RIGHT. IS THAT WEIRD?
HEY, I LOVE THAT, ACTUALLY.
THE STORM, BY CHLOE PRICE.
SOME PEOPLE MIGHT READ STORM AS NEGATIVE, BUT ME? IT'S ***POWER,*** AND THE PROMISE OF WHAT'S TO COME.
IT'S ***PERFECT,*** CHLOE.

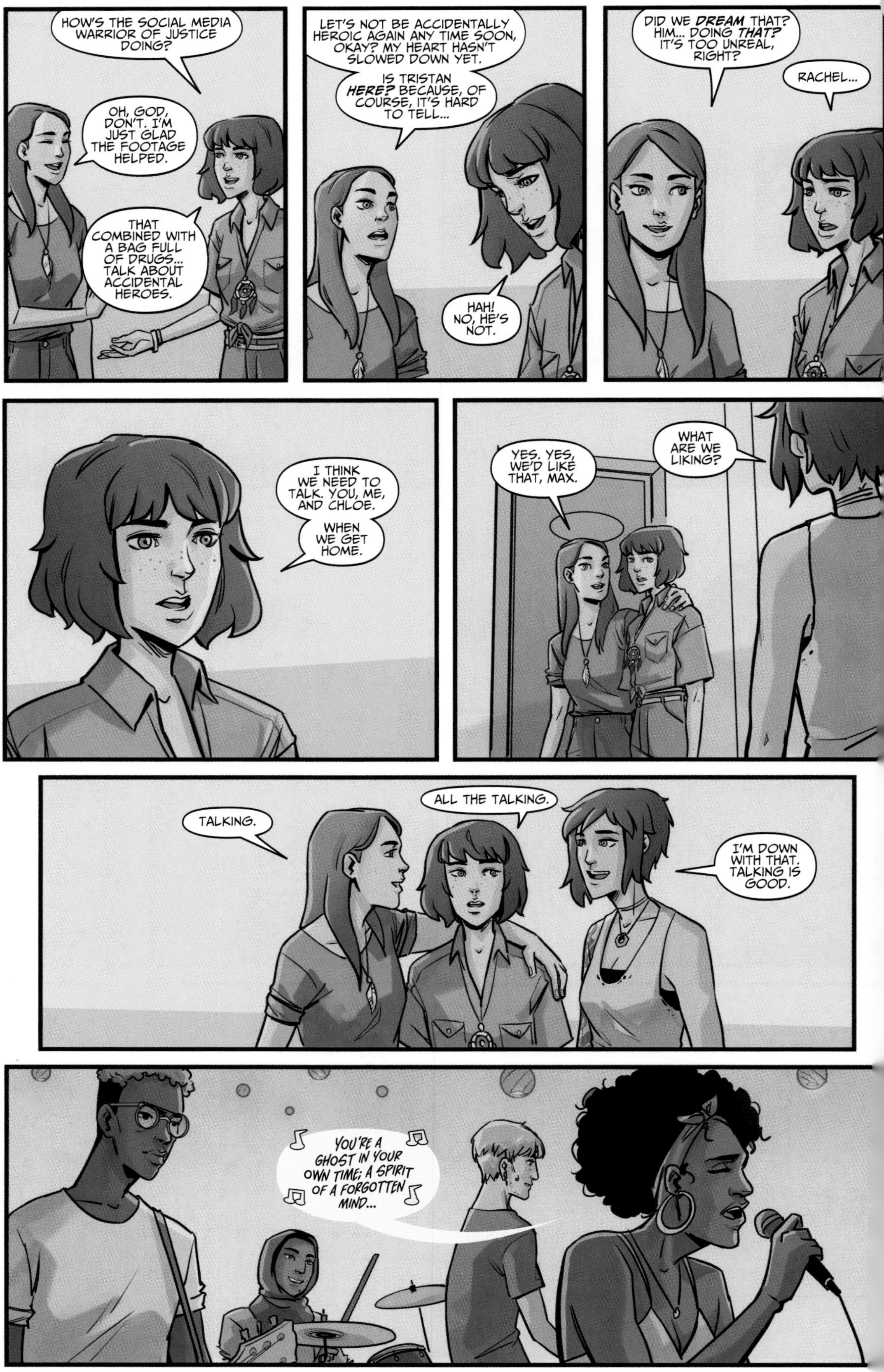
HOW'S THE SOCIAL MEDIA WARRIOR OF JUSTICE DOING?
OH, GOD, DON'T. I'M JUST GLAD THE FOOTAGE HELPED.
THAT COMBINED WITH A BAG FULL OF DRUGS... TALK ABOUT ACCIDENTAL HEROES.
LET'S NOT BE ACCIDENTALLY HEROIC AGAIN ANY TIME SOON, OKAY? MY HEART HASN'T SLOWED DOWN YET.
IS TRISTAN HERE? BECAUSE, OF COURSE, IT'S HARD TO TELL...
HAH! NO, HE'S NOT.
DID WE DREAM THAT? HIM... DOING THAT? IT'S TOO UNREAL, RIGHT?
RACHEL...
I THINK WE NEED TO TALK. YOU, ME, AND CHLOE.
WHEN WE GET HOME.
YES. YES, WE'D LIKE THAT, MAX.
WHAT ARE WE LIKING?
TALKING.
ALL THE TALKING.
I'M DOWN WITH THAT. TALKING IS GOOD.
YOU'RE A GHOST IN YOUR OWN TIME; A SPIRIT OF A FORGOTTEN MIND...

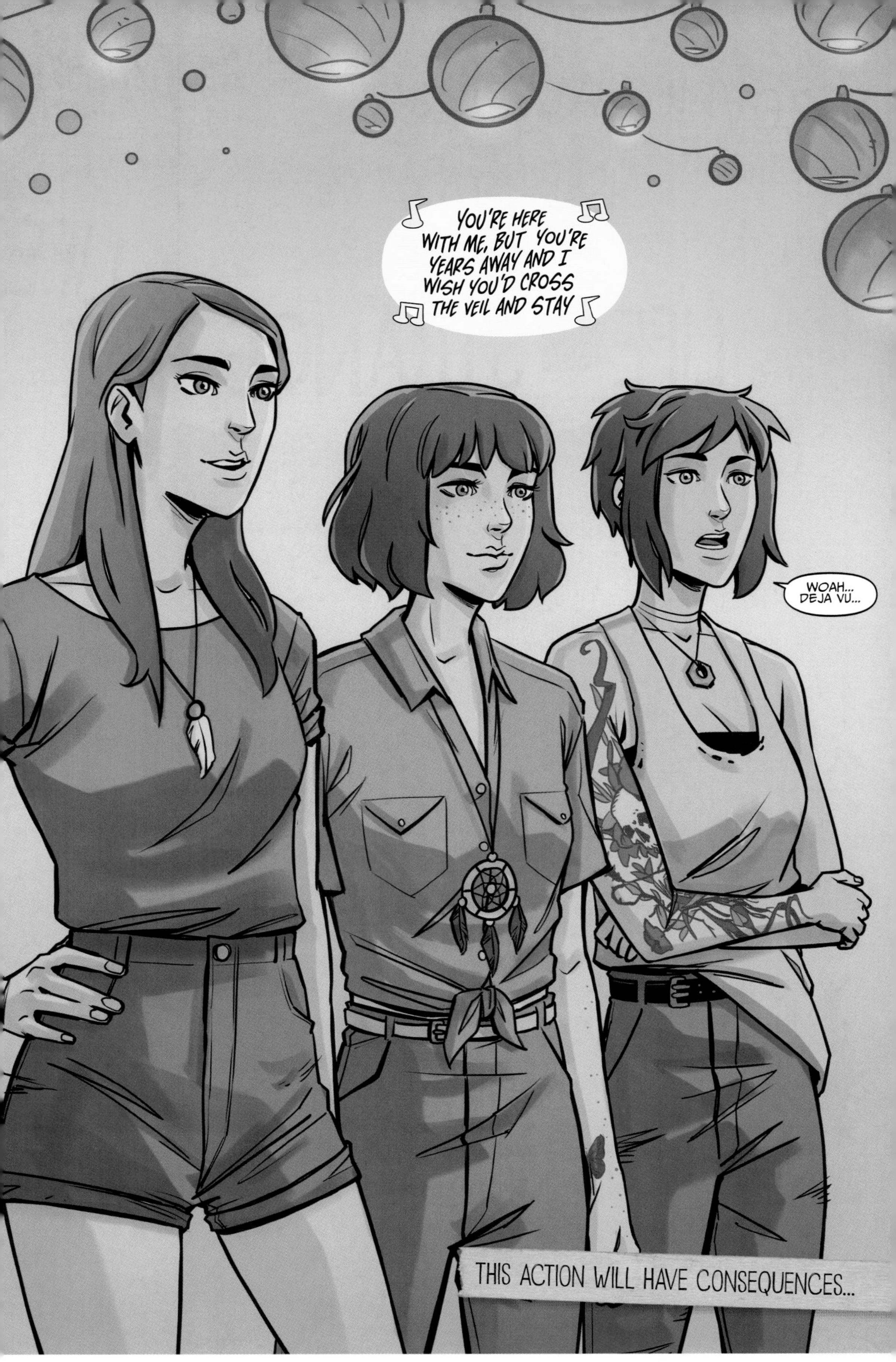
YOU'RE HERE WITH ME, BUT YOU'RE YEARS AWAY AND I WISH YOU'D CROSS THE VEIL AND STAY
WOAH... DEJA VU...
THIS ACTION WILL HAVE CONSEQUENCES...

COVER GALLERY

ISSUE #5

Emma Vieceli • Claudia Leonardi • Andrea Izzo
LIFE IS STRANGE
COVER B
WILL OFFER

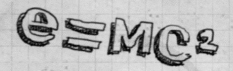

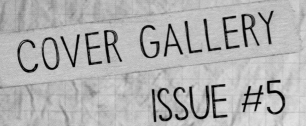

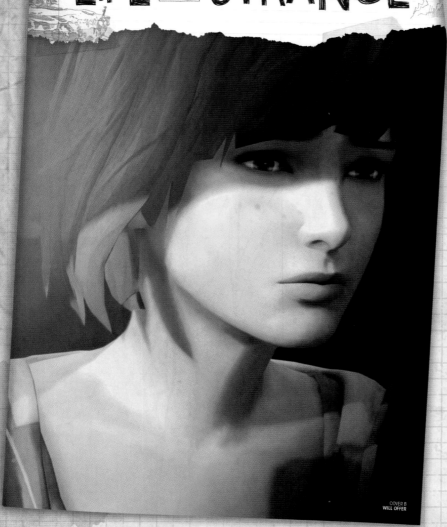

COVER B - WILL OFFER

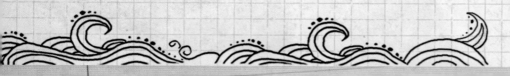

COVER C -
T-SHIRT ART

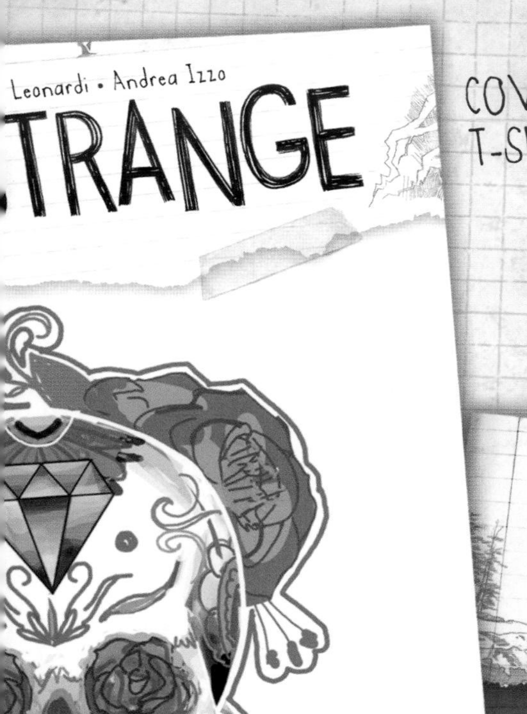
Leonardi • Andrea Izzo
STRANGE
COVER C
T-SHIRT VARIANT

COVER D - CLAUDIA LEONARDI

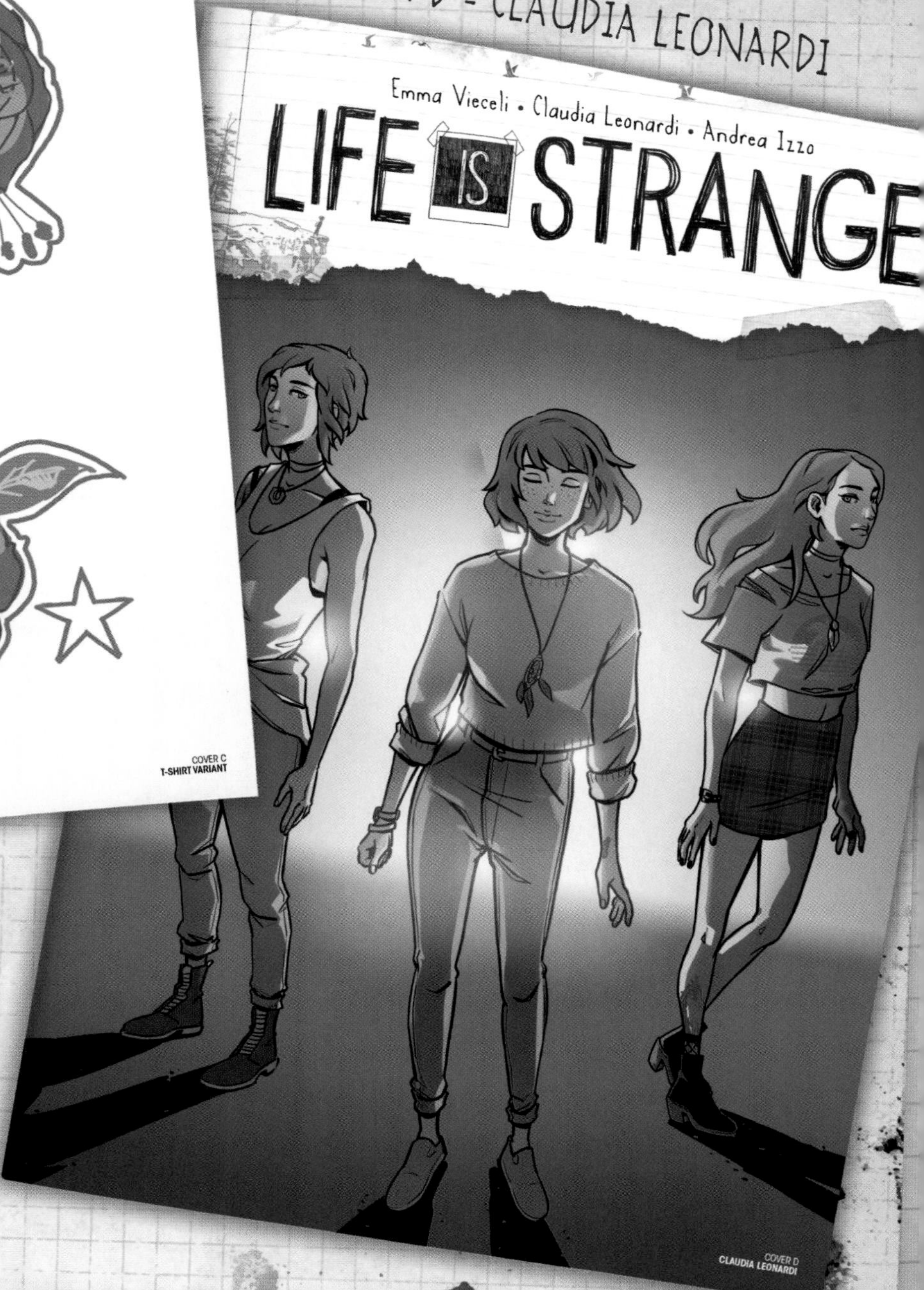
Emma Vieceli • Claudia Leonardi • Andrea Izzo
LIFE IS STRANGE
COVER D
CLAUDIA LEONARDI

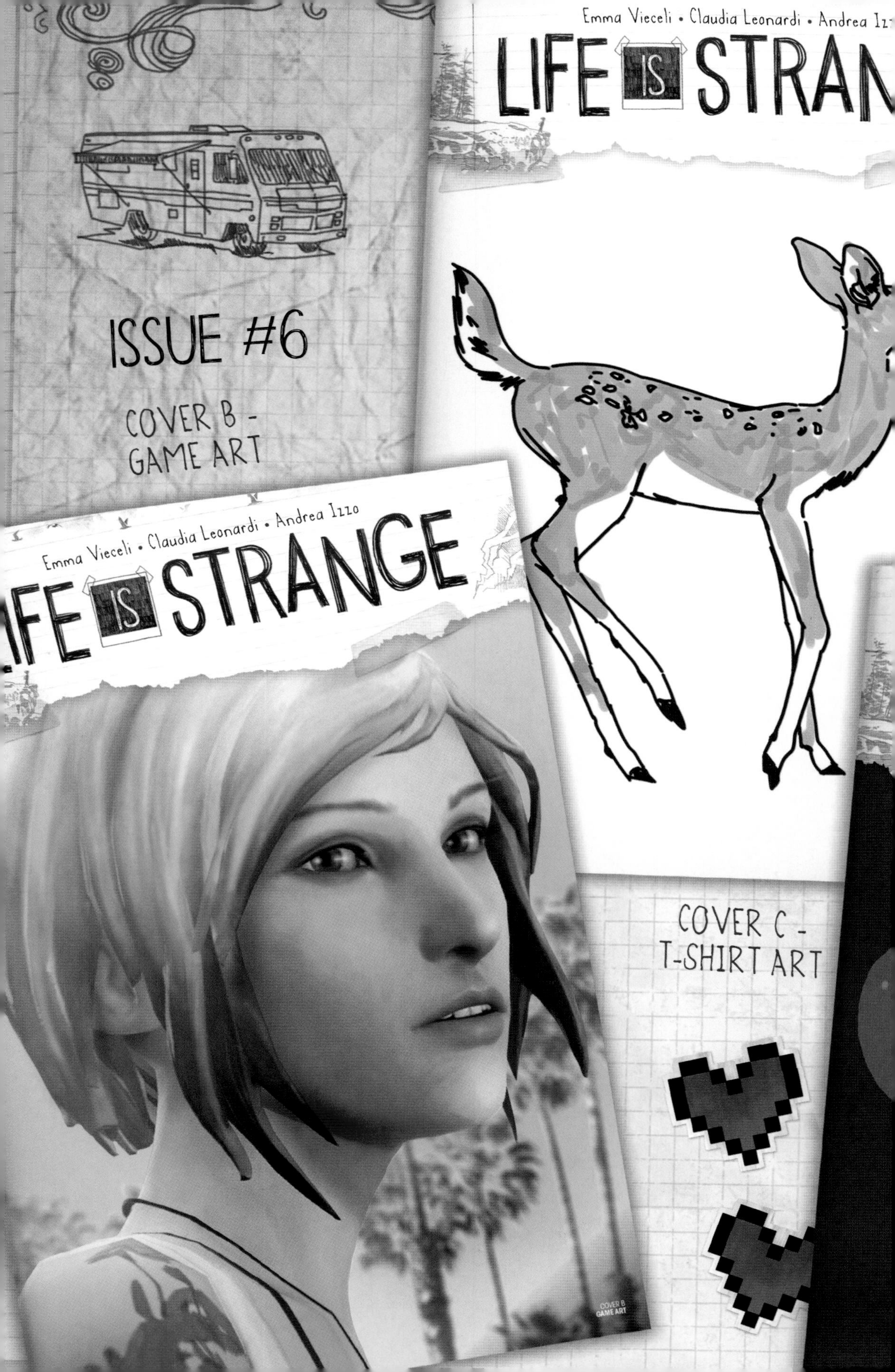

Emma Vieceli • Claudia Leonardi • Andrea Iz
LIFE IS STRAN
ISSUE #6
COVER B - GAME ART
Emma Vieceli • Claudia Leonardi • Andrea Izzo
IFE IS STRANGE
COVER C - T-SHIRT ART
COVER B GAME ART

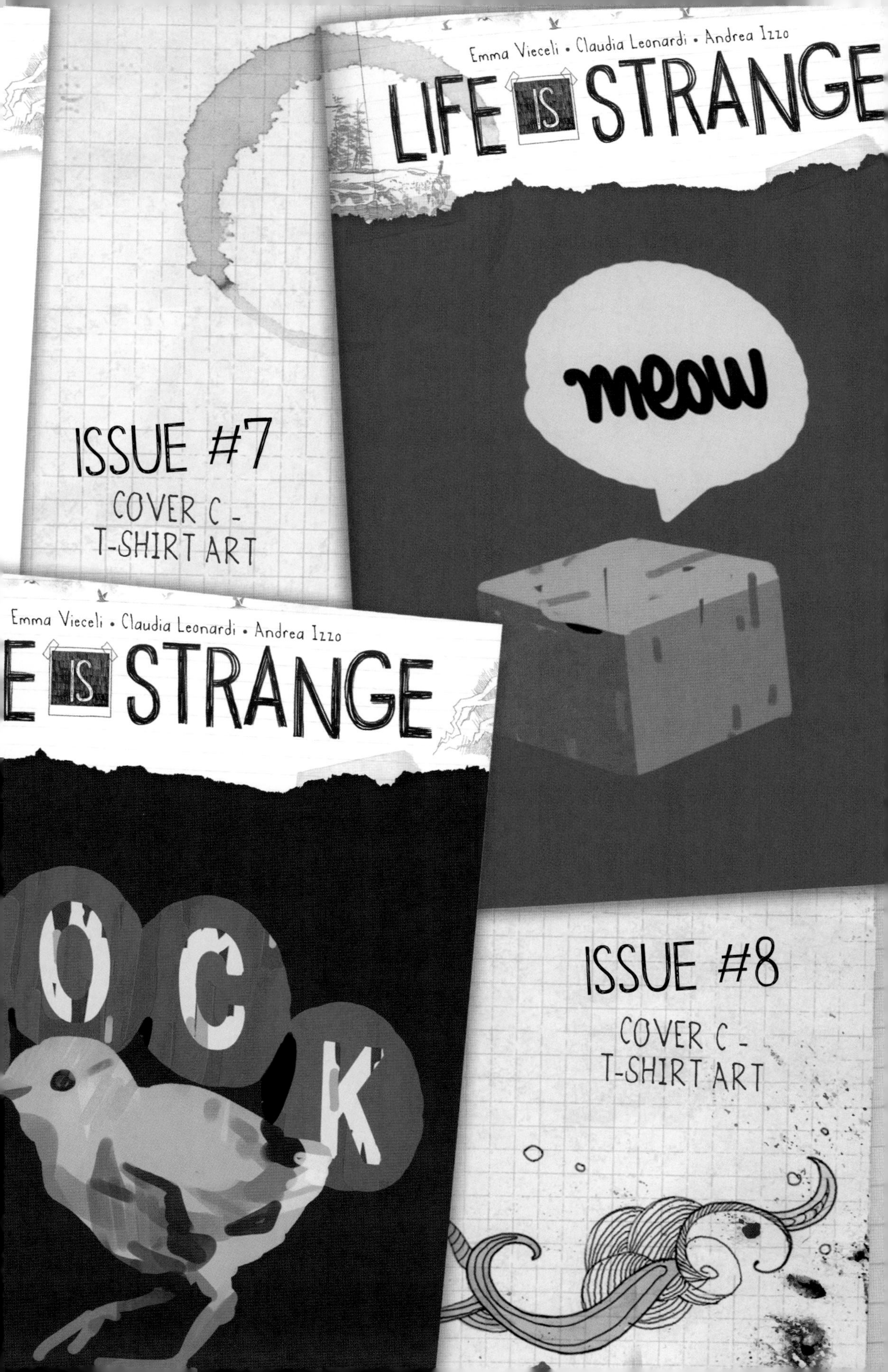
ISSUE #7
COVER C - T-SHIRT ART
Emma Vieceli • Claudia Leonardi • Andrea Izzo
LIFE IS STRANGE
meow
Emma Vieceli • Claudia Leonardi • Andrea Izzo
E IS STRANGE
O C K
ISSUE #8
COVER C - T-SHIRT ART

CHARACTER SKETCHES

BY CLAUDIA LEONARDI

CHLOE

WE HAD BEEN PLANNING A TWO YEAR TIME JUMP FOR T SECOND ARC FOR A WHILE, S NATURALLY WE HAD TO AGE THE CHARACTERS UP. CLAUD EXPLORED POSSIBILITIES FOR HOW THE CHARACTERS COUL HAVE LOOKED. IN THE END WE DIDN'T WANT TO CHANGE THE GIRLS' APPEARANCES TOO DRASTICALLY, BUT HERE'S AN INTERESTING LOOK INTO WHAT COULD HAVE BEEN!

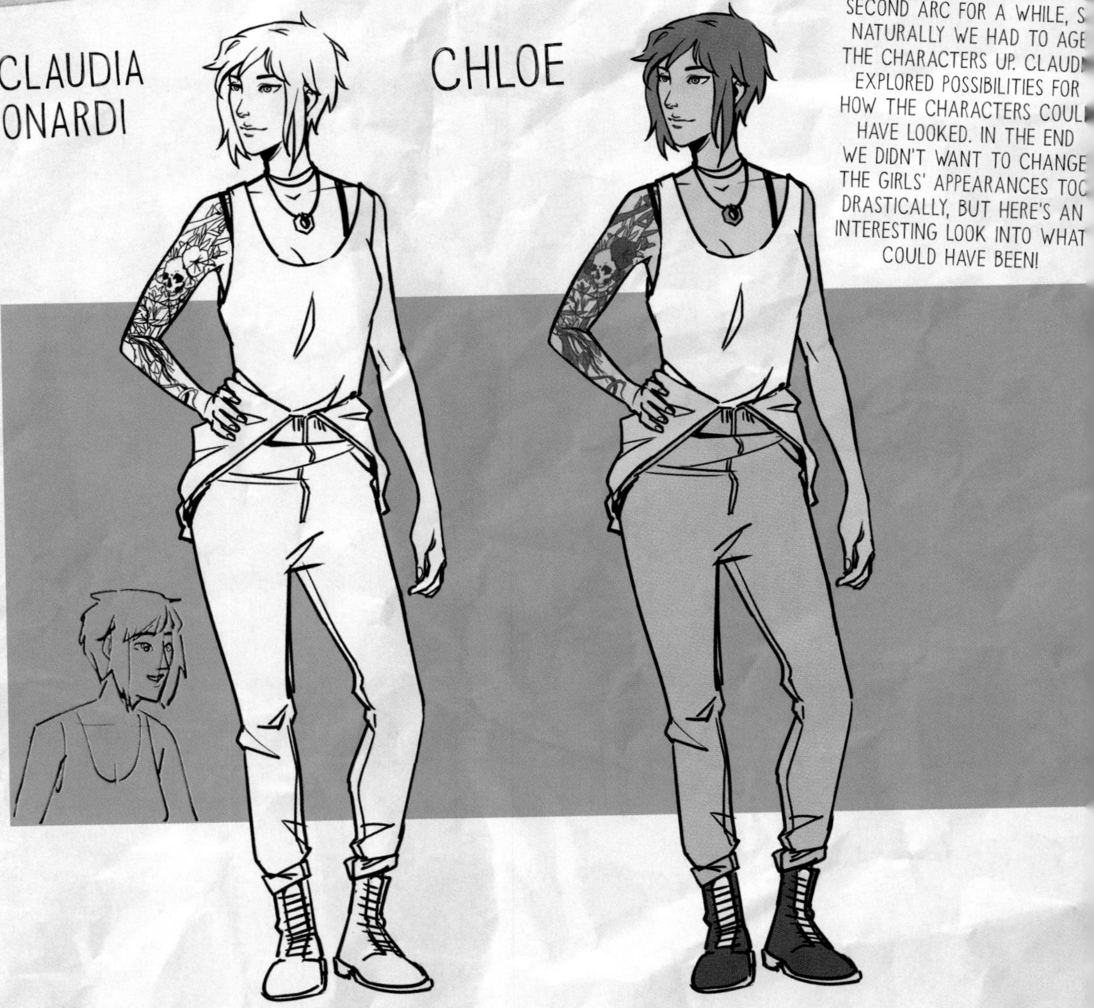

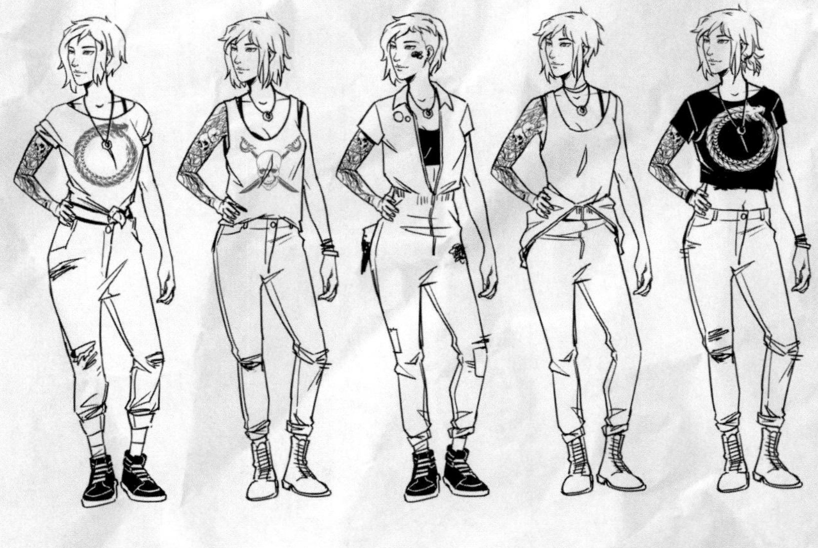

MAX

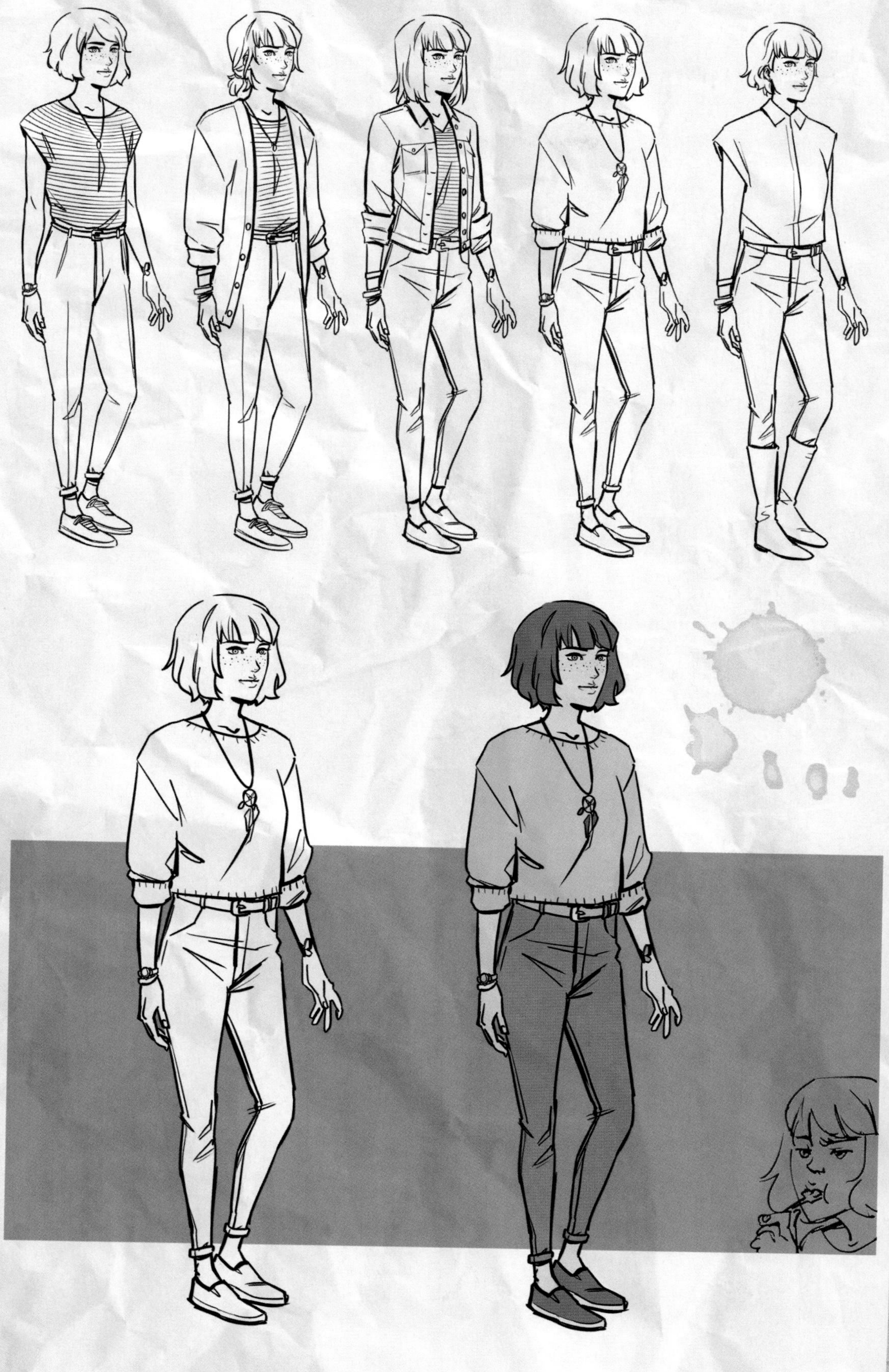

CHARACTER SKETCHES

BY CLAUDIA LEONARDI

RACHEL

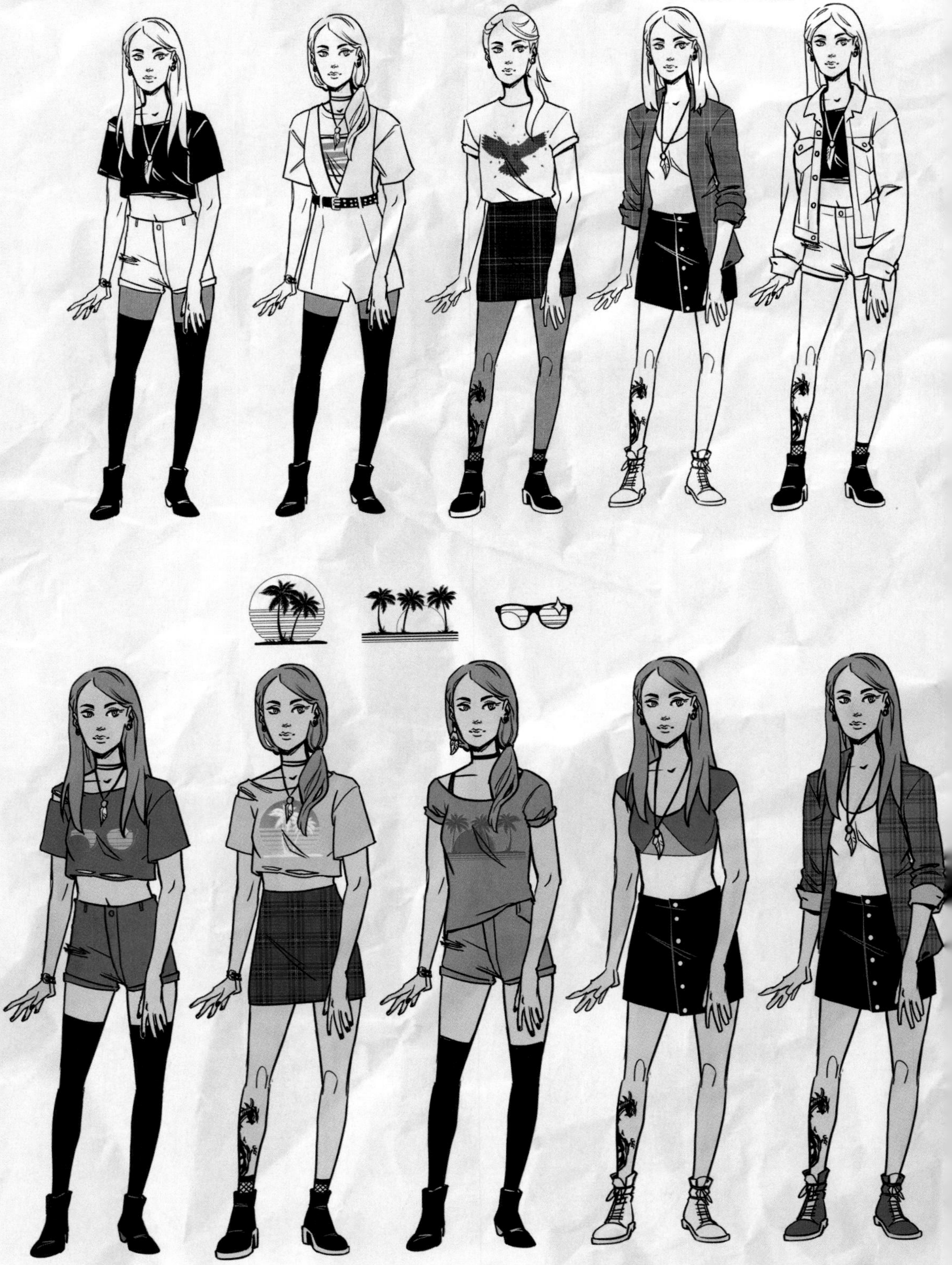

TRISTAN

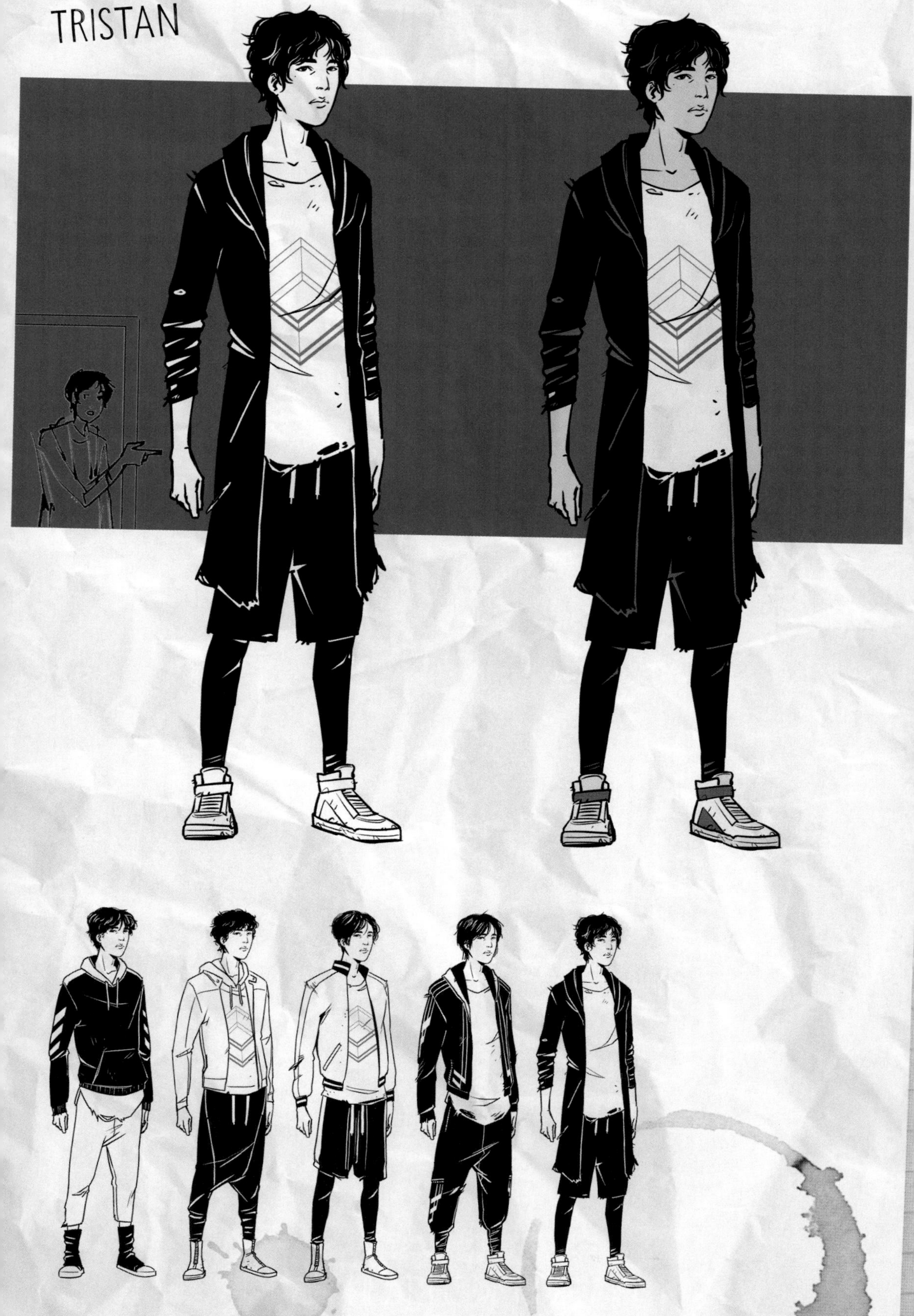

VOLUME 3 COMING SOON

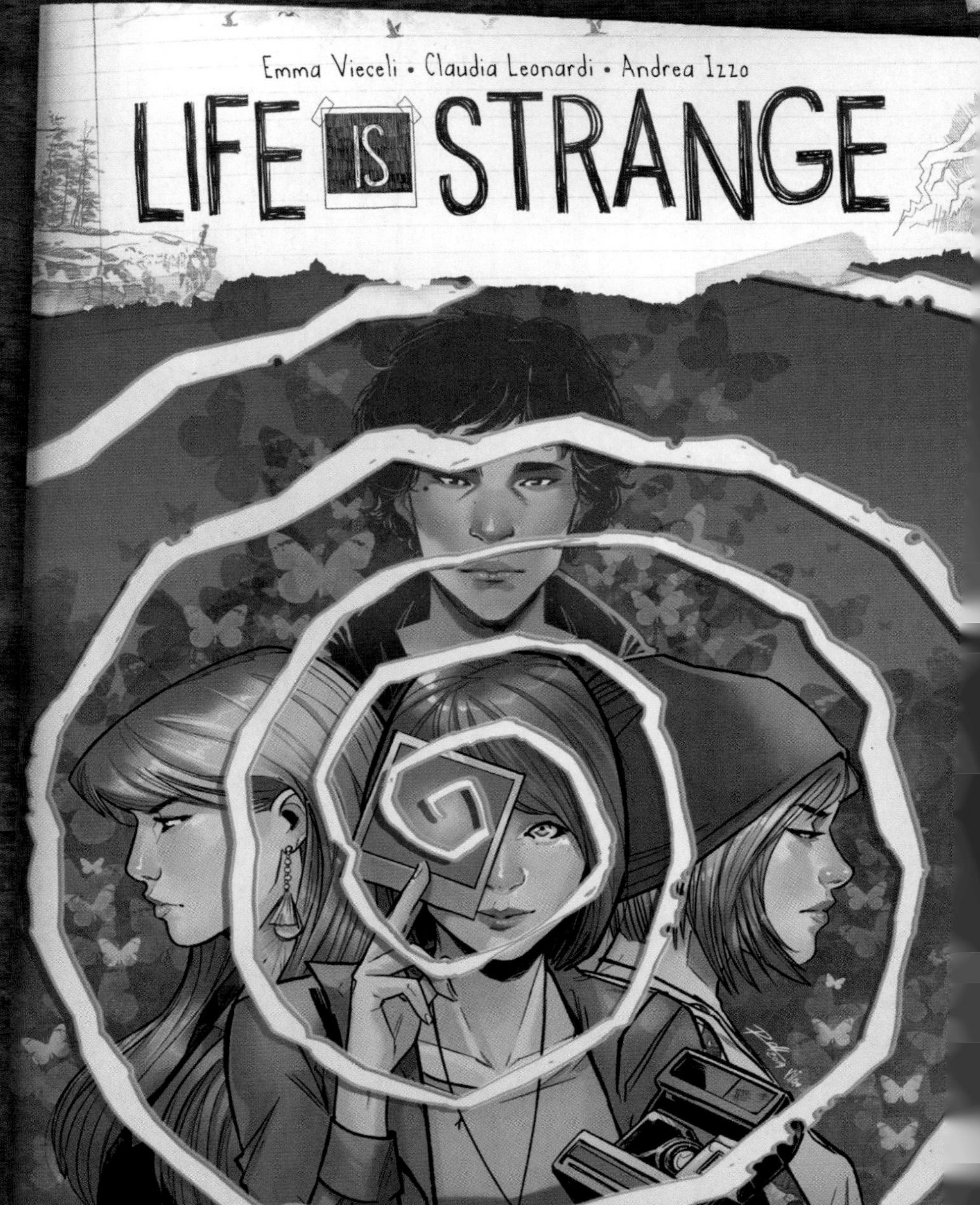
Emma Vieceli • Claudia Leonardi • Andrea Izzo
LIFE IS STRANGE

COVER BY ROBERTA INGRANATA

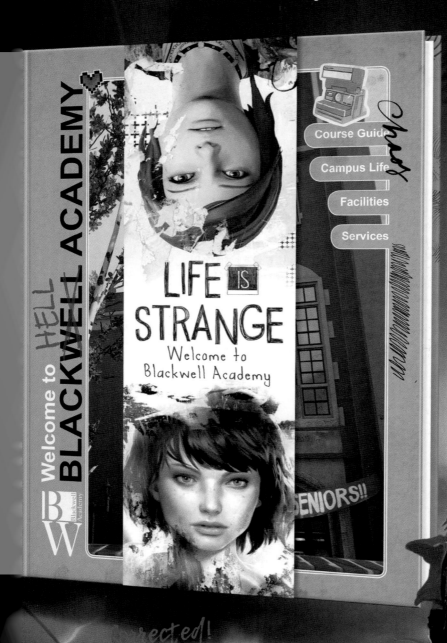

ACKWELL ACADEMY

ent guide to Blackwell Academy and Arcadia Bay

Course Guide

Campus Life

Facilities

Services

Welcome to HELL
BLACKWELL ACADEMY

LIFE IS STRANGE
Welcome to Blackwell Academy

BW Blackwell Academy

SENIORS!!

corrected!
As defaced by Max and Chloe

OUT NOW!

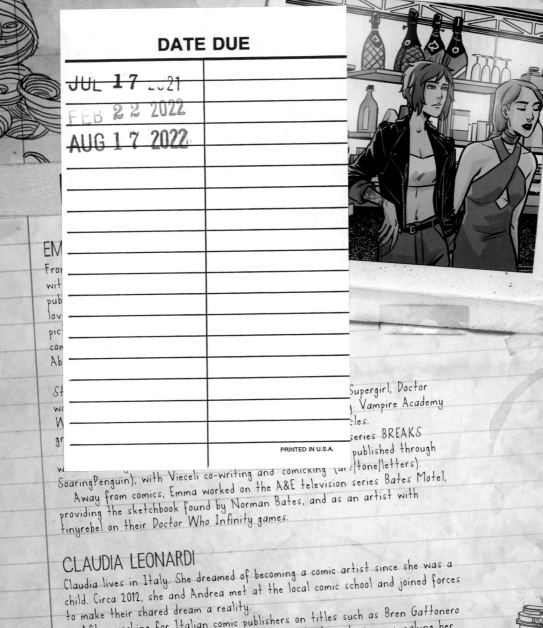

EM

Fro
wit
pub
lov
pic
con
Ab

St… Supergirl, Doctor
w… Vampire Academy
W… cles.
gr… series BREAKS
… published through
w… and comicking (art/tone/letters).
SoaringPenguin), with Vieceli co-writing and comicking (art/tone/letters).

Away from comics, Emma worked on the A&E television series *Bates Motel*, providing the sketchbook found by Norman Bates, and as an artist with tinyrebel on their *Doctor Who Infinity* games.

CLAUDIA LEONARDI

Claudia lives in Italy. She dreamed of becoming a comic artist since she was a child. Circa 2012, she and Andrea met at the local comic school and joined forces to make their shared dream a reality.

After working for Italian comic publishers on titles such as Bren Gattonero and Zeroi, plus indie productions as penciller and inker, she is now making her international debut with *Life is Strange*.

ANDREA IZZO

Andrea Izzo was born in 1984 and loves music and videogames. In 2012, he graduated in digital coloring at the International School of Comics in Reggio Emilia.

He worked as a digital colorist for many indie publishers, colored the Italian comic Zeroi and the whole series of comic strips *Sturmtruppen 50 anni - A Koloren*. He also colored the illustrations of an Armed & Dangerous expansion, the card game BANG! and 3 Segreti - Crimini Nel Tempo.

Now he is the colorist of the official videogame-based comic *Life is Strange*. He got the platinum trophy in *Life is Strange* and he hates canned tuna.

NEXT LEVEL GRAPHIC NOVELS
FOR THE GAMER IN YOU!

SEA OF THIEVES
$16.99 • ISBN: 9781785869891

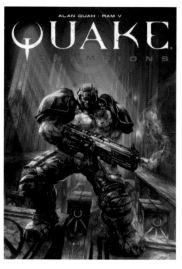

QUAKE CHAMPIONS
$16.99 • ISBN: 9781787731752

WOLFENSTEIN
$16.99 • ISBN: 9781785863417

EVIL WITHIN 2
$16.99 • ISBN: 9781785863295

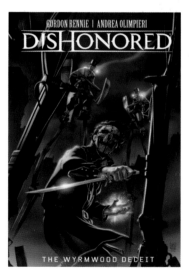

DISHONORED: THE WYRMWOOD DECEIT
$16.99 • ISBN: 9781785852336

TEKKEN VOL. 1: BLOOD FEUD
$16.99 • ISBN: 9781785861284

One of the best comic books based on a
video game, if not *the* best."
Multiversity Comics

After being forced to leave her beloved Chloe and timeline behind,
time traveler Max Caulfield arrives into a new reality to find not only
alternative Chloe, but also Rachel, now very much alive!

Based on the fan-adored, BAFTA-winning video game *Life is Strange*, *Waves* continues the ad
of Max in one of the many alternate realities from the critically acclaimed game, and find
struggling to fit into an unfamiliar new reality. In this reality Rachel was never murdered and
dating Chloe! And Max discovers a mysterious boy with a unique talent...

"Phenomenal."
Outright Geekery

"Striking, unique artwork
and a strong script, this is a
compelling take on friends
and relationships."
Comic of the Day

"Complex and
Compelling."
Comicon.com

COVER ART
CLAUD
LEONAR

Collects Life
Strange #5

$16.99 US / $22.99 CAN / £13.99 UK

ISBN:9781787730885

AVAILABLE NOW

LIFE IS STRANGE

LIFE IS STRANGE

TITAN®

TITAN-COMICS.COM

9 781787 730885
51699

NEXT LEVEL GRAPHIC NOVELS FOR THE GAMER IN YOU!

SEA OF THIEVES

QUAKE CHAMPIONS

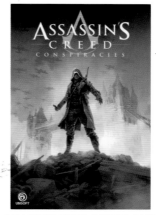

ASSASSIN'S CREED CONSPIRACIES
17 VOLUMES AVAILABLE

WOLFENSTEIN

EVIL WITHIN 2
TWO VOLUMES AVAILABLE

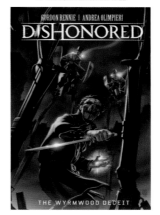

DISHONORED
TWO VOLUMES AVAILABLE

TEKKEN VOL. 1: BLOOD FEUD

FREEWAY FIGHTER

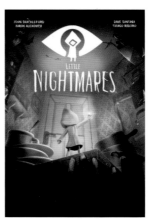

LITTLE NIGHTMARES

"For those hoping to see more of Chloe and Max this comic is a worthy sequel!"
COMICBOOK.COM

Time traveler Max Caulfield has been keeping a secret from her close fri Chloe and Rachel. She's not from their reality! Now Max thinks she may hav a way home, back to her own Chloe... and so it's time for the truth to com

Based on the fan-favorite BAFTA award-winning video game *Life is Strange*, 'Strings' picks up of the endings of the original game and follows Max into a new alternate reality. Here, Rach died, and she and Chloe are a couple. Here, too, is a young man with an unexpected new pov ability to disappear - who may offer Max the ability to return home to her original timeli

"Make sure you read this."
The Xbox Hub

"This book is the shizzle. Two thumbs up and aces."
Mass Movements

"Life might b this is hel"
The GWW

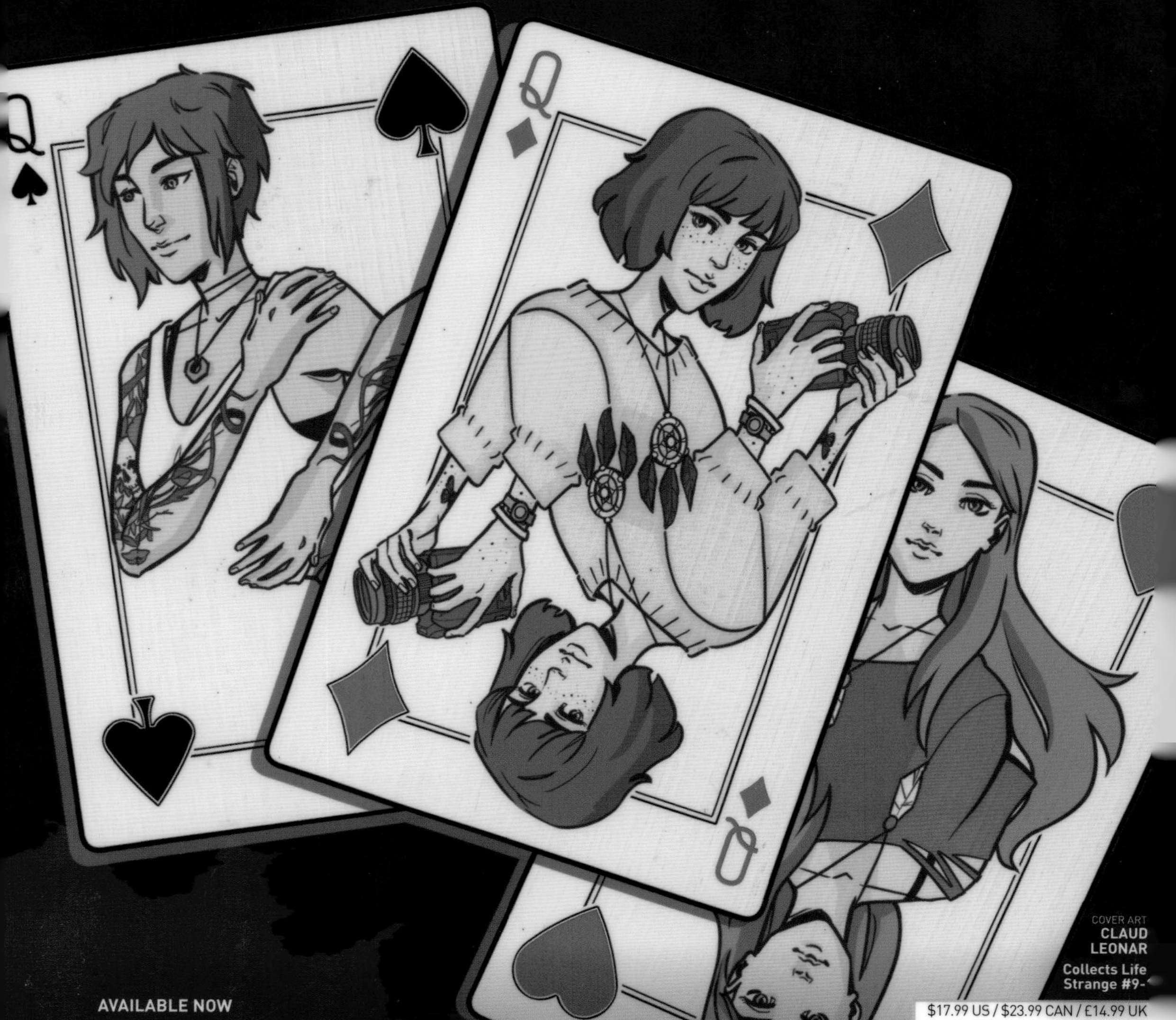

COVER ART
CLAUD
LEONAR

Collects Life
Strange #9-

AVAILABLE NOW

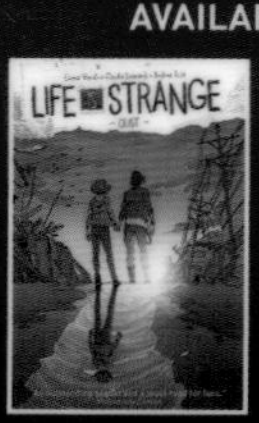
Vol. 1: Dust

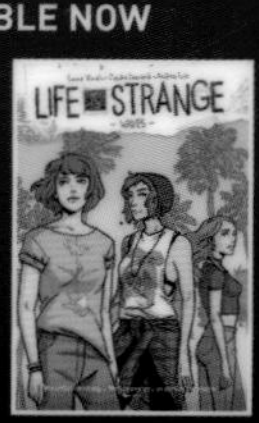
Vol. 2: Waves

$17.99 US / $23.99 CAN / £14.99 UK
ISBN: 978-1787732070
51799
9 781787 732070

TITAN COMICS
TITAN-COMICS.COM
SUGGESTED FOR MATURE READERS

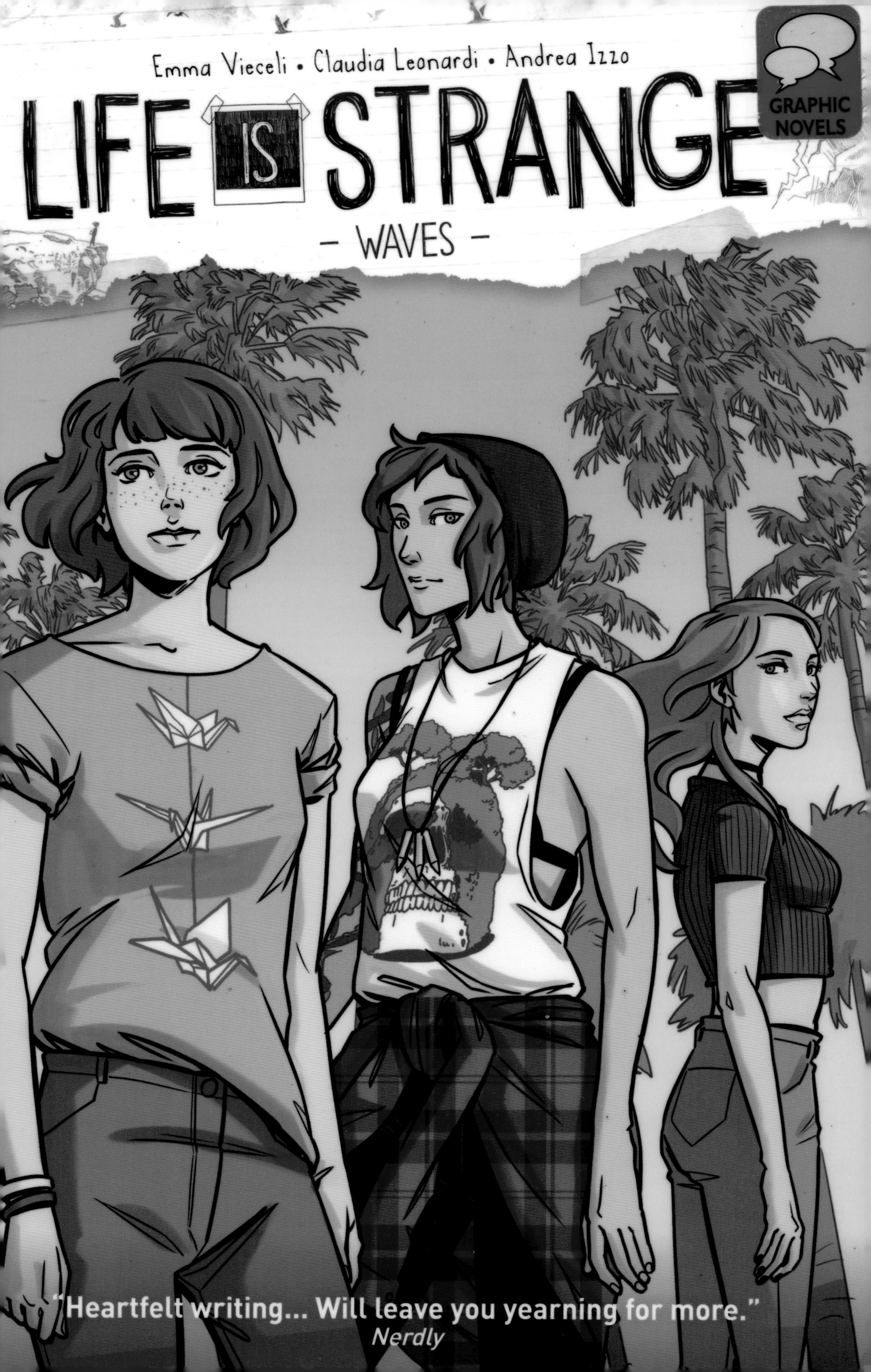
Emma Vieceli • Claudia Leonardi • Andrea Izzo
LIFE IS STRANGE
GRAPHIC NOVELS
– WAVES –
"Heartfelt writing... Will leave you yearning for more."
Nerdly

CHECK OUT THESE BRAND NEW GAMING GRAPHIC NOVELS!

Emma Vieceli • Claudia Leonardi • Andrea Izzo
LIFE IS STRANGE
- DUST -
"An outstanding sequel and a must-read for fans."
Multiversity Comics

LIFE IS STRANGE VOL. 1
$16.99 • ISBN: 9781785866456

Bloodborne
THE VEIL, TORN ASUNDER
KOT | KOWALSKI | SIMPSON

BLOODBORNE VOL. 4
On Sale January 2020
$16.99 • ISBN: 9781787730151

KANSARA
HORNE
WATCH_DOGS
RETURN TO ROCINHA

WATCHDOGS: RETURN TO ROCINHA
$16.99 • ISBN: 9781785864049

O'SULLIVAN & KOKAREV
DARK SOULS
THE AGE OF FIRE

DARK SOULS: THE AGE OF FIRE
$16.99 • ISBN: 9781785861659

ASSASSIN'S
CREED
THE FALL & THE CHAIN
UBISOFT

ASSASSIN'S CREED: THE FALL & THE CHAIN
$19.99 • ISBN: 9781787731509

CHRIS SORRELL
JASON WILSON
MEDIEVIL
OFFICIAL PREQUEL FROM THE ORIGINAL GAME'S CREATORS!

MEDIEVIL: THE GAME PREQUEL
$12.99 • ISBN: 9781787734197

AVAILABLE IN PRINT AND DIGITALLY AT:

TITAN-COMICS.COM

COMIXOLOGY • iBooks • amazonkindle • Google Play • kobo

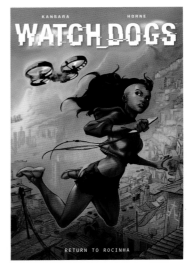

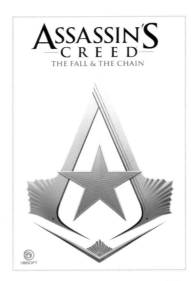

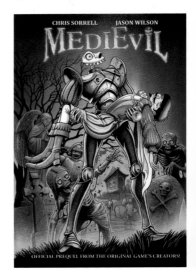